DOES GOD MAKE THE MAN?

Does God Make the Man?

Media, Religion, and the Crisis of Masculinity

Stewart M. Hoover and Curtis D. Coats

NEW YORK UNIVERSITY PRESS

New York and London

NEW YORK UNIVERSITY PRESS
New York and London
www.nyupress.org

References to Internet websites (URLs) were accurate at the time of writing. Neither the author nor New York University Press is responsible for URLs that may have expired or changed since the manuscript was prepared.

Library of Congress Cataloging-in-Publication Data
Hoover, Stewart M.
Does God make the man? : media, religion, and the crisis of masculinity /
Stewart M. Hoover and Curtis D. Coats.
pages cm   Includes bibliographical references and index.
ISBN 978-1-4798-1177-9 (cl : alk. paper) — ISBN 978-1-4798-6223-8 (pb : alk. paper)
1. Men (Christian theology) 2. Protestant men—United States. 3. Masculinity—Religious aspects—Christianity. 4. Masculinity in mass media. 5. Mass media—Religious aspects—Christianity. 6. Christianity and culture—United States. I. Title.
BT703.5.H67   2015
248.8'42—dc23   2015017602

New York University Press books are printed on acid-free paper, and their binding materials are chosen for strength and durability. We strive to use environmentally responsible suppliers and materials to the greatest extent possible in publishing our books.

Manufactured in the United States of America

10 9 8 7 6 5 4 3 2 1

Also available as an ebook

CONTENTS

PREFACE

This is the latest in a series of works offering an ongoing scholarly inquiry into meaning-making among media audiences. As we explain in these pages, prior accounts have looked at families, women, education, and digital cultures. This book emerged as a kind of extension of these earlier efforts. It is also situated in an emerging scholarly discourse devoted to rich and disciplined studies of the interactions between religion and media. A growing network of scholars from the fields of media or communication studies, religious studies, anthropology, cultural geography, history, art history, ethnic studies, postcolonial studies, gender studies, and a range of other disciplines has brought increasing attention to what was once a "repressed" field of inquiry.

Much exciting work awaits the scholars who engage this emerging field, and its breadth necessarily implies that a wide range of theoretical and methodological resources must be brought to bear. We like to think of this volume as a demonstration of how careful qualitative audience analysis has much to contribute to our understandings of contemporary media cultures. The media seem almost to invite large analyses, with the current momentum toward "big data" in digital and media studies only the latest iteration of a sensibility that too easily and too facilely looks beyond the trees to a large and undifferentiated forest. The kind of work here, which looks in depth at the ways individuals negotiate meanings in an age dominated (at least discursively) by media practice, is an essential element in a thorough analysis of how people live their lives today. These are "small data," but they are rich data, and they provide insights that would be impossible to glean any other way, and they serve to problematize and enrich much of what we think we know by looking at larger and more quantitatively derived frames of reference.

This book thus addresses a lacuna in the way we think about media, but it also addresses a number of lacunae in the ways we think about religion and about gender. There have been gaps in research on media and gender and men and religion, and this book is an initial step toward filling them. But the scholarly and conceptual issues here are complex ones, and we realized early on that there is great potential for being misunderstood. We are not gender essentialists, nor do we look at religion through a confessional framework. We do think of the media sphere as essential and inevitable and believe that both religion and "gender trouble" will be with us for a long time to come. Thus it does no good to continue to overlook their interactions.

Our purpose in this book, first and foremost, is scholarly. We intend this to be a serious inquiry into these issues, employing academic rigor to bring new insights to what are important and fraught public and private issues. We would never claim that our work here is neutral or unbiased. No scholarship is or can be. We do claim some perspectives that we believe enrich our analysis. As feminists, we look at things through the lens of the historical struggles for women's rights and see this work as furthering understanding of those struggles. We are convinced that the academy has traditionally undervalued religion as a field of scholarship and that one of our own fields—critical cultural audience studies—has historically had a special blind spot when it comes to "the religious." We hope to be read as attempting to address these issues by demonstrating a certain way through them.

This book will, of course, be read from a variety of perspectives. We look forward to what we hope will be a lively dialogue with readers. We intend to engage this dialogue not to defend a particular position but to collaborate with broader communities of discourse in building knowledge about the important questions herein. That is what scholarship is for, and in our view there can be no higher purpose.

ACKNOWLEDGMENTS

This book would not have been possible without the efforts of many people who participated in the creation, conception, and execution of the research on which it is based. As part of a series of studies of media audiences conducted at the University of Colorado's Center for Media, Religion, and Culture, it was supported by a grant from the Lilly Endowment, and we thank Drs. Craig Dykstra and Chris Coble of Lilly for their interest in and commitment to this research and Professor Lynn Schofield Clark of the University of Denver, who was co-investigator, with Stewart Hoover, of the overall research. At the University of Colorado, we thank Professor Paul Voakes (who was dean at the time) and the staff of the School of Journalism and Mass Communication (now superseded by a new College of Media, Communication, and Information), especially Center for Media, Religion, and Culture Administrative Assistants Doña Olivier and Kimberly Donovan.

Audience research in the Center is conducted by its faculty and student associate researchers who participate both as interviewers and as contributors to the Center's ongoing research seminar, wherein field research is analyzed and interpreted. We acknowledge Dr. Monica Emerich, Dr. Kimberly Everheart Casteline, Dr. Rachael Liberman, Dr. Robert Peaslee, Dr. Benjamin Thevenin, Colin Lingle, Rianne Subijanto, Doug Crigler, Theo Zijderveld, and Caley Cook, all of whom conducted interviews. In addition, we thank Center Associate Director Professor Nabil Echchaibi, visiting scholar Professor Jeffrey Mahan, and Dr. Kyle Kontour and graduate students Rolando Perez, Annemarie Galeucia, and Magdalena Ayala for their insights during the research analysis meetings. At NYU Press, we thank our editor, Jennifer Hammer, for her abiding interest in the project, and we are also grateful for the advice and feedback we've received from countless colleagues at academic and other presentations, and the input of anonymous reviewers at NYU Press and the *Journal of Communication*. We also thank our respondents who participated in this project, and we offer a special thanks to one of the respondents who read early iterations of this book and offered valuable feedback.

Finally, it is almost ironic to note here that a project such as this one cannot succeed without the support of the domestic sphere. In our cases we wish to thank our spouses, Karen Hoover and Heather Coats, for sticking with us through what became a very long process.

Stewart M. Hoover
Arapaho Ranch, Colorado

Curtis D. Coats
Jackson, Mississippi

Introduction

Media, Religion, and "the Crisis of Masculinity"

"The new American man doesn't look like his father," noted National Public Radio's *All Things Considered* while introducing a special series, "Men in America."[1] The program's producers presented a wide-ranging overview of men, masculinity, and fatherhood that showed how questions of masculine identity remain unsettled today. The breadth of covered topics illustrated the scope of contemporary concerns about masculinity—single fatherhood, the sources of masculine identity, gender relations in the domestic sphere, work and career, the essences of "manhood," and racial and ethnic differences. Equally interesting were the ideas expressed on the program's comment boards, where a diverse, lively discourse raged as comment posters searched for central points of conversation in a fluid field of ideas, claims, and experiences.[2]

This book enters this unsettled landscape with an account of how American Protestant Christianity and media influence white, middle-class, heterosexual men's ideas about masculinity and their roles in their families and in public life. Religion is thought by some to exert a positive influence on men and masculinity, encouraging positive roles in family life and even in broader civic spheres. Media, on the other hand, are thought by many to be a negative influence. This book, based on extensive interviews, focus group studies, and participant observations with both Evangelical and non-Evangelical Protestant men, concludes that the picture is not so simple. There is more to both the challenges and potential solutions to the puzzle of masculinity than simple inputs from either religion or the media. The puzzle of American masculinity is complex and has been made more complex by social and political events that have, in recent years, been increasingly interpreted and understood through lenses of gender.

Such events have included recent acts of horrific violence at Sandy Hook Elementary School and in Isla Vista, California. Each of these events was interpreted in gendered ways, and each connected to the comparatively mundane realm of politics where increasingly gendered—and specifically male-gendered—accounts of purpose, value, and effect seem to have achieved a new focus in recent years. This gender trouble, to borrow from Judith Butler, was particularly obvious in the 2012 presidential election. What had been expected to be a close and indeterminate race instead delivered an outcome that was seen by many as predictive of even more social change to come. It was seen as the confirmation of a decades-long shift in the political culture of the United States, away from one defined by a dominant cultural establishment and toward a multicultural future. Women and people of color were the decisive factors in many of the battleground states and were seen by most observers as representing an emerging core of American politics.

In the political discourse surrounding the election, the theme of masculinity emerged with a surprising force and intensity around the implications of its outcome for the prospects and interests of *white men*. The white male voter had been predicted to be at the core of the Republican coalition, with some pundits assuming that the intensity of this group would carry through into a winning turnout for the Republican ticket.[3] Others were not so sure, and in the end, the intensity seemed to be on the other side. The fact that political strategies in the election had so clearly identified these men as a target group can, in part, explain how central they became in the postmortems. But regardless of their significance to the politics of the moment, the discussion of men, their interests, and their prospects clearly pointed to a much broader and deeper discourse about them and their roles. They are, of course, a marker for the sociocultural establishment. American conversations about gender and power over the past thirty years have assumed the centrality of men in dominant white culture. Thus, when that culture begins to lose influence, we can assume that men are centrally implicated in that loss.

But the discussions of men, politics, race, and culture in the months following the election also seemed to take for granted a discourse with some specific themes: themes of shifting relations of power concerning gender, themes of a decline in men's prerogatives and influence, themes of a continuing crisis that some men feel in relation to their roles and positions in society. These themes can be seen in a sampling of the headlines that circulated in the wake of the election. "What are white guys afraid of?" asked Catherine Poe in the conservative *Washington Times*.[4] "What is that creaking noise you hear? It is the sound of conservative white men trying to fight off change—and failing," observed Rich Benjamin on *Salon.com*.[5] Probably the most widely noted and commented-on of the post-election ruminations were those of the conservative male voices Rush Limbaugh, Glenn Beck, and Bill O'Reilly. For them, it was a time of lamentation, not just over the outcome of this one contest but also over what it represented to them: another stage in the ongoing decline of the influence of men, and of white men in particular, in American society.

Derek Thompson, writing in *The Atlantic* online, noted: "White men are now a clear minority of the electorate. Old Christian white men—the bread and butter of the GOP—hardly comprise [*sic*] one-third of voters."[6] Much of this discourse pointed to the centrality of white men to the shifting demographics of the American electorate. This shift, of course, has two dimensions. As Thompson and other critics were quick to point out, and most conservative voices acknowledged, there was the simple reality of where the votes were. But there is a second, more subtle, and in many ways just as significant dimension of the cultural image of white-maleness and its prospects in a changing culture. Nationally, more than a quarter of the white men who voted (and majorities of white men in some states and in many localities) voted for President Obama in 2012. But theirs was not the story that the culture wished to tell itself. Instead, it was a story of declining influence and the declining prospects of white men as a central force in defining the culture.

This discourse about race and about masculinity needs to be seen as layered over a number of prior public iterations of these same issues. Questions of men, men's prospects, and men's prerogatives have emerged in other ways and other places in American politics in recent times. Both the George W. Bush and Obama administrations focused on the so-called masculinity crisis facing society's men and fathers, pursuing this emphasis through programs directed at men, fathers, and boys. In fact, the idea that contemporary American men find themselves in a crisis has a long history, finding expression in initiatives and movements stretching back to at least the nineteenth century in the United States.[7]

Other themes emerge in the contemporary discourse of a "masculinity crisis." One is the particular challenge this "crisis" poses for boys and their social and moral development. In a rather traditionalist turn, many voices suggest that boys are especially affected by the crisis of masculinity and that a range of social problems are at least made more severe to the extent that fathers are absent.[8] Others claim that one of the outcomes that need to be addressed is the impact this situation has on broader society. It is thought by some that men have a special role to play in the area of work and vocation and particularly in conveying values of work and vocation to the next generation.[9] Still others extend a prescription to the broader context of civil society, civic engagement, and democratic practice, claiming that these are particular spheres of activity that men have vacated and should re-inhabit.[10] And yet other voices connect the problem of masculinity—and its solution—with what they see to be the traditional institutions and folkways of the culture. Religion, for example, is thought by some to offer particular value and potential solutions.[11] Others point to deeper, more essentialist dimensions of the culture as resources, suggesting, for example, that men and boys today suffer because the "rites of passage" that once defined manhood are no longer practiced.[12]

Media loom large in these contemporary discussions about the crisis of masculinity. Those sources that lament the loss of traditional institutions, the decline of religion, and the absence of rites of passage often point to a media sphere that is complicit in the contemporary crisis of masculinity and, indeed, a perceived decline of men. On the one hand, media, according to these views, convey only the most negative and trivial stereotypes of men and fathers, while at the same time encouraging the overall culture's orientation toward women, women's rights, and women's prospects. On the other hand, media are seen as a distraction from the real work of helping men find their true place in the culture. Media lure men with escape and distraction, drawing them away from the kinds of disciplined action that are their essential role in the culture. At least, that is the critique.[13]

This conversation draws together important and compelling contemporary themes. Gender continues to be a central concern of modern life, as changes in the workplace continue to reorganize gender relations in private and public spheres. Religion persists as an important dimension of American cultural geography, but its expression in public and private life remains controversial. Further, the language of "crisis" brings issues that were once private into the public realm of policy and professional action. The overall issue of whether and how the world "outside" invades the private sphere of domestic life is therefore centered. Finally, across the culture there has been a growing concern with civic engagement, citizenship, and vocation. The larger conversation has been centered on Robert Putnam's ideas about social capital articulated in *Bowling Alone*.[14] The "crisis" discourse asks what specific role men should play in reinvigorating social spaces and reanimating social capital.

Looking into this "crisis of masculinity" occurred to us as a natural extension of our research on media and meaning-making in the contexts of home and family. Our work has centered on households and the ways they use the various available communication channels to make meanings about themselves, their lives, and their world. We've been especially interested in questions of religion and spirituality in these relations, looking at how traditional and formal religious involvements relate to media and at how people make innovative religious and spiritual sense out of entertainment media that may or may not have a religious or spiritual intention. This book extends this work in two ways. First, it focuses on white, heterosexual Christian men and the ways in which their religious commitments and media consumption intersect with their gender identities. Second, it considers how these men's gender identities intersect with their private lives as husbands and fathers and their public lives as workers and citizens.

Against the traditionalist "crisis of masculinity" discourse, the findings here contest the idea that religion yields more stable masculine identities that will, by extension, yield a more stable and "good" society. Christianity is central to the identities and life experiences of the men in this study, but it does not simply instill positive gender identity or encourage public involvement. Further, media are as central as religion in the narratives of these devoted Christian men. This centrality of media does not create the toxic masculinity feared by conservative critics. Rather, media often reinforce Christian masculinity in ways that religion does not seem to. The men in this book do not engage media, Christianity, or the general "crisis of masculinity" discourse in the ways suggested by conservative critics. Instead, theirs is a complex interaction within public, mediated, and private spheres that cannot be reduced to a simple prescription for a "good" society.

At first glance, this argument might seem to resonate with the critiques offered by champions of the "crisis of masculinity" discourse. Christianity has lost its authority in directing "godly" men, and media have taken up the slack, with dire cultural consequences, so that argument goes. However, while there are similar threads here, our argument moves in a different direction. Religion has lost some of its authority and media have taken up the slack, yet the overwhelming majority of men in this study still cling to an essentialist patriarchy, albeit one that looks different from that of their fathers. Media and religion play important, if ambivalent and sometimes contradictory, roles in the persistence of this essentialist patriarchy, and both media and religion are involved in the turn inward toward what we call the "domestic ideal," and away from traditional ideas of public engagement.

Two of our respondents, Glenn Donegal[15] and Denton Calhoun, help to elucidate further the contours of the "crisis of masculinity" discourse and our argument about it. Both men were surprising in some ways because they defied some tried-and-true expectations about conservative religious men in relation to gender, family, media, and public life. A convert from Catholicism to Evangelical Protestantism, Glenn was clearly negotiating an identity amid a range of often contradictory structural forces. Glenn's wife was the primary breadwinner in their household, a fact that challenged his received ideas about the natural way of life in the home. He believed deeply in a traditional view of gender relations, and he clearly struggled with changes in those realms, though he and his wife had mostly settled the issues concerning her career and their own relationship. Glenn was a recovering alcoholic who attributed his recovery to his religious conversion. His struggles with addiction led him to talk about personal responsibility and morality, and he clearly looked to religion and religious organizations (e.g., the Evangelically based Promise Keepers and Focus on the Family) for support for his ideas about manhood. He strove to integrate into his own relationship with his wife and children religiously inflected ideas from these organizations about male "headship" in the home, a project that seemed to be more an aspiration than an accomplishment. Ironically, Glenn was surprisingly universalistic in his own religious quest, claiming to have received insights from Eastern religions along with those from his deeply felt Christianity. Glenn was remarkably judgmental about issues of personal and public morality, and he had high and puritanical standards for what qualified as responsible social life. He felt deeply that responsible manhood involved civic engagement, where men are, through their character, responsible for the stability of the social world. He was particularly critical and judgmental about media and popular culture, seeming to feel that they were both a waste of time and a negative moral influence. At the same time, Glenn talked with some passion about men needing to rethink their traditional role expectations and values, suggesting that most men would benefit from rediscovering their "feminine" sides.

As we reflected on Glenn's story, we came to see how extensively media were integrated into his values and his consciousness. Not only were many of the resources important to his life mediated (Focus on the Family broadcasts, tapes, and publications; the LeHaye/Jenkins *Left Behind* books and films; Promise Keepers publications and events, etc.), but also some of his most important icons and models of masculinity were also mediated (the western-movie actor John Wayne, for example). At the same time, he clearly saw "the secular media" as representing an important challenge to his deeply held values about character, self-reliance, and responsibility. The media sphere thus played an important role in structuring his world, but largely in a negative way, he thought. It was significant, then, that Glenn also saw one media example as positively meaningful to him and his sense of himself as a father and community citizen. Glenn identified with the 1960s-era comedy-drama *The Andy Griffith Show* as a powerful expression of manhood and father-hood.[16] Glenn's view of *The Andy Griffith Show* was clearly demarcated by his own experience as a father and by broader themes of a culture struggling to contend with the aspirations of the women's movement. What made Andy such a good model to Glenn was the very fact that Andy was a single father. Thus, he was a father who inhabited both the imputed "male" and "female" characteristics that Glenn saw as necessary to effective masculinity on the one hand, but, on the other hand, this complementarity was modulated by Glenn's desire not to deny the importance of women and their essential contribution to social life. Glenn's hope for the recovery of a sense of male prerogative (called "headship" by many contemporary conservative Christian voices) thus found a kind of satisfying expression in a father who could be both a mother and a father to his son.

Glenn was struggling to negotiate a sense of himself against a backdrop of received cultural values of manhood and masculinity. That backdrop was one partly defined by religion and partly by the broader culture. It was also one that was structured by a mediated public sphere that provided him with both problematic and unproblematic resources. Glenn was clearly involved in what Anthony Giddens[17] might call a "reflexive project of the self" wherein he was working to construct narratives that incorporated the received backdrop with emerging realities and claims. He found some of these claims compelling, like egalitarian gender relations in the home, in spite of his more traditionalist impulses. Glenn, then, represented a negotiation having to do with issues of importance to the "crisis of masculinity" discourse, and he also showed how complex this situation is. His interview also suggested to us that our emerging sense of media households as places of meaning-making needed to focus on men and masculinity as a next step.

Partly because of what we learned from Glenn Donegal, the emergent public discourse concerning the crisis of masculinity took on some additional depth and resonance for us. At about the same time we'd talked with Glenn, there was a round of publicity from the Bush administration announcing a new initiative to be headed by First Lady Laura Bush intended to address the needs of boys in relation to this "crisis."[18] The latest layers of this discourse in public discussions having to do with masculine prerogative, military service, and gun violence have provided new definition to this discourse, but the basic themes remain the same.

We have described some of its claims already, but we can think of this discourse about a crisis of masculinity as arising from, and pointing to, an emergent generic argument about contemporary men. It links people like Glenn Donegal to media figures like former *Fox News* host Glenn Beck in a set of claims and conditions surrounding men as they negotiate their identities today. Ironically, this argument also links people across the political spectrum like Beck, Bill O'Reilly, and Mitt Romney to Barack Obama and the Nation of Islam's longtime leader, Louis Farrakhan. The outlines of this argument can be seen in Glenn Donegal's narrative of self. Through his eyes we can see men today contending with a situation in which their traditional roles and prerogatives have been thrown into question by a combination of forces in the labor markets, in the cultural success of the women's movement, and in the political success of multiculturalism. They might see current trends as significant losses in areas of domestic life and family where fathers should have an important role to play in their children's lives. But there are broader losses as well. In this view, men have traditionally had a responsibility in civil society, contributing efforts to citizenship, career, and vocation. These men also contend with a broader cultural context that provides mediated sources that are both positive and helpful, even though media generally are seen as largely negative.

This generic argument is not universal, of course, but it has found some important and influential proponents. There is also a growing network of scholars, public intellectuals, and advocacy organizations that has taken up this cause. At the center of this discourse in the Bush administration was Dr. Don Eberly, who has provided a spirited and coherent argument about the problem of masculinity, its relationship to fatherhood and the needs of civil society, and its sources in religion and the media. Eberly has much in common in this view with Dr. James Dobson, the founder of Focus on the Family, who through his long career has also articulated an extensive theory of normative masculinity and fatherhood.[19]

Eberly held several positions in the Bush administration and more recently in two organizations, the Civil Society Project and the National Fatherhood Initiative. He is a leading voice on civil society in conservative circles and identifies with what has come to be known as a "neo-traditionalist" view of masculinity, fatherhood, and family sociology.

Central to this conservative view of civil society is the role of "virtue" and a focus on morality. In the words of Gertrude Himmelfarb, a revered voice to this movement, "When we speak of the restoration of civil society, it is a moral restoration we should seek."[20] For Eberly and other neo-traditionalists, men are particularly implicated in the maintenance of moral culture and therefore must be at the center of this moral restoration. In this view the problem lies in the rise of the "Republic of the Autonomous Self, where the individual is the only real sovereign, where 'mediating' structures have been leveled, and where rules proliferate, yet lack legitimacy." Eberly points to a "good society" based in revitalized civic consciousness and voluntary associations.[21]

Eberly, Dobson, and other neo-traditionalist social critics identify the *family* as the place where civic vocation is formed, though the family cannot go it alone—or so the thinking goes. Voluntary associations, what Eberly calls "the seedbeds of citizenship," work with the family, but the family is the primary unit of value in civil society.[22] This line of reasoning connecting the family with the larger project of civil society and civic vocation has deep roots. Eberly and others cite Edmund Burke's idea of families as "little platoons" and Tocqueville's notion that families are the "first link" in a chain leading to civic engagement. But they see a growing problem for families in fulfilling their role in civic engagement and civil society. Eberly argues that the role of the family as a moral center has suffered from the withdrawal of the normative role of "parents, priests, and pedagogues."[23] The key parent in these regards, he contends, is the *father*. What he calls "father absence" is at the root of the withdrawal of families from their central moral role in crafting the good society.[24]

This neo-traditionalist argument contends that men and fathers have much to gain from religion as they rise to their responsibilities in relation to civic engagement. Their role should address social problems emerging in the next generation, including alienation and declining respect for authority.[25] One can find concerns about feminism lurking behind much of this critique. Lamenting the rise of identity politics and decrying the emergent social idea that "the personal is political," Eberly and others see men as lacking the social capital that should be available to them in community and culture, such as through voluntary associations, and they decry the eclipsing of traditional standpoints and cultural anchors, which has left men without positive models.

> A society of too few mature fathers ends up with what Dr. Frank Pittman calls "toxic masculinity," where essentially weak, insecure, and poorly fathered men chase after a socially destructive masculine mystique. Men who have not fully felt the love and approval of their fathers are men who live in masculine shame. Says Pittman, "[M]en without models don't know what is behind their shame, loneliness, and despair, their desperate search for love, for affirmation and for structure, their frantic tendency to compete over just about anything with just about anybody."[26]

Eberly links his analysis to the broader discourse about "social capital"[27] and argues that religion is one of the most important voluntary associations that should be supporting progress toward the good society: "A national consensus is beginning to emerge on certain key public concerns such as family disintegration and out-of-wedlock childbearing. Moreover, notwithstanding the reservations of some, religion is likely to have a stronger voice in the public square, both as a legitimate well-spring of personal values and as perhaps the richest source of renewed social capital in communities."[28]

But there is an even more fundamental role for religion in this project. Religion should support fundamental truths about male identity, according to this view. As Eberly puts it, referring to an imagined past where male identities were rooted in "God-centered masculinity," "Here, we find the man as he was meant to be, mirroring the true character of God. Here we find the paternal male who generates, not destroys life—the benevolent provider and defender, not the aggressor or predator. Here we discover the man who finds his strength and purpose as a father and friend, a protector and provider, and mentor and a moral example. . . ."[29]

As religion plays a positive role in this outlook, the media play a negative role. Eberly speaks for many, and not just on the right end of the political spectrum, in his view of the relationship of media and popular culture to identity, masculinity, and civic engagement.

Many of the most corrupting viruses are now being borne along not by sinister politicians but by an entertainment and information media culture whose omnipresence is displacing the core social institutions that once shaped and molded the democratic citizen. Whereas parents, priests, and pedagogues once presided over the socialization of the young, now television, film, music, cyberspace and the celebrity culture of sports and entertainment dominate this process of shaping youthful attitudes and beliefs. It is popular mass culture that largely informs our most basic understanding of society, our public life, our obligations to each other, and even the nature of the American experiment.[30]

In remarks on the issue of fatherhood, President Obama has also routinely included critiques of media: "Don't just sit in the house and watch 'Sports Center' all weekend long. That's why so many children are growing up in front of the television. As fathers and parents, we've got to spend more time with them, and help them with their homework, and replace the video game or the remote control with a book once in a while . . . ."[31] "It's up to us to say to our daughters, don't ever let images on TV tell you what you are worth, because I expect you to dream without limit and reach for those goals. It's up to us to tell our sons, those songs on the radio may glorify violence, but in my house we give glory to achievement, self-respect and hard work. It's up to us to set these high expectations. And that means meeting those expectations ourselves. That means setting examples of excellence in our own lives."[32]

This larger societal discourse about the crisis of masculinity has assumed greater focus in both scholarly and lay settings.[33] These observers, both scholarly and popular, have suggested that men today suffer from the effects of what Joseph Pleck has called "sex role strain."[34] While there are different versions of this argument, the central idea is that as a result of the social evolution of gender roles over the past several decades, men have been left without definitive ideas about roles and identities and without helpful models for what should now be normative masculinity.[35] As one journalist put it, "[S]ociety used to assign certain characteristics to men, including power, aggressiveness, professional success and autonomy." Today, shifts in gender roles have put such expectations into question. "This has left some young men wondering what it means these days to be a guy."[36]

The normative discourse of masculinity and fatherhood articulated by Glenn Donegal and then by Don Eberly, James Dobson, President Obama, Glenn Beck, and others answers the question of this "crisis" by suggesting that what is missing and what is needed is a new concentration on masculinity and fatherhood as a *moral* project, and that its object is to create (or they would argue "re-create") a place for men at the center of social life. Men's centrality is both natural and essential, and their role is to provide models and resources to their children and to succeeding generations through leadership in vocation, in civil society, and in civic engagement. As this thinking goes, men have a natural place, and their roles have been displaced.

Religion is seen to have a positive role to play in addressing this situation. For many, religion is a center of social and moral values that provides moral support to men as they rise to their obligations. Others articulate a more complex role for religion, which they feel should play a more important role in civil society and at the same time should provide a theological justification for a renewal of masculinity. Additionally, all seem to agree that the role of the media in these regards is unquestionably a negative one. It can be blamed for distracting men from their role by absorbing their time and attention; being the source of influences and attractions of sensation, sexuality, and irresponsible living; providing negative, even antisocial models and images of masculinity, and replacing the normative influence of fathers by dominating the time, attention, and values of children.

There are, of course, other social contexts of discourse about masculinity both in relation to religion and in relation to media. A growing popular and scholarly literature focuses on men's spiritualities and men's religious sensibilities. John Eldredge's bestseller *Wild at Heart*[37] is typical of the popular genre, laying out an argument for the recovery of the essentials of masculinity within a framework of faith (but not necessarily religious institutions). In *Numen, Old Men*, Joseph Gelfer[38] details a growing scholarly record looking at men, religion, and spirituality. In it, he describes a wide range of perspectives, from those stressing an elemental masculinity to those which hold that gender is constructed through cultural and social influence. Both the popular and scholarly literatures raise important questions about the easy assumption that religion should be thought of as playing a positive, determinative (and singular) role in masculinity.

Eldredge and other popularizers, for example, talk matter-of-factly about the perceived failure of religion to address the concerns and interests of men. Likewise, Gelfer and others[39] identify much in the research and other scholarly literatures that raises a question about how the whole issue of religion is to be thought about. At the same time, many of these sources raise questions about the notion that media play a necessarily negative role. Neither the popular nor the scholarly literature, it seems, can get very far in describing the nature of contemporary masculinity without referring to media. Television and film seem to provide powerful and probative models and symbols for the way men think about their lives, just as John Wayne and Andy Griffith did for Glenn Donegal.

These claims of a crisis of masculinity suggested by Eberly and others (with all of the implications for public and private life) suggested to us that it was time for a careful inquiry about masculinities, so we began talking about them with white, married, heterosexual couples and individual men. We wanted to find out where and how these men get their ideas about masculine roles and identities. We wanted to ask them about their perceptions of responsibilities as fathers and as influences and models in their families and their communities. We wanted to find out how they thought about questions of career and vocation in relation to their ideas of manhood and civic responsibility. We also wanted to look directly at the questions of religion and the media. In terms of real, lived lives and everyday experience, how do media and religion serve the needs of men as they think through who they should be in their families and beyond?

In this process, we met Denton Calhoun, an exemplar Evangelical respondent whom we discuss here to introduce themes we will develop in the coming pages. Denton was twenty-eight and lived with his wife, Nancy, and their four-year-old son in a middle-class home in a small town in the American South. Denton and Nancy were raised in conservative Christian households, and they had gravitated toward churches that were theologically conservative. They held social attitudes and beliefs about gender roles and relations that were traditional, though not without some negotiation. Denton expressed a traditionalist, patriarchal, and essentialist view of gender relations in marriage but tacked toward a softer expression of his patriarchy than he thought others did. He said, "I would even say that if you push the traditional thought too far, you could do it in a way where you would be crossing the line in my mind as far as putting women down [is concerned]. I would hopefully not go that far. . . . There are definitely some people who push it so far, you know, the woman being submissive to the man. . . . I would just look at it as different roles with equal importance."

While Denton believed that this expression of "headship" had Biblical roots, he had an ambiguous view of his religion, which is a theme we will explore in chapter 1. He and Nancy were by all accounts devout and active in their nondenominational Evangelical congregation and clearly identified "Christ-centered" faith as important to them. At the same time, many of the trappings of formal religion, even formal Evangelicalism, bothered him. He was suspicious of subcultural "buzzwords," for example "born-again" or "Evangelical"; Evangelical media texts, for example *Left Behind* and *The Purpose Driven Life*; and self-appointed

Evangelical authorities, for example Pat Robertson. Christianity, to the Calhouns, was radically simple and personal and could not be judged by its popularity in this world. Given his general suspicion of organized religion and of religious authority, it might not be surprising to learn that Denton had found little in church that helped him decipher what it meant to be a man and a father. What was there seemed not to move him very much, morally or spiritually. When asked what his church specifically teaches about being a man, he responded, "Um, again, I'm trying to think of it exactly, I mean real specific teachings? I don't know." Denton was aware of the general discourse about Christian headship, aware of key texts and para-church organizations devoted to masculinity, for example *Wild at Heart* and Promise Keepers, yet he was both suspicious of and uncertain about what religious authorities had to offer him generally and about developing as a man.

As he reflected on the role of his faith community on his self-understandings of masculinity, the media began to appear as a source of influence. Like many of his Evangelical and non-Evangelical peers, Denton had an ambiguous relationship with media. At the same time that he articulated the vibrant critique of popular media we have come to expect from religious conservatives, he did watch a good deal of television and was a loyal viewer of the situation comedy *Friends* (long in reruns) and a number of other popular programs, many of which contained what he considered negative moral messages. Denton also readily recalled shows, characters, and themes in secular, mainstream media (especially films and television shows) that expressed what he considered positive characteristics of masculinity. He mentioned a Biblical character only once—Jesus—and this was in reference to the film *The Passion of the Christ*. Further, his discussion of Jesus was not in reference to characteristics of masculinity. For these references, Denton drew on Jack from *Lost* and others like him, similar to the way Glenn drew on John Wayne and Andy Griffith. We consider these ambiguities around media more closely in our analysis in chapter 2.

While Denton was ambivalent about the roles of media and Christianity in his self-understanding of masculinity, he was certain that his primary roles were to be a godly husband and father. Everything else he did—work, career, church, citizenship—served these primary roles, creating a carefully constructed "domestic ideal" that we will explore in chapter 3 and its implications for public life in the Conclusion. Denton was ambitious in his career, but he wasn't "called" to it, he said. His calling was to provide for his family, to be a godly father and husband. Further, he did see his work as a sort of "mission field," but not one ripe for proselytizing and not one that should interfere with his central duties to provide for and protect the domestic sphere. Work was purposeful, but largely insofar as it helped him provide and protect his family.

When asked to reflect further on whether a religiously inflected notion of vocation or calling would be relevant to him, Denton demurred. His ideas of work and vocation were less high-minded, save those that might have been in pastoral or mission work, and again revolved around work's relation to home:

> DENTON: I think they would definitely say that everybody has a calling, and some people's calling would be in something like missions and other people's calling would be for the factory line or whatever.... [For] me specifically, I guess I wonder to some degree what that is, but . . . I don't spend a lot of time worrying about that. I think God has me where he wants me, and when it's time to go somewhere else, we'll go there. I do get irritated when people sit around, sit around, sit around, asking, "What's my calling?" Well, if you just do something, there's your calling. . . . .At this stage in my life, I certainly see a large part of my calling as being a father and a husband. Ultimately that's much more important than a calling to work at an ad agency.

For Denton, Christianity (both his local community and the broader Evangelical sphere), media, and even his father provided complex and contradictory models for his self-understanding of masculinity. He was committed to his Christian faith and faith community, but he was suspicious of many aspects of it and ambivalent about what this faith offered him as a father and husband. He was critical of the media, yet he readily found media symbols that resonated with his sense of masculine self and media texts from which he derived much pleasure (even while recognizing their negative characteristics). Even his father, a man Denton loved and sought to emulate in some ways, could not escape Denton's ambivalence, for example in commitment to work and provision for family, yet whom Denton also criticized as being too detached, working too much, and being emotionally or spiritually disconnected from his family.

In many ways, Denton's narrative echoes the neo-traditionalist masculinity proposed by Eberly and others—a commitment to church and family and criticism of the media. But Denton's narrative was also much more complicated. He had profound ambivalence about institutional religion, a complex relationship with media, and a commitment to family that superseded concern for "the public." Denton's—and Glenn's—relationship to the broader neo-traditionalist discourse was, thus, more complicated than we might have expected.

To what extent is what we've learned from Denton and Glenn typical of other men in other physical, religious, and cultural locations? We undertook to find out through a series of interviews, observations, and group discussions around the United States with white, heterosexual Protestant men.[40] These conversations gave us additional insights into the sources of male identity in contemporary life, the influences of various authorities on these questions, the ways that men are negotiating gender relations in daily life, and the ways they think about career, vocation, and civic engagement. We have also learned about the ways in which contemporary religious and media cultures frame, condition, and contribute to these negotiations.

These conversations took place in a narrow range of households. Nearly all of our informants were from two-parent heterosexual households. All but one of the respondents discussed here were white. All identified as Christian, and nearly all were of the middle class. This selection was intentional. These interviews reveal the households implied by the political discourse on male gender that followed the 2012 election. To an extent, our purpose in carrying out these inquiries was to test an implicit syllogism in much of the public commentary (particularly from a neo-conservative perspective). Much of this prescriptive language has assumed that masculinity is best expressed in fatherhood, and in fatherhood as contributing to "stable" domestic life for children. A range of critical literature on gender and family rightly points out that definitions of what is stable in family relations deserves careful and critical reflection.[41] At the same time, the received prescription often outlines a role for religion for men, fatherhood, and family life. Again, these notions have been subject to critical scholarly and public scrutiny. In looking at white, heteronormative and Christian households we by no means argue for the normativity of either. Our project is quite different. We see this inquiry as a kind of "critical test" of received ideas and values. If public voices such as Don Eberly's and James Dobson's are right, then their normative view of masculinity should be most settled for two-parent, heterosexual, Christian, middle-class, white households. Evidence that things are *not* settled in the ways assumed is then significant. And as should be obvious from our conversations with Denton Calhoun and Glenn Donegal, there is much evidence that the received view deserves some careful rethinking.

"The Masculine" in These Pages

In our conversations with the men and women in this book, there is much talk about the relationship among ideas of gender and a range of contexts. We talk about how family, church, faith, spirituality, friendship networks, the media, and the broader culture relate to their ideas of what it means to be a man. In this way our work is very much consistent with a great deal of other work focused on these questions. We know a great deal about the relationship of broader contexts to ideas of what it means to be a woman or a man in contemporary life.

In the midst of these conversations, though, we found ourselves looking at the central question of what our informants *say* masculinity is. There is a lot of talk about threats to male prerogative, challenges to traditional ideas of manhood and masculinity, and aspirations to positive or normative values of the masculine. But at its core, what is this thing "masculinity"? We know that normative ideas of the masculine have been in flux and in negotiation for at least five decades. Feminism has had the profound effect of identifying ways that women must think of themselves as people with unique needs, goals, and challenges. As a variety of writers on masculinity have noted, this feminist critique has often found its distinctiveness in contrast to "the male" or "the masculine."[42] And as many of those same writers have noted, this vision of the masculine as a contrast has not provided men or those interested in masculinity in and of itself a substantive or extensive description. So it is with much of the discourse in our interviews. Men, women, and couples here have found it easier to describe men in relation to women than to identify precisely what it is to be "a man."

But a picture does emerge, one that we call "elemental masculinity." We describe what we mean by this term because there is much potential for it to be misunderstood. First and foremost, we stress that our use of the term is empirical, not normative. The idea of elemental masculinity emerges from our data. Across the board among our interviewees, from conservative to progressive, the men with whom we spoke expressed a remarkable consensus that three basic things define masculinity. In a way, they clearly saw these as the residual essence of men's roles and identities when the elements of maleness that might be socially problematic (aggressiveness, nonrelational attitudes to family and personal relationships, etc.) are discarded. What was left for the men in these pages can be described as "provision," "protection," and "purpose." It is obvious that the notion of "elementalism" evokes longstanding debates in gender theory over "essentialism." There is a sense in which our informants thought of these ideas as essential, as natural. They did not search for a first cause for these dimensions of manhood. These dimensions were, for them, a given. It is important to note that we've found these ideas even among men who've had ample exposure to debates about "nature versus nurture" and who accept that gender roles are constructed and imposed by social and cultural context, men who would describe themselves as feminists as well as men who are traditionalists who wish to be "soft" traditionalists. For all of them, there was still a core of what it means to be a man, and these three ideas are the core. Ideas of provision, protection, and purpose thus function on a normative level of discourse where they may well (and indeed do) find themselves in conflict with the practical realities of modern life, domestic relations, and aspirations for the nurture of children (three large themes of our discussions).

But while our informants treated their elementalism as essentialist, we do not argue that our work is a defense of essentialism. Far from it. We see this work as an elaboration of constructivist views of gender, providing a rich and layered account of how ideas of gender are negotiated in modern life. We are not saying that provision, protection, and purpose are essentially "male." Rather, we are saying we found that nearly universally among our informants, these impulses were seen as definitive across a range of sources and contexts where ideas of maleness and masculinity are brought to bear.

These ideas, even as expressed here, are not exactly a "hard" essentialism as might be described in some more scholarly[43] or more popular work.[44] These men (and women) saw these elementals as the particular gifts or talents that men can uniquely bring to domestic space. They were often careful to make this distinction themselves, and particularly to distance themselves from the notion that these unique male talents should devolve to unique male prerogatives in dominance or power. For them, it was simply that, all things considered, women needed to do some things and men needed to do some other things.

Debates over essentialism in gender studies center on the prospects of women in domestic and work life. Much of the research looks at whether there are essential differences between the sexes that reveal themselves in systematic outcomes in life. The literature here is extensive, and the debates remain spirited. We'd like to describe our work in relation to this literature in order to make what we think is an important distinction between essentialism and our "elementalism."

A series of articles in the *British Journal of Sociology* has focused on the work of Catherine Hakim, a sociologist who has produced a prodigious literature on women and work life articulating a paradigm she calls "preference theory."[45] Hakim describes her work as focusing on preferences in work and career choice, and she has provided some important and comprehensive accounts of the domestic negotiations over women's work prospects, using large (largely European) databases. She has demonstrated that domestic relations in women's work life can be described in three broad categories: women whose preferences are "home centered," women who are "work centered" (each about 20 percent of households), and a large category (60 percent) of "adaptive" households where work–life preferences are much more in a process of constant negotiation.[46] While Hakim distances her work from other paradigms of gender and work, it is nonetheless difficult not to think of her work as falling in the broad context of "rational choice" theory. Indeed, she has been broadly influential among those who wish to focus on the potential for positive gender outcomes of the neo-liberal market.[47]

Hakim's primary interlocutor in the *BJS* debates has been Rosemary Crompton and a series of collaborators.[48] Crompton and her associates wish to shift the focus away from the expression of preference toward questions of structural constraints and determinants. Their argument is that while there is strong empirical evidence for Hakim's suggestion that women choose to focus on the domestic or on career and that women's choices and negotiations are fundamental, Hakim seems to miss that such preferences can themselves be the result of structural factors. Hakim's approach is thus essentialist in that it seems to assume that there is something prior to or outside of structural constraint that determines women's choices to work inside or outside their homes. This argument links as well to questions of agency versus determination in social relations. If one assumes the level of agency proposed in Hakim's preference theory, it necessarily suggests that the explanation for systematic gender differences in choice must have its roots in some version of essentialism. Hakim has mounted a spirited defense of her work seeking to distance herself from hard essentialism.[49] It is nonetheless hard to see her measurement of "preference" without recourse to some fundamental explanation.

For our purposes here an essential distinction between the two perspectives is over what is meant by a "preference." Crompton and others who focus on structural factors as determinative would argue that a "preference" is something more ideological than Hakim seems to accept, a choice that is determined by structural factors. This determination happens through the mechanism of the articulation and circulation of social norms and values that intervene in the construction of preferences and then in choices.[50] For Hakim, "preference" is instead only a *behavior*, a measurable choice to work inside or outside their homes, or negotiate something in between. If structure is to work itself out in preferences and choices, it would do so through its construction of appropriate societal norms and expectations. This notion is where the linkage to our conversations comes in, as we are clearly involved in an elaboration of the circulation of and negotiations with social norms in the lives of our informants. Hakim dismisses attention to social norms: "There is only a weak link between societal norms and personal preferences. (We can agree that it is a good idea for everyone to stop smoking, yet choose to smoke ourselves.) Societal norms are non-causal attitudes; they are part of the social furniture but do not predict individual behaviour. Personal preferences are causal attitudes and strongly shape behaviour. In the absence of major contextual constraints, they can become the primary determinant of behaviour."[51]

This is an essential, even fundamental, distinction. What do we do with discourses that are focused on the level of norms and values? If they do not necessarily predict behavior (and they do not necessarily do so, even for our informants), then what is their role and status? We are collecting "stories we tell ourselves" from these informants, contributing to what have been called informants' "plausible narratives of the self."[52] These narratives constitute a repertoire of self-knowledge and aspiration that underlies much of one's conceptual relationship to other domains, constraints, sources, and outcomes. These narratives can be seen to underlie choices in politics and personal life, connect with senses of the self,[53] and express identity. They are also important to senses of happiness and well-being. In short, any part of the complex of behaviors, interactions, and ideas that circulate around socially situated individuals that is conceptual rather than behavioral clearly plays a role in identity and preferences. That is the point of the discourses we will present here.

We are not measuring choice, or outcome, or happiness or satisfaction per se; we are interpreting the way individuals *talk about* their negotiation of meaningful spaces of interaction in ways that contribute to their senses of themselves, of their options, and of their location in the web of social relations that define their lives. We are not measuring directly what choices are made or what behaviors result from those choices, though we do see evidence of these choices in our interviews. These accounts are performances, though, and we consider them to be part of gender performance in Judith Butler's sense. They are therefore also significant for what they tell us about larger discourses of norms, values, and ideals of gender. If such performances are important to the constitution of gender (and we argue that they are), then these accounts are also significant in that way. Further, they are significant to the political discourses with which we began the discussion. Accounts such as these are deeply linked to the discursive possibilities that define the moral discourse of the contemporary political sphere.

These accounts are important in what they can tell us about their formation in broader social contexts, including the media, which is a major theme of our project here. Our view of elementalism is broadly interactionist, drawing on the work of Goffman, Denzin, and others. We are pursuing the agenda in relation to masculinity, gender, and media suggested by Gauntlett in his account of Butler's significance for media studies: "The call for gender trouble has obvious media implications, since the mass media is [sic] the primary means for alternative images to be disseminated. The media is therefore the site upon which this 'semiotic war' (a war of symbols, of how things are represented) would take place."[54]

Our category of "elemental masculinity" is not focused on demonstrating that the ideas of provision, protection, and purpose are essentialist. These categories are more like ideals, norms, or values in our discussions. They are poles or dimensions against which other claims on time, attention, and belief are measured and tested. They are discursive and narrative, a "gender performance" fitted to the particular demands of these households at this point in time with this set of challenges, constraints, and aspirations orbiting it. They may be, as we've said, a kind of residual of traditionalism, left over when other, more problematic dimensions of masculinity have been discarded in the process of social progress toward egalitarianism.

Of course, they might be "essential" in some way. Something like this was argued in Harvey Mansfield's controversial book *Manliness*.[55] Mansfield, an intellectual historian, set out to recover some sense of what remained of masculinity after the gender revolution of the past fifty years by looking back at the classics. Lamenting the loss of something essential, he claimed that something that looks like our provision, protection, and (particularly) purpose was at the root of the classical sense of the masculine. Does this concordance with Mansfield mean that our informants are also on some level essentialists? It is true that they probably think that if they were to follow Mansfield and look back far enough in sacred texts (classical or theological) they might well find an essence very much like provision, protection, and purpose. That is, however, not our argument. We would see their articulation of these elements, and Mansfield's, as a kind of measure of where we are in the evolution of changed relations in the gendered domestic sphere. These elements are the way that our informants articulated their senses of what it is men should be thinking they are about. Certainly, these senses are rooted in history and perceived essentials. That is, in fact, the point. That the men and women we interview claim as their own these dimensions of elementalism, articulated in the way they do, as central to their senses of who they are tells us much about where we are in the historical process of rethinking gender in modern life. Our work moves beyond essentialism, though, by lodging this discourse of elementalism in the potential sources of meaning—family, religion, the media, and broader social and cultural contexts. Further, we ask whether some of these sources have, in fact, failed.

It should be obvious as well that we take a somewhat skeptical and analytic view of the crisis of masculinity. Even though it appears without quotation marks in our title, we use this term advisedly throughout this book. It is clear that there is a crisis of masculinity to the extent that broad themes in the culture focus on changes in the nature of masculinity and male identity and identify these as broadly unsettled and in flux. That we lack languages and consensual frameworks can be a discursive crisis and thus an identity crisis, and there is evidence of this in these pages. Whether there is a crisis in some absolute sense is another question, and one that, while we do not fully answer it here, we believe we can speak to, and we do—in the final chapter.

1

The New Christian Patriarchs

In the Introduction, we laid out the overall agenda of this book. We will explore longstanding and emerging issues of white masculinity, manhood, fatherhood, and men's roles in society, relating them to resources and influences found in religion and in the media sphere. We have met two men, Glenn Donegal and Denton Calhoun, who expressed ideals and values related to their roles as men, which they saw as rooted in an elementalist, patriarchal masculinity. These roles—provision, protection, and purpose. We also noted that these men implicated religion and media culture in these elemental roles and values. In reflecting on media culture and religion, we observed that the situation is far more complex than is often appreciated.

In this chapter, we consider the role of religion—particularly white American Evangelical Protestantism and "Liberal" or "Ecumenical" Protestantism[1]—in men's lives. We explore the extent to which men's religious beliefs and faith communities provide them with salient resources for masculinity, both at a normative and a practical level. There is strong evidence that Evangelical communities provide a normative discourse, articulated under the general category of "headship," but religion may provide fewer resources for how to *live* or even *talk about* being a man within a broader, more egalitarian cultural discourse about gender. This gap may seem surprising given the patriarchal nature of Evangelical religious spaces and the flourishing religious publishing industry focused on patriarchal manhood. Yet, as we will see, Evangelical men are ambivalent about the role of religion in supporting their senses of masculine selves.

The ambivalence for Ecumenical Protestant men is even more pronounced. A strong majority of these men noted and celebrated the more egalitarian gender commitments of their faith communities yet lamented that these institutional commitments had left them without the normative scaffolding for masculine identity or the spaces within which to develop such an identity. For them, religion had very little to offer at all for "being" men, except to challenge conservative notions of patriarchy. While this situation suggests the gains of feminism in these communities (again, something they generally embraced), these men also expressed a sense of loss that their religious communities simply didn't know what to do with men. This lament was especially strong in the men who held to elementalist notions of masculinity.[2]

At this point, we'd like to expand on these findings and reserve a more summative and detailed account of them (and of other emergent issues) for later in the book. Much of the discussion will focus on Evangelical men, beginning with further exploration of Glenn Donegal and Denton Calhoun. We focus on Evangelicals because these are the men for whom religion is said to play a powerful role in masculine identity. And, in fact, religion does seem to play such a role, but not in clear-cut ways suggested by neo-traditionalist commentators.

First, many conservative masculinist observers anticipate that religion should work to provide important theologically or doctrinally rooted ideas to men and women about how they should live their lives.[3] We expected, then, that both Evangelical and Ecumenical Protestant men would have heard focused discourses of masculinity from the pulpit, at least. As we noted in the Introduction, men like Glenn and Denton had difficulty remembering such direct teaching about masculinity. This deficit is surprising given their commitment to and involvement in their faith communities. It is also surprising given that their beliefs coincided very clearly with widely understood Evangelical beliefs. Both of these men, for example, reflected on the prerogatives and roles men should enjoy in the Christian home. For both of them, these prerogatives and roles were in line with the notion of "headship." But the sources of these ideas were less clear, and the exact application of these ideas was not clear. More important, there didn't seem to be a clear connection between fundamental religious teachings and specific attitudes and behaviors that necessarily followed. Both could paraphrase the standard Biblical "proof text" on headship in Ephesians 5, but neither could point to sermons about it or even remember reading it recently. Thus, for both Glenn and Denton, what Don Eberly called "God-centered masculinity" is not drawn directly from religious *teaching* so much as it is seen and practiced through a set of behaviors and relations defined in the contexts of their domestic lives. Observing that masculinity is grounded there does not deny that religious authority or power is in play. In fact, following Bourdieu's ideas about doxa,[4] it may point to an even more powerful religious field precisely *because* this "natural" gender order "goes without saying and therefore goes unquestioned."[5] It is thus notable that church leadership seems to be giving little rhetorical or theological effort.[6] The mythology of headship is still so pervasive in Evangelical circles that talking about male authority is deemed largely unnecessary, but it is clear that some of these men long for this type of discussion from the pulpit, which suggests that, for these men, the presumed natural gender order no longer "goes without saying." The lack of such discussions plays a role in the critiques of religion levied by men against their faith communities. In sum, while headship seems to exist in the realm of doxa in Evangelical church leadership, some Evangelical men are anxious about what they see as the creeping kudzu of feminist heterodoxy, which causes them to long for a practical gender orthodoxy about how to navigate gender dynamics in their modern lives.

Second, Glenn's and Denton's domestic lives were central to the way they thought about themselves as men. The fact that they were husbands and fathers was profoundly definitive. They articulated compelling narratives of moral and spiritual purpose in the context of the home. While these narratives appeared concrete, they seemed also to be more aspirational than realizable. More importantly, perhaps, Glenn and Denton pointed us to the domestic sphere as a normative sphere of action. For example, Denton's view of fatherhood and of his own father was modulated by his sense that he wanted to do things differently. In particular, he wanted to spend more time with his family and devote less attention to career than his father had to his. Yet he was also driven in his work, aspiring to more purposeful work, thereby leading to a tension. Again, such expressions are not surprising and are so commonplace in the culture that they hardly seem notable. However, neither of these men articulated much of an aspiration to action outside the home (beyond paid labor or involvement in church). There was little call to (nonreligious) service in communities, for example, which would be of concern to voices across the political spectrum. Further, to the extent that this attitude exhibits some crisis in or of the public sphere, it is as much a *religious* attitude and commitment as it is anything else. It appears that these men see the home and a domestic ideal as their primary fields of action. In important ways, this commitment follows the "subjective turn"[7] in Western religion and spirituality. Heelas and Woodhead suggested a turn inward toward the self as the locus of authority. We suggest a complementary turn inward toward the domestic as the location for gendered self-formation. Evangelicals are not alone in this turn (nor is the turn universal among Evangelicals), but it is more pronounced in men like Denton than in his Ecumenical Protestant counterparts.

Third, both Denton and Glenn held the view that there is something essential—even elemental—about masculinity and manhood. Each of them articulated a view of gender clearly modulated by two important conditions. The first condition was the framework of their own lives and their own marital relationships. That is, each spent much time discussing their roles in the home and the tensions therein depending upon that role, for example as the primary wage earner (and thus pulled from the home) or as part of a dual-income family (and thus unable to be the sole financial provider). The second condition, of almost equal importance, was a self-conscious reference to broader social discourses of gender. Each very much wanted to avoid appearing to fall into stereotypes of sexism. Each was clearly conscious of the ways their ideas might be viewed through the conceptual and discursive standards of the feminist movement. For each of them, this concern with sexism was mitigated by the assumption that some essential characteristics of manhood and masculinity are now in negotiation with feminism and with the realities of their own domestic arrangements.

Finally, for each of them, the idea of work or career took on special meaning. As we've noted, domestic life was of primary concern for both Glenn and Denton. In Denton's case, in fact, the domestic could be seen to be in conflict with work and career, both in his account of his father and in his own case. Work was secondary for Denton but was vital in at least one important way: work was the way in which Denton could be a provider. For both Glenn and Denton, this idea of provision was central. And, as we shall see, they are not alone in this idea. If there is one elemental dimension to masculinity that is shared across the voices in this book, it is this idea of provision. The home and the domestic sphere might be at the normative center of life, but work is important because it is the means by which the home and the family are supported financially. The men in this study are driven by this idea, and it is an idea that extends into the realm of purpose. Men—even Denton—want their work to be purposeful, but for most, the purpose is primarily to provide for their families.

From the neo-traditionalist point of view, men like Denton and Glen—committed Christian fathers and husbands—are models for normative masculinity and the good society. The idea that religion is an important framework for their identities as men, that they draw from religion clear and focused senses of who they should be as men, and that this framing should lead to a kind of engaged masculinity fits with the normative domestic ideals we considered earlier. Talking with Glenn and Denton raised some questions about this easy definition of the situation. Our conversation with a group of men at a large "emerging church" from the western United States raised even more.

In this group, we found a number of themes that are significant to our study and with which we found ourselves contending in many of our other interviews as well. Like Glenn and Denton, these men subscribed to elementalist manhood. There are, simply, taken-for-granted characteristics of what it means to be a man. Defining the extents and limits of masculinity, though, is also subtle, complex, and shifting. There also seems to be a taken-for-granted sense of what religion has to provide masculine identity. Such provisions are also subtle, complex, and shifting. And, as we shall see, essential characteristics of masculinity and essential demands of religion—or at least religion as expressed through churches—may well exist in a tense relationship with many men's experiences. This tension stands in contrast to the received idea that traditional religion might well be a settled contributor to traditional masculinity.

In the following excerpt, the interviewer has been discussing the popular literature of masculinity represented by John Eldredge's *Wild at Heart*. Sources like Eldredge, in fact, convey religion's relationship to manhood as ambiguous and contested. In pursuing this issue, the interviewer introduced the idea—present in many of these sources and in wider discourses—that the church might well be too "feminized." The men generally agreed with this notion but elaborated on it in significant ways:

COLIN: I think women relate more emotionally with the faith than a lot of guys do. Like my grandmother goes to church every Sunday, and my grandfather stays at home. My aunts are more inclined to go to church than their husbands are. And, you know, the husbands will go—it's not to say they don't believe; it's just that they don't—they're not as emotionally invested.

DAVIS: I wonder though if this feminization of the church is not part of social trends. I wonder if like—because you look at the church in the old times, it's a very patriarchal institution, just like anything else. And I wonder if we just have that [missed] role of men in the church, or if there is a role of men in the church, is it a reaction to the feminist movement? And maybe males internalize the notion that we've, you know, we've gotta become, we've gotta become wimps because we can't be a traditional male anymore because that's not going to work in this certain new viewpoint that we have.

What we call "elemental masculinity" is clear here. It is expressed along two lines. First, it is something that is simply empirically experienced in the way men and women behave differently regarding church. Second, it is something that is more generically in conflict with the goals and expectations of church and religion. This point is even more clear in the following, also from this group interview:

HARRISON: If you think about how church is set up, I don't even sometimes understand why guys go to church. Because you come into this building, and you sit and then you sing songs together, and then you have some guy telling you what to do—or telling you what [not] to do—but a lot of times it is telling you what to do or what to think. And then you have to sit there very silently and very spiritually and reverently. And then they'll pray, and maybe you'll need to go do an altar call—

GREG: And then you pay for it—

HARRISON: And then you pay for it. Exactly. These are not manly things to do. If you look at what Christ did, he gathered along some friends, and he [and they] went out and did things together.

The last comment combines elementalism with something else that is thought to be an essential male characteristic: that men are bound together by *purpose*. They get on with it. We see this theme surfacing again and again in our interviews. But the larger theme throughout is the way religion is directly in conflict with this sense of purposive action. Religion, this thinking goes, is fundamentally about domesticating men, about subverting their elemental impulses in service of normative ideals of belief and behavior. As one man put it, church is like a "lady heaven" where all dress up, sit quietly, and focus on what others are wearing.

The male ideal contrasts with this for these men. They saw aspects of Jesus's ministry as a model:

HARRISON: And he'd teach along the way. . . . If church was like that all the time, it would be more of a manly type thing. You know, if [the pastor] took a couple of us, and was like, "Hey, let's do church in the mountains for a couple of days." We'd be like, "Yeah, let's do it!" And, you know, we'd get more out of that.

And these men were pretty clear that some basic characteristics are essential to what it means to be a man, characteristics that are contradicted—even actively subverted—by church.

GREG: But for guys, think about what you give up in the church—your natural instinct to conquer, right? We're "outties." And the natural instinct for man is to have sex with as many people as possible. And all of the sudden it's like, no, don't do that.
FRANCIS: [whispers] one woman.
GREG: And it's—don't be loud, don't be obnoxious, don't go hike on a Sunday morning and play sports. Come sit here on a little uncomfortable seat and sing songs. I think guys have to give up a lot more to be a part of religion in the church aspect.

It was not just church per se that was the problem for these men. Para-church activities and ministries focused on men have emerged in both Evangelical and Ecumenical Protestant churches. These were not satisfactory, either, in that they conflict with elemental characteristics. One interviewee here noted these trends in megachurches in particular, where ". . . it's become an encounter group. Where it's like bang a drum and I cry about it, and do all this ridiculous stuff. . . ." Using rather crude traditional language (he called men who are drawn to this type of religiosity "pussies"), he underscored a dynamic that we will continue to see, in less strident form, in the men we will talk with in this and later chapters. Whatever the successes of the feminist movement in encouraging a careful rethinking of the immutability of so-called natural differences between men and women, clear and fixed beliefs remain,[8] and these beliefs, to greater and lesser degrees, are significant in the way men think about religion and church. However, as we will see, as men have more domestic responsibilities, this critique of church becomes considerably softened.

This group interview was significant both for what it revealed about the persistence of elementalism, which is in seeming conflict with the domesticating project of religion and the church (but not of Jesus's "true" message, in the view of these men) and for the details of this elementalism it revealed. Again, while these themes were put in particularly unequivocal terms here, they continued to reveal themselves as we moved into our conversations with couples, in households, and indeed with Ecumenical Protestant men as well. Not surprisingly, these men articulated some familiar ideas about essential differences between men and women.

When the interviewer returned to the question of "encounter"- or "therapy"-oriented religious ministries for men, the group's consensus was that those approaches were more naturally appropriate to women, agreeing with the idea that "when we talk about relational stuff, people think of women, right? That's often considered a feminized quality." One of the men drew the comparison more concretely.

ELLIOT: I think, you know, men, we lead by example. We share by example. We share by doing. And so where women can express things verbally and talk and communicate and that sort of relational aspect, men need a more physical contacting type of relationship where you're walking next—kind of walking side by side with someone.

They also expressed another theme we'd find among our Evangelical men, a kind of resistance to settled clerical authority. This is, of course, consistent with a broad decline in the influence of religious authority, but with these men it took on a certain specific gender valence, best put by this interviewee as he talked about how men's expectations of church differ from women's:

> GREG: I also think men, at least I, require you to earn my ears. You gotta earn my respect and earn the fact that I'm going to listen to anything you've got to say. Just the fact that you're a pastor of a church doesn't mean [that] anything you say has any merit to me whatsoever. I feel like you almost have to earn that. And as a guy, it's a little bit harder.

Despite these criticisms, these men did find some significant sources of self in traditional religion. These were men who were committed to and active in their faith community, even the church they criticized. There were models and insights, but they were all seen through an elementalist framing.

> GREG: We've talked a lot about the church and how does the church affect our view of manhood and masculinity. But I think that's very different from comparing it to . . . the Bible. . . . How does actual religion affect you? I think going to a church that is very feminized is much different than reading stories about a guy who sat in jail and was burned alive for God or things like that. All of [a] sudden it's—I view that—I respect that. I get that. It challenges me. It shows me some of what being a man means. It's not necessarily cleft chin, big biceps, but it's standing up for your beliefs and sacrifice.

This argument circles around the issues of feminization and elementalism to find within Christian and Biblical traditions images of men and masculinity that ring true. There are things in these traditions that evoke these ideas of what men "essentially" are. And, these are powerful and functional ideas, at least to the voices we hear from here. Further, these men found ways to interpret these Biblical ideas of masculinity in functional frameworks for their lives. Here, one of them takes the implicit notion of masculine aggressiveness and reformulates it in a more generic and denatured form relevant to daily experience. He implies that men's essential natures, in fact, present specific gifts to the practice of religion and evangelicalism.

ELLIOT: And that whole manliness replacing aggressiveness with boldness. You don't have to be fighting somebody, but you're not back-
ing down either. You don't apologize for your beliefs, which I think
Christians do an excessive amount [of]. Apologize for believing in
truth, that not everything can be true, you know? I think, you know
in conversations, I have a hard time because as soon as you say, "I
believe this, and that's wrong," a lot of people say, "Well, no one else
tells me that . . . . I'm just shutting down." Someone else is going to
tell me that I can be right in some aspect or way. . . . I think we're losing out on some of that strength.

A clear sense of boldness and purpose emerges from this conversation. These men saw these as important elements, ones that were often
not welcomed in church but that were nonetheless Biblical and functional. There is another dimension here, too, that we will see consistently with at least our conservative Evangelical interviewees. That is
the idea that men have a particular gift or role to play. That gift is at the
center of the important idea of "headship" that will dominate many of
our conversations with men and couples in the coming pages. As we do,
it is important to keep in mind the symbols and images that underlie the
notion of headship.

From this conversation it seems that headship is rooted in this sense
of purpose and boldness. These men described an essential male characteristic that involved decisiveness and action. They were critical of
church (and the broader society) for not honoring this characteristic.
These men also articulated the essentialist sense that this and other
characteristics were natural and taken for granted. The contexts of action also are worth noting. The preponderant view here seemed to be
that the church is not the most logical setting for men to express themselves and their essential natures. There are other contexts (of which—
presumably—the home is one) where men might well be more active
and make their presence felt. Following these voices, we might also con-
clude that positive manhood might be about "things that matter."

The problem for the church or religion here is a profound one. These
men clearly felt a sense of autonomy in relation to religion. The authority of the church or of church leaders did not seem to play a big role for
them. They felt strongly that it was up to them to decide what is right

and wrong for them (something, it appears, that they believed men do much more easily than women). Thus, the notion of headship carries this valence of meaning as well. It is the essential quality of boldness, purpose, and decisive action that equips men to lead. (However, it is notable that leadership rarely engaged civic duty or responsibility.) This self-reliance in faith and in social spaces is a clear theme for them, and the challenge for religion and the church is to present them with opportunities for leadership or headship. Otherwise, they may well tend to view the church and religion as a challenge to their headship. Church demands that they balance the essentialist notion of "men as leaders" with the traditional institutional demand that participants be followers. That clearly does not sit well with these men. Rather than religion serving as a seamless whole, it is clearly a situation of seams and fissures.

Against this background, we will turn now to the bulk of our interviews, which we conducted with a different cohort of men. The men above were almost all single (save one), in their twenties or thirties, and members of a group for single men at a large, urban "emerging," though still clearly Evangelical, church. These men are not the central focus of this study, though, which is more about "settled" men and men who are fathers. However, what these single men had to say is important as a background to what we will hear from more settled men. They demonstrate a sense that life today is about negotiating elemental ideas about masculinity against social forces—including religion—that aspire to subvert or domesticate those essentials.

The men we hear from next echoed the negotiations expressed by the emerging church group. But for them, this negotiation moved beyond church and religion to a more pressing set of conditions and contexts: home, marriage, and family. This situation is significant to this study. Rather than being a situation of easy accommodation between "religion" and "men," the situation is more complex. These men show that the interests of religion and men can be described as being in conflict—even for conservative men. The idea that religion should exist in an easy relationship to men's roles as husbands and fathers deserves some extensive rethinking as well.

Each of our Evangelical men and families had an active personal and family history with church. All of our Evangelical respondents were active in their faith communities at the time of the interviews. Some of our interviewees were also pursuing seminary education with an eye toward professional or lay ministry. So this group was quite familiar with and invested in church, from denominational congregations to megachurches to alternative, "emerging" forms. As we shall see, most of these men spoke with some confidence about the issues men face in relation to church. Most were familiar with the extensive Evangelical popular culture concerning gender and masculinity, from the Promise Keepers organization to the works of John Eldredge. They were also able to articulate the commonplace traditionalism regarding masculinity and gender one might expect from Evangelical men. However, as with the single men above, we found this traditionalism to be nuanced in fascinating ways in these conversations, ways that put in question the received idea that religion is somehow a taken-for-granted force in the construction of male identity. Nearly all of our informants did convey that in their church experience, what we might call a stance of "hard patriarchy" is the norm.[9] This rigidity is particularly articulated, for them, in the case of church leadership where lead pastors were male and where women were assigned subsidiary roles. There were no women pastors in any of their religious experiences.

We were fascinated to hear their responses to the question of how these and other messages about gender were conveyed. We asked each of our informants what their church "teaches about being a man." Recall Denton's response, which was typical:

> I'm trying to think of it exactly, I mean real specific teachings? I don't know. Maybe I missed it. I mean generally I think they would take a Biblical approach toward the sexes. This past week they were talking about nominating people for elders and encouraging the congregation—if they knew of someone. And they specifically said a man, and that, probably five years ago, that wouldn't have struck me as odd or [I would not have] even noticed that he specifically said a man to distinguish from a woman. But I think in this day and age where things are progressing toward equality of the sexes and a little more free or liberal thought, if you want to call it that, you know, that's probably a distinction he had to make.

So for Denton, the basic message was a clear (yet barely spoken) one and one about which there had been little internal controversy in the church. At the same time, though, he acknowledged that the broader culture had developed different ideas to which the church must respond. Yet the response was subtle. The question of gender in leadership was not preached about, nor was it couched in a critique of broader feminist trends. Rather, it was simply mentioned in the job description.

It is also telling that for Denton, as for many of our informants, it was nearly impossible to talk about masculinity or male roles per se. Talking about men and men's roles automatically meant talking about women. It was nearly impossible to speak about either in isolation. Asked about women's roles in his church, he replied:

> Yeah, you know, I have a pretty old school take on that probably as well, probably more from my upbringing more than anything. And I think—a combination of my upbringing and what the Bible teaches from what I can tell—that I wouldn't say that [a woman's] role is to teach men. And I'm not so strict about that, that if I'm in a situation where a woman gets up, then I'm like, "I'm outta here because this is gonna ruin me. . . ." But as a principle, certainly if I was involved in decision making, that would probably be the main guiding principle in terms of what the role of women should be in the church. And that's one I assume the church takes because I've never seen a woman up there doing a sermon, as long as we've been there.

While Denton could not recall an actual moment when any ideas about women in leadership were expressed from the pulpit, it was clear to him that these gender norms were a well-grounded tenet of his congregation, norms that only recently even needed to be expressed. It may be that, for men like Denton and for churches like his, ideas about gender are not expressed regularly because they haven't needed to be. It might well be that for him some variation on these ideas would have caused him to rethink his relationship to this particular church. If he is typical on the point of his experience (and he seems to be, given our other interviews), then it may be that the social messages about gender—even in relation to religion and church—are conveyed or reinforced in other ways and in other places. Only recently, according to Denton, had the church needed to "speak" gender, and this speaking included the mention of a single word, *man*, in a job description for church leadership, not a more robust defense of normative patriarchy. Whatever someone like Denton thinks, and whatever commitments his congregation may have had related to gender, they were aware that the world outside had changed and the struggle for orthodoxy/heterodoxy had begun.

While such tension and the necessary "speaking" of gender in the religious institutional setting may be fairly recent for these men, the speaking of gender in the home is not a new development, as was clear in our conversation with Tim Brewer, who was typical of our Evangelical cohort. Tim was a self-employed business owner and an Evangelical living in the American South. He shared with all but two of our Evangelical men a commitment to the idea of male "headship." In spite of the general lack of explicit teaching about headship, most of our Evangelical respondents thought it was rooted in Biblical precepts. When asked to reflect on his ideas about women's roles in relation to headship, Tim stood both on received precept and on what sounded like contemporary, egalitarian principles:

> I don't know where to quote it off the top of my head, but most people stop at "women be submissive to your husband . . . ." And that's what they quote. But the next line is, men be submissive to your wife as you are submissive to . . . so you know I think in that role, it's respect, but it's equal respect, equal love. It's pretty much equal everything. It's not like, women don't speak in the church. It's not like that, which some churches are like that, but ours is not. But my wife can have her opinion, but she knows—she just wants me to listen to her—but I still have the final say.

No one would describe Tim as a feminist, obviously, but he did find that his traditional ideas about masculine prerogative were increasingly at odds with broader social evidence and experience. He was even attracted to some of the broader discourse about egalitarianism. Some basics had not changed for him, though. This idea of a "final say" extended beyond the home and the church to the public and political spheres as well. Asked about gender beyond church and home, he said:

> You mean as far as women CEOs [are concerned]? I actually think it's pretty cool. The thing a lot of people need to realize when they talk about that there shouldn't be female presidents [is that] they have to answer to

a board. So, and not that the boards [don't have] females, but if there was a Chairman of the Board that was a female, I don't know of any. So, I still think you could put—I think they are great in that role, but a President of our country? I don't think so [*laughs*]. I don't really have anything to—I guess I'd have to think about why because I can't just tell you. I don't know if that's enough for you to say that. . . . You know I think if you look at the Biblical principles, that would be why.

There are hints here of the landscape that defines gender issues for Tim. First, as with Denton, there is a sort of unstated but taken-for-granted set of definitive principles (both of them call them "Biblical principles"). These principles seem to have been important in comparison with their actual experience of church where, while each was confident that the church's commitments were consistent with traditional narratives of male authority, at the same time there was little actual preaching or teaching on manhood, masculinity, or gender. So, the taken-for-granted ideas, which seemed also to be sourced in broader social contexts, were important, yet unstated. Second, Tim clearly had experience with, and referenced, broader cultural narratives about gender, narratives that stress egalitarianism more than they do male prerogative. He felt compelled—along with most of the men in this cohort—to embrace these egalitarian ideals and negotiate them *within* headship, which leads to expressions of what W. Bradford Wilcox[10] called "soft patriarchy"—a patriarchy that listens, nurtures, and compromises but that has the "final say" and that has a definitive place in authority structures both in the domestic and the public sphere.

The dynamics in this landscape are clear. On the one hand, Tim's religious culture was one that instantiated traditionalist ideas about gender. On the other hand, there is a broader set of social and cultural conditions that contrast with traditionalist ideas, which were perceived by Tim to be normative in broader, secular media culture. Further, this normative presence of feminism had forced his religious culture to respond and had caused him to renegotiate the gender dynamics in his personal life, resulting in the perceived "crisis" of masculinity felt by these men and their antagonistic relationship with culture.

How messages about gender get circulated in this system is still in question. The traditionalist discourse we started with seemed to be saying that religion had a positive, self-evident role to play as an inculcator of masculine values. Most of the men in our Evangelical cohort agreed. But the situation is more complex, as we have shown. Religion also has a tendency to feminize men, or so men in this cohort thought, even though Evangelical institutional structures exude male power. Religion also has a tendency to not talk about gender or masculinity in a way that is satisfactory to these men. Certainly, religion has given them some resources with which to navigate broader cultural shifts in gender dynamics (e.g., the idea of headship), but it has not gone far enough, these men thought. They longed for clearer models and conversations about gender to better negotiate some egalitarian notions into their daily lives *and* to equip them with language that makes headship seem less sexist and more relevant to broader culture. In the end, these men wanted essential masculinity to "work." They hoped religion could provide resources that would help them integrate normative headship into their everyday lives as men, particularly in their everyday *domestic* lives as fathers and husbands.

For all of our interviewees, as we've said, masculinity cannot be described in a vacuum. It requires resources and symbols from the culture. But it also must be seen in relation to women and women's prospects, and in relation to the decisions these men must make on a regular basis as husbands and fathers. For our Evangelical interviewees, these decisions took place within an elementalist framework. They saw certain essential characteristics of what it means to be a man. They saw those characteristics as having a relationship to religion, but their expression in church and in pastoral authority was ambiguous, even conflicted. These essentials are widely accepted and taken for granted, and they often don't need to be explicitly expressed. They are just "known." The relationship of religion to these ideas was less ambiguous for these men to the extent that they believed they drew them from authoritative scripture and must negotiate them into their lives in a way that reflected and supported Biblical teaching. But it is clear that broader cultural discourses played a pivotal role, causing negotiation *and* a measured embrace of the egalitarian impulse (an embrace that is also interpreted through Biblical teaching). Further, as we will see later, the broader (and perceived "secular") culture—and particularly media culture—is not only the source of the egalitarian impulse. Rather, media culture also provided them with salient practical resources for negotiating headship, perhaps even to a greater degree than their faith communities did, and media provided resources that expressed their elementalist ideals about masculinity (albeit resources typically stripped of their religious character). The broader cultural context, which is in many ways a media context, thus provides new influences and pressures on these elementalist ideas, and men must work to negotiate these pressures and influences in their own lives.

For most of our interviewees, the most important of these pressures from the broader media culture were those that moved in the direction of gender egalitarianism. It was rare for us to find a respondent who did not express a desire to have a more egalitarian and respectful-of-women's-prospects relationship. For many of them, this impulse was further instantiated by the concrete reality that their wives either have careers or desire to have them. This situation is, in some cases, a matter of economic necessity. In others, it is a matter of preference, attitude, and basic values. For nearly all of our interviewees, though, it was important to accommodate a view of women's roles that varied from that of previous generations while maintaining certain limits to these prospects through the idea of headship. Some described a preference for a more traditionally gendered relationship, but all understood that such relationships are less and less the norm in modern life.

So as our Evangelical interviewees encountered the questions of masculinity, gender relations, and normative values, and as each attempted to realize these negotiations in concrete belief and behavior, we could see among them some patterns of belief and action. As has been suggested elsewhere, Evangelical narratives of gender should be seen not as monolithic but as defined along lines that differentiate among dimensions of the lived situation. Coats[11] has argued that Evangelical attitudes about gendered domestic relations can be placed along a continuum from "strong traditionalism" to "egalitarianism." Men on the "traditionalist" end of the spectrum express patriarchy in absolutist terms, grounded in a literalist interpretation of scripture. Egalitarian Evangelicals take an opposite view, grounded in a reinterpretation of the same scriptures. Coats divided this continuum into several cells. There is "interpretive traditionalism," which takes a more nuanced view at that end of the continuum, less certain than strong traditionalists. These men are open to personal interpretation and are less convinced that there is a singular Biblical view. There is also "cultural traditionalism," which does not apply to the Evangelical men in our study, but it is a location on the continuum for men who express a form of negotiated traditionalism without religious rhetorical scaffolding, which will be applicable to some of the Ecumenical Protestant men in our study. On the "Egalitarian" end, Coats also identified egalitarians who were more "apolitical" in their views, basing their views about gender less on a commitment to objectively feminist or gender-balance ideals. For these people, egalitarianism was practical and normative, but it was not a political project and, often, not one they felt compelled to address directly in their communities either because there were more important religious matters (e.g., other core messages of importance in scripture) or because they did not want to be at odds with their faith community (i.e., it was not a fight worth fighting at that time).

It is notable that any point on this spectrum can be elementalist with regard to gender. Various forms of traditionalism are certainly grounded in gender elementalism, but egalitarianism can be also, as is evident in certain strands of feminism and in some within our cohorts who expressed some degree of elementalism *and* egalitarianism. Thus, the conversation about gender operates on three axes: gender hierarchy along the spectrum of traditionalism and egalitarianism, the practical/normative registers of gendered practice and understanding, and elementalist/non-elementalist ideas about gender. The overwhelming majority of men in our study (around three-quarters of all respondents) expressed some form of elementalism concerning the ideas of provision, protection, and purpose. Elementalism was much stronger in both number and in certainty among the Evangelical men in our study. Other differences between Evangelical and Ecumenical men centered on the resources available to them on the practical/normative register and on the extent to which they expressed hierarchical views of gender. Of the first (the practical/normative register), Evangelicals tended to have available a wider range of normative symbols regarding gender, but both Evangelicals and Ecumenicals said they lacked practical symbolic resources for navigating changing gender dynamics in everyday life. Of the second, Evangelicals expressed gender hierarchies more frequently than their Ecumenical counterparts.

This more nuanced interpretive landscape gives us a way of looking in more detail at the Evangelicals with whom we spoke. Most of them were strong traditionalists. They were not authoritarian dictators. They aspired to be what Wilcox called "soft patriarchs."[12] They thought of themselves as "tender warriors"[13] or aspired to a kind of "tender leadership."[14] John Little, an Evangelical seminary student living in the American West, was such a traditionalist with a soft side:

> The Bible teaches of the ideal man, if we're talking just about men. Because you look at Ephesians and you know, the spiritual head is supposed to stand against what's wrong and being firm as to not back down . . . press ahead, so taking in challenges. You know press ahead, and you're not giving in to the oppositions. But also we're supposed to love our wives as Christ loved the church. We're supposed to love our children and bring them up in the church. So it also gives an example of the tenderhearted part of God. Men, we're supposed to be, not just all hard, go-getters but tender, loving, taking care of our families. We're supposed to be focused on God. We're supposed to be pressing on, taking challenges on. But also we're supposed to be loving and kind and caring, fruits of the spirit. All that plays into who we should be in Christ.

John's description of the "ideal man" arose from Ephesians but incorporated more characteristics of masculinity (those "essentials" we've been noting in many of our conversations) than are explicit in that passage. Men are to "press ahead" and "take on challenges." To underscore an emergent point about the overwhelming elementalism here, no informant connected a Biblical proof text to any of these other traits. These elements are, for many men, natural, taken for granted. The proof text instead functions to give men direction in how to implement these *natural* traits. The key dynamic for the late modern men in our cohort, though, is the softening with regard to relationships. Men are to be tough but tender, echoing the direction of contemporary culture. This shift might be evidence of progress of women in achieving a greater balance of power in conservative households.[15] It might also represent the indirect influence of a pervasive publishing industry and the Evangelical para-church network, for example Promise Keepers, that promotes these ideas. What is interesting here (and why it might be an indirect influence) is that, like John, few of the men in our sample reported direct contact with such organizations or even with localized men's groups in their churches. Nor had many read much of the Evangelical literature about gender (though some admitted to having the books on their shelves and to being aware of their basic ideas). Yet somehow these ideas filtered into their expressions of masculinity even though these men could not pinpoint the resources for how to be "soft" yet in some ways "hard" in their faith communities. That is, there seemed to be a call from these men for a more direct message about masculinity. Nonetheless, this move toward "softer" valences of masculinity could be seen as an attempt to accommodate feminist gains in broader culture and in their specific religious culture in an effort to seal what Michael Messner called "patriarchal bargains" and to rhetorically bind male and female roles in a kind of equivalence.[16]

In situations of change, fissures and contradictions emerge. For these traditionalists, whether of the "hard" or "soft" variety, change was clearly happening. And it is this kind of change, experienced and negotiated in the context of daily life, that seems to be the consistent theme of most of our interviews of both Evangelical and Ecumenical men.

The theme of change, and accommodation to it, is even more obvious in the case of our interpretive traditionalists. These were a smaller number among our respondents, but they were distinct—and telling—in their view of the way male prerogative should be seen in light of scripture and traditional practice. These men were clearly drawn to a more egalitarian view of gender relations but in the end felt that the Ephesians passage enforced male authority with a kind of ultimate finality. They were less certain than the strong traditionalists, however, of what this finality meant. All of them suggested that whatever traditionalist views they had were also held by their spouses, who expected that kind of "leadership" from them.[17] Some felt that this dynamic had Biblical roots, that men who were truly "following Christ" would find that their spouses would not only respect but also expect their role and prerogatives as men.

Mark Simms, an Evangelical who attended a nondenominational church in a large western U.S. city, articulated this view, as well as the broader notion that scripture-based gender roles were not about power but merely about different—and morally equivalent—gifts and responsibilities.

As far as [their roles] in the home [are concerned], men and women are equal, but they have different roles. . . . [T]he woman's role . . . or the woman is supposed to respect her husband, and the man is supposed to love his wife. . . . He would have more of a leadership role when it comes down to, you know, final decisions but not often coming down to that . . . more [its] being a collaborative effort. And if he really is loving his wife like Jesus loved the church and laid down his life for the church, then she's not going to have a problem respecting him basically. So, the summary would be men and women are equal in value but have different roles.

The outlines of the "traditionalist" view, shared by both the stronger and more interpretive voices, were that men do have the ultimate prerogative for leadership and decision making. Both the strong traditionalist and interpretive traditionalist men believed that men were wired this way—essentially, naturally, divinely. At the same time, though, in practice this leadership should be collaborative, rather than dictatorial, and as long as men are acting authentically as Christians, women will not object. Finally, though there does appear to be an implied imbalance of power in this situation, these men (and presumably their spouses) consider the reality to be one of equivalent, but different, roles.

What set those Coats calls "interpretive traditionalists" apart, though, was their reluctance to embrace fully either the spirit or the letter of what this leadership or headship implies when push comes to shove. Mark went on to say:

I still can't ignore some of the things I think the Bible says. But I'm not. . . . I could be wrong. I'm not really hard-nosed about it anyway. And I'm a guy, so all my views are naturally not valid [laughs] because, of course, a guy can say that because it doesn't matter. . . . I have nothing at stake. Brenda might agree with me on it. Actually, it will be interesting for you to ask her because I think she comes down harder on my side than I do.

Peter Traylor, an Evangelical attending seminary in a large western U.S. city, echoed this reticence, focusing on the notion that his wife and family actually expected headship from him, something he was reluctant to see in traditional terms. If headship is a God-given role, then it is important, and will be expected, but Peter was reluctant to see any personal legitimation of power in it. "Yeah . . . just looking at Joshua and how he was taking over for Moses and just . . . being strong and encouraging for whatever task you have and just being diligent at it. Just, um, being a good leader, like the people followed Moses because he was a good leader. I don't look at myself as like the leader of this household, but I do feel like as a father, you know, and the husband . . . that my wife and kids are looking to me as a leader."

Emory French agreed with this view and presented a complex account of negotiating such roles in his relationship with his wife. Emory, an Evangelical attending seminary who presented a narrative of recent commitment to Christianity, addressed an issue that is at the core of the question of male headship, the question of exactly what men are to exercise headship over. As we will see later, this question of "turf" becomes an important way that actual power and authority are negotiated in these relationships.[18] There is a range of things about which couples must make decisions, including finances, educating their children, work, and where they will live. Like others we interviewed, Emory chose to stress his role in less concrete realms. Instead, for him (as for many others) headship was most relevant with regard to the couple's and family's religious lives. He said:

> I take the lead with regards to worship. It wasn't always that way. At the beginning when I was the new Christian and I didn't know what to do, I didn't want the responsibility of it. I didn't understand it. I was a little embarrassed, you know trying to talk to God out loud. Um, so that was something that I would ask her to work with me on. She never would usurp what she considers the authority. She's always been submissive to God, and I never understood how it works, but she is. And so if I asked her to pray, she would, but she would always return it to me . . . that that was my place in the household . . . that I was to be the spiritual leader. . . . I realized how powerful that is. Because it's a strange, inexplicable mystery that God really listens to the man in the family. . . . [Y]ou don't realize it until you start praying and you see the miracles happen. He just, you know steps in, and things go. My wife prays all the time. I know that, and I know it's earnest. And I know that she's really talking and relating. But for some reason if I sit down and pray in earnest and, you know, am repentant and am broken and humbled and, you know, like a true Christian

does, like the spirit of Christ would, miracles happen. . . . It just makes a difference in our family. It makes things different. Now whether that's—coming from my past, my secular New Age spiritist past—um, whether that's because there is a God who really does listen and who is the God of the Bible and it's structured that way. That's the way He set it up.

This interpretation of headship—that it is actually about spiritual headship—avoids the inevitable conflicts over what we might think of as the harder and more critical issues of life and relationships. For families such as Emory's, of course, their spiritual lives are, in fact, ultimately important. And the way in which Emory reported negotiating this relationship with his wife is also important. It is not so much that there is a received, doctrinal empowerment that flows from scripture; it is that scripture seemed merely to state the obvious to him. It confirmed what Emory and his wife had discovered in real life—that male headship is the natural order of things, demonstrated by experience. The Bible merely confirmed what is natural and essential. The distinction here is important to Emory and to others. All understood and accepted that a kind of ordained order was described in Ephesians. But they were also aware of the implication that this ordained authority is dismissive of or abusive to women. This view is in part due to their awareness of the changing mores in the culture with regard to gender relations, which they appreciated. A number of Evangelical men (even some strong traditionalists in our cohort) criticized older generations and regressive contemporary congregations for their abusive positions toward women. For some of these men, their negotiations were rooted in experience and in their imagination of power relations in their own lives. For the interpretivists, this awareness led them to think creatively and carefully about how and where to find headship in the dynamics of their daily lives. Mark, Peter, and Emory found it to be the case that they were in effect pushed to lead by their respective spouses (and by divine responsibility).

This discussion should not suggest that strong traditionalists are not creative or that they are abusive per se. The discourse of "soft patriarchy" was pervasive in this cohort across the traditionalist spectrum. The difference highlighted here is related to the degree of certainty about gender, the measure of personal experience in interpretation, and the rhetorical tactics interpretive traditionalists employed in their narratives of traditionalism, for example that the expectation of headship often came from their wives. The difference here may be that these interpretive traditionalists simply were more reflective of the "plausible narrative of self" they presented to the researcher in this setting, more aware of the broader cultural discourse or more sensitive about cultural relevance.

In sum, a commitment to some form of patriarchal authority was the norm among the Evangelicals we interviewed. All but one shared a sense that there is an elemental nature to manhood and that social arrangements at church and in marriage must in some ways deal with this reality. Few could think of specific church or clerical teachings addressing their roles as men, but all felt there was a strong, taken-for-granted narrative of masculinity that defined it in their faith contexts. Their faith commitments, after all, reflected the natural order, so they thought. They expressed these narratives in relation to their domestic lives, which gives important insights into the ways that they think about their roles as men, as husbands, as fathers, and even as citizens and workers. The ideal of male authority was thus diffused into their thinking in a fundamental way. And *diffused* is the operative word here. The sources and outlines were harder to pin down for these men than we expected. All could reference the key passage in Ephesians, but its exact implications were less systematic and less addressed by their religious experience. The notion thus had a kind of symbolic, normative importance that transcended its sources in important ways. Further, these men searched for practical ways to implement and talk about this normative notion in their everyday lives, a search that yielded mixed results in their religious lives.

Though this synopsis addresses the overwhelming majority of Evangelicals we interviewed, we would be remiss if we failed to discuss the two outliers who add complexity and evidence of difference within Evangelicalism. Where our Evangelical traditionalists wanted to hold on to the notion of male prerogative, two Evangelicals we interviewed were committed to an egalitarian view of these relationships. Jasper Hall and Aiden Jones dealt with scriptural authority in a different way from that of the traditionalists, reading it descriptively rather than prescriptively. As Aiden put it, "I think those [scriptures] are referring to a very specific place and a specific time back in the ancient Middle East. I don't necessarily think they translate well into the current situation." He described his own faith history in a series of churches that were more gender-traditional than he was now comfortable with.

> Previously to all the churches before this one, gender was actually a big deal. Growing up, there were definite gender roles. The church I grew up in, like they had rules that women could not be Elders, they could not be Deacons, they could not have leadership positions—most of the leadership positions were in charge of other women and children. Um, definitely all the leadership was exclusively male. And they sort of taught that the man was supposed to be the spiritual leader of the home, that sort of thing. And so, that was definitely where I was raised. And my family is still there; I'm not [laughs]. I am definitely more of an equality guy.

It is interesting to note Aiden's sense that in his prior churches the issue of gender was central.[19] His current ideas were more egalitarian and presumably questioned the extent to which gender should be so definitive. Jasper Hall agreed that making gender so central to religious authority is a displacement of priorities:

> I think there are just a few things that I see as being important religiously, in a religious context about being a man. And one of those—I think you begin with, in the Christian context, your relationship with God and more specifically with Jesus, and the notion of submission—submission to something that is bigger than yourself and to an authority that is outside of yourself. And I would describe that as being primarily revealed in Scripture and particularly in the Gospels with the example of Jesus, the sort of life that He lived and so forth. So, I would begin there.

Turning to the question of gender relationships, Jasper saw these issues as more or less deemphasized, or at least less central, in scripture: "In relationships, I think there are just a handful of specific instructions Biblically that relate to that. In particular in marriage, the notion of submission but not—typically you hear 'wives submit to your husbands'—but the verse just prior to that says 'submit to one another,' telling the husband to submit just as it tells the wife to submit, so I think there is Biblically the idea of partnership and coming alongside one another in a marriage."

Jasper read scripture very differently from the traditionalist stereotype in other ways, too. Fathering, to Jasper, was also something that involved a sense of submission and humility. "And I think that is sort of my message really, one of humility to men," he said. Jasper was also unusual in his view of women's leadership, even in church. He, of course, recognized that he was not in the majority in holding this perspective, and he was hesitant to make gender a political issue in his congregation: "I think some women are in a sense born to be leaders and are gifted with the sort of abilities that make a good leader. For those women, I think it's fabulous to have those roles in religious institutions, cultural, political, whatever, so that really doesn't bother me. I don't have any problem with that personally, but I certainly live in a spiritual community where that view would not be shared."

We see here a range of views of male prerogative and gender relationships. These latter perspectives, while in the minority among our interviewees and presumably a minority among the larger universe of Evangelical men, are significant not to the question of the preponderance of opinion but to the question of the extents and limits of discourses of gender related to church and to faith. They show that ideas about gender are not monolithic but that a variety of conceptual and rhetorical turns are available to men as they position themselves in relation to church, faith, marriage, domestic space, and—perhaps significantly—broader discourses in the culture. That none of them articulated a view that we might think of as "hard" traditionalist or "hard patriarchy" in domestic spaces suggests that social mores are in fact shifting here. Even strong traditionalists sought to soften their tone about gender negotiations in domestic life, confirming widely accepted evidence from social research.[20]

The responses from our Evangelical cohort also give us insight into the forces that may come into play in influencing attitudes and behaviors. We can see here, in the background, a set of commonplace and taken-for-granted assumptions about the nature of the sexes. We can also see the influence of a longstanding set of commitments to certain traditionalist ideas of gender within this religious worldview. We can see that the source of those ideas, at least as expressed by the men in this study, is not actually in objective teachings by doctrinal or clerical authority. Instead, masculinity is something that has been widely accepted and perhaps not often explicitly addressed because "it didn't need to be." This grounding of masculinity opens the question of sources and circulations outside the boundaries of specific faith communities and thus opens the question of how the broader culture—including media culture—might well be involved. We can further see the suggestion here that an important contributor to this situation is the actual experience of daily gender relations, wherein men who are increasingly open to more egalitarian ideas about headship encounter women who are similarly situated. As we will see in the following chapters, there is a more complex set of ways that actual experience is involved in these ideas, ways that are rooted in long-progressing fundamental changes in the structure of American domestic life.

For all their critique of the church and religion, we can describe the Evangelicals we interviewed as having a rather focused and salient narrative of masculinity compared with that of their Ecumenical Protestant peers. Certainly, their narratives had fissures, but most of them would agree about a number of things. They would share the focused sense of faith journey that defines Evangelical experience. There was commonality in the way most of them described manhood or masculinity. They identified with a version of it broadly consistent with Wilcox's "soft patriarchy," articulated for many of them around the notion of "headship," with all of its concomitant tensions and contradictions.

In spite of the broad agreement over theology and the commonality of opinion about these broader questions, there was a good deal of dissatisfaction with (or, at least, ambivalence about) church and religion. To put it broadly, most of them thought that men were not well-understood or accommodated in church. They would agree that church provides little objective pedagogy about what it means to be a man and how one lives masculinity. In particular, they felt that men's natural need to feel a sense of purpose, to do things rather than just talk about them, was left out of the practices of lay church life. They saw church as domesticating, even feminizing, in this regard.[21] We must also note, of course, that a good deal of this discourse is made complex because it is permeable to the broader sociocultural context. They were conscious of this context and wanted to modulate some of their more essentialist ideas about what it means to be a man. They lived in a world—made more real and more instantaneous by its media and mediation—that had some clear ideas about gender, and these men wanted very much to resolve their ideas of the masculine within this broader context of values and discourse.

Ecumenical Protestant Men

There was broad agreement from the Ecumenical Protestant men we interviewed that the church and religion had failed to provide clear messages for men. Typical was Jack Jones: "I think the tradition of Christianity does a really crappy job of teaching what it means to be a man." The difference from Evangelical men is a difference in focus. Where Evangelical men articulated a *religious* narrative of masculinity, the Ecumenical men we interviewed did not. Their focus, instead, seemed to be much more on the broader sociocultural context and its support of more egalitarian, less masculinist, ways of looking at gender identity. Jack Jones again:

> I think at least for me, the things that teach me to be a man are less, or at least the sources I consider most important, are less from the spiritual perspective and more from the familial and friend perspective of that kind of experiential knowledge. You know, certainly my college would say that men are, and I accepted this for a while, that men are the providers for the family, they are the strength of the family, they are the . . . they're power brokers basically, which is a good way of looking at that. They are the ones that control pieces. Obviously I don't really buy into that a great deal given my current role and hearing some of my friends from that time.

Furthermore, many of these Ecumenical men explicitly identified the difference between them and others.[22] That is, for most of them it was important to distance themselves from the religiously modulated narratives of manhood that they identified quite explicitly with conservative religion. They also tended to think these conservative narratives were clear and explicit, as opposed to the Evangelical men who live in these spaces and think otherwise. "That is not me," Ecumenical Protestant men seemed to be saying, making this distinction an important marker of their identities as men. Most of these men clearly supported the notion that gender relations should be egalitarian and collective (at least in their narratives) and that equality between the sexes should be pursued, without messy conditions such as headship. They articulated narratives of egalitarianism, and these narratives lacked a specific religious timbre. The dynamism was somewhere else. They stressed the notion that religion had taught them how to be a person, not how to be a man, that gender differences should be deemphasized in favor of what the genders have in common. Where Evangelical men looked to their faith as a source of their ideas about manhood, the Ecumenical Protestant men looked elsewhere. The general sense was that their faith in the Gospel encouraged openness and egalitarianism and thus in a way deemphasized masculinity. More focus on egalitarianism meant less focus on "being a man."

However, whereas most of these men embraced the egalitarianism in their faith communities, a majority of these egalitarians also lamented that such equality veiled what they saw as differences between men and women. Note Ricky McDonald, an Ecumenical Protestant attending seminary in a western U.S. metropolitan setting:

INTERVIEWER: Now, can you remember an experience in your church that helped shape your life as a man? I know we touched on this a little before.

RICKY: [*pause*] I guess my stopping and having to think so long means no, which is striking to me. Is that a question you should answer no to? I would hope it wouldn't be. But, there are two ways to try and avoid gender stereotypes, right? Either . . . at least one of the ways is to pretend they don't exist. Pretend there's no such thing as gender and everybody's just the same and it doesn't matter if you're a man or a woman. Now that's probably, certainly what the church was trying to do. Um, fighting to have women pastors, you got up and they were just as good as male pastors, so you didn't talk about what the difference was. They were just up there doing the same thing, so it didn't matter. So you really didn't get those messages at all. Yeah, it's striking to me.

Some of the Ecumenical Protestant men, in fact, sought a religious experience that allowed them to be egalitarian *men*, not simply egalitarian *people*. That the church could not supply such an experience was, to borrow from Ricky, "striking." For many there was even a lurking (and not far beneath the surface) desire for the recognition of gender difference, rooted in the same sorts of gender elementalism found among their Evangelical counterparts. This similarity became clearer in some of our group discussions where the egalitarian narrative seemed to leave them with a feeling that their senses of self lacked definition or that their religious identities simply had little to offer their gender identities. There was often a longing for a stronger masculine narrative of identity. A way of saying this is that—against the backdrop of a general acceptance of egalitarian ideals—there was a kind of turn back toward tradition, a desire to figure out what it meant to be an egalitarian *man*. This longing for a religiously infused, egalitarian masculinity was expressed most clearly in a group of young Ecumenical Protestant men from the upper Midwest:

> INTERVIEWER: Okay. Is there a role that you think [religion] should play or that it could do a better job of or maybe not, maybe not at all, maybe religion shouldn't have a bigger role? Whatever you think?
>
> ROBERT: I think this is the hardest question so far. I don't have an exact role. I really draw a blank. I guess I struggle with my spirituality. Everyone does, I mean, but I really struggle with tying it in to my masculine qualities and who I am as a man and kind of connecting the two. And I want them to connect more. I don't know how. So what role should they play? I don't know. I want them to be more connected I guess you could say, but I don't even know how. I kind of draw a blank.
>
> INTERVIEWER: That's fine. Any other thoughts there about what role it should play?
>
> TREVOR: I agree with Robert [with regard to] not having a picture in mind of an ideal that I would—that doesn't get much play, but if it got more that would be good.
>
> ROBERT: Yeah.
>
> TREVOR: But with this one, I don't have actually a whole lot of examples or images in my mind of how it might look if it were better, which is telling.

A spatial metaphor might be useful in describing the differences we saw between the Evangelical and Ecumenical Protestant informants. For the Evangelicals, the field of conceptual play for the articulation of male identities was more contingent on there being some form of male exceptionalism at the center, thus the ongoing consideration of the meaning of headship. For the Ecumenical Protestant men, a broader conceptual field of play was possible and encouraged by their religion. Thus, a variety of views, from traditionalism to egalitarianism, could be expressed with legitimacy (though none of the various views had the same unifying symbolism as the Evangelical notion of headship).

We should not overlook the potential contribution that the lived contexts of their religious lives made to these ideas and beliefs. It is clear from our interviews (and can be assumed from social research) that Evangelical and Ecumenical Protestant men experience very different structural contexts of religion. Evangelicals are far less likely to see women in significant positions of leadership. For Ecumenical Protestants, women in leadership positions are far more common. For Evangelicals, progress that women may be making in leadership is still contested to an extent that it is not (at least superficially) among Ecumenical Protestants. To return to a point above, Evangelical religious structures exhibit hard patriarchy and patriarchal orthodoxy (if not doxa). Ecumenical Protestant structures exhibit egalitarianism and gender heterodoxy. That means that the issue of gender hierarchy is relatively absent in Ecumenical Protestant religious structures. It also means that the religiously inflected discourse of headship in domestic relations is absent for them. The Ecumenical men in our cohort, in fact, found odd the whole idea that one would consider such a framework. This perspective was the case even for those men who expressed patriarchal ideals. *Headship* was simply not in their lexicon (except as a negative ideal for the egalitarian men).

This is not to say that in another context and in other conversations these Ecumenical men would not express elementalist, patriarchal ideas about what it means to be a man. In fact, it was clear that the egalitarian solution was not fully resolved for many of them. There were some significant similarities to the Evangelicals. Nearly half of the Ecumenical Protestant men we interviewed, in fact, dwelled on the cultural traditionalist end of the spectrum. Twenty-two of the Ecumenical Protestant men expressed some form of essentialism (including half of those who were egalitarians). Broadly speaking, these men agreed with their Evangelical counterparts that some fundamental things define what it means to be a man. Most would agree with the notion of male purpose or purposive action. Most would agree that men have a primary role to provide for their families. They would agree that protecting the family is the man's role. Thus, along the spectrum of egalitarianism and traditionalism discussed above, these men tended to move between cultural traditionalism and egalitarianism. And along the axis of gender essentialism, many of these were very similar to their Evangelical peers, though a much larger minority (nine of thirty-one) tacked toward constructivism.

For example, we get a sense of the more essentialist valence (particularly about the notion of purpose) from another focus group of Ecumenical Protestant men from the upper Midwest.

KEVIN: [white, married, father of three] Do you think of Jesus as being masculine though?

[*pause*]

MATT: [white, married, father of two] I don't have to, but I certainly can.

KEVIN: Do you though when you think about—

LARRY: [white, married, father of three] Well, I think the whole dying on the cross thing is more masculine than it is feminine.

OLIVER: [white, married, father of three] Knowing that was going to happen and going ahead. Knowing you're going to take a bullet and taking it, you know?

LARRY: But that's just me. You know, going out in the wilderness and starving and resisting temptation and all that—

OLIVER: Right, because just because he was compassionate and all that doesn't mean that he wasn't a man. Knowing that he was going to go on the cross and choosing that anyway, that was as masculine a decision as anyone could make in my eyes.

This sentiment about purpose (as it relates to a male savior) is strikingly similar to one made by Clark Caldwell, an Evangelical Southern pastor:

You go to *Braveheart*, and you see a man who has a cause. He has a passion; he has something he is willing to die for. And I think that's probably—if you're going to say what's the core difference between a man and a woman, a woman by and large will be protecting her children, and she may be willing to die to save her children. But she's going to try to do everything she can to protect her family; whereas a man, he may be willing to die for a cause that he just firmly believes in and that's kind of the *Braveheart* mentality. You go out. You believe something strongly. You're willing to stand up and paint your face blue and do whatever it takes because injustice needs to know that it's wrong. So sometimes men seem to need to stand up and fight for a cause.

We see a tension in many of these Ecumenical Protestant men in their identities and everyday lives. This was a tension that can take on religious dimensions (as we see in the discussion of Jesus above) but tended not to for these men. It was a tension that, at some turns, embraced egalitarianism yet, at others, espoused an essentialism that also veered toward traditionalism. To better capture this tension, we turn to an exchange between Richard and Vince, part of another focus group of young Ecumenical Protestant men from the upper Midwest, who discussed the book *Wild at Heart*:

RICHARD: [white and single with no children] On this issue of adventure, journey, and heroism, last year on internship, I read a book that a lot of people from a lot of conservative churches have been reading—Eldredge's *Wild at Heart*, which gives these sort of three fundamental characteristics . . . like you need an adventure to embark upon, a battle to fight, and a beauty to win. And he was quite explicit in saying that that's what draws us to *Braveheart* and other things. And that's why [Eldredge's] son, um, like draws pictures with guys with big swords. And like, overall, there's an awful lot that I had a hard time with and that I expected that I would, but he makes the point like there's a vividness and like, uh, a full-bloodedness that has been sucked out a lot of times. He was talking particularly in churches and kind of the models [of] what a Christian man is supposed to be, but I think it's related to this media question, so I would agree with him insofar as, like, he bemoans the insipidness of what life is for a lot of men where it's just this blasé office type, no goal, no exertion, no effort, no purposefulness, no honing of skills and person.

VINCE: [white and married] As you bring that up, I'm thinking about *Fight Club*.

RICHARD: Hmm.

VINCE: As really taking up this question of, you know, what does it mean to be a twentieth-century man? I don't know that it necessarily comes to a plausible outcome, but it deals with the question and takes it up in a really serious way, and I enjoyed that.

INTERVIEWER: And you see a parallel with Eldredge's claim that there are these elemental kinds of functions or desires out there that we're drawn to?

VINCE: Mm-hmm.

INTERVIEWER: What did you not like about Eldredge?

RICHARD: I think he makes it pretty binary. His wife has written, I think, a complement where [it's about] what is a woman? One that wants to be taken on an adventure, to be wooed or fought for. And then he grounds it theologically, like this is how men become people after God's own heart, that this is really reflective of the nature of God.

It is hard to describe the general situation with regard to Ecumenical Protestant men and their ideas about masculinity without noting the sense in which their discourses of religion and masculinity have a decidedly political frame around them. They drew a political distinction between themselves and their conservative brethren. There was a consistent tendency for them to want to differentiate themselves unequivocally from conservative ideas and to see their own ideas of masculinity in terms of distance from their notional senses of what conservative and masculinist claims might be. They wanted to push against the language that Evangelicals described as headship in the context of domestic relations and the gender binaries expressed by Richard above. They wanted to differentiate themselves from masculinist and "macho" social identities and practices beyond the home. It was important for them to say what they were *not*. Barry Aaron, an Ecumenical Protestant from a city in the western United States, was typical. "I find that some of the men that I'm most uncomfortable with are the men at the Evangelical churches. They are very head-of-the-household, 'I'm the man; I'm the religious leader of the family.' I can't handle that."

And this distinction was not just about labels; it was about the language and teachings. Brandon Lane specifically referenced the discourse of headship in talking about what he saw as negative teachings in churches: "We're called to be the spiritual leader of the household. That I got from the Bible study that was very conservative. I think I told you I left because it was too conservative." This was the common view, one that self-consciously differentiated from what they understood conservative or Evangelical practice to be.

It is important to note here that the Evangelical and Ecumenical Protestant men we interviewed actually inhabited very similar situations in their private lives and shared some strikingly similar views about gender essentialism. In spite of their differing views on headship and egalitarianism, both groups were contending with the realities of contemporary domestic gender relations, working spouses, or spouses who were primary breadwinners, for example. Among the Ecumenical Protestant men, interestingly, there were stay-at-home fathers, but most were in situations where their female spouse either was not employed outside the home or was employed only part-time. Thus the predominant discourse of egalitarianism could not be said to have necessarily moved them toward, or to have been derived from, their domestic situations (with the notable exceptions of the stay-at-home fathers). For both groups, their ideas of headship or equality seemed to be rooted elsewhere, in what we might think of as a notional normative realm of ideals.

In talking about the roles and prospects of women, these Ecumenical Protestants wanted to lodge their ideas in, and refer to, commonplace discourses in the culture, instead of in religious language. There was a general recognition of the difficulties that women face in the workplace and a general acceptance of the tendency for women to more frequently be homemakers. A key difference here was that, in place of a narrative of headship, these men tended to explain these roles as the practical outcome of different expectations and preparedness between men and women. Notably, these role expectations were tied to gender essentialism. If Evangelicals tied their essentialism to the male head, Ecumenicals tied theirs to the female heart. That is, gender role expectations were connected to the emotional/affective element of femininity, thus equipping women better for domestic roles, or so these men thought. The practical effect here is often the same—women are the primary domestic caregivers. The normative or, at least, rhetorical difference, however, is notable and speaks to the different ways in which more traditionalist Ecumenical Protestant men embodied and "spoke" gender in ways that distanced them from what they saw as the harder lines of patriarchy expressed by their Evangelical peers.

Their experience with religion was one source of their egalitarian views. Also, religion and church gave them symbolic resources to soften their edges, though as Richard noted above, this could have a tendency to feminize church and men. Generally speaking though, the men in this cohort expressed this "softening" as good and necessary. As Mike Andrews put it, church "kind of took that macho-ness out of being a man. . . ." And for the vast majority of men in this cohort, including Mike, this was a good thing. This "softening" was strongly grounded in the framework of their commitment to domestic and family life, in that it was seen by them as particularly important in their roles as fathers. And they identified these qualities and these messages as being in contrast with the broader culture. "You know, be compassionate, be empathetic, be understanding, those sort of things, which aren't exactly today's typical male qualities," said Jeremy Billings.

The Ecumenicals shared with the Evangelicals a sense that few explicit practical lessons in religion or church were directed at helping them understand what it means to be a man. And many shared with Evangelicals in a more diffuse way a sense that there are, after all, elemental characteristics of manhood and masculinity. As opposed to the religious language that is available to describe what headship might be, these men found themselves thinking about masculinity in terms of what they were *not* to do. Ricky McDonald, a self-described liberal Mennonite, reflected self-consciously on the political nature and sources of his church's teachings, in making this point:

> I think on the kind of more left side of the church, that the pacifist emphasis makes it tricky to figure out what a man is. As you combine that with the general kind of Leftist, feminist sensibility—you know what a man's not supposed to be. You're not supposed to be war-like; you're not

supposed to be aggressive. You're not even really supposed to be angry. I think that's where a lot of the abuse maybe comes from because you're not allowed to be angry because that's a sin, so it just blows up eventually because it all gets held in, and there's no way to express that. So you have all these negatives of being a man, but there's no real good real sense of what being a man is and I think sometimes quite explicitly. . . . [M]y feeling in college was, it was as good to be as womanly as you could because that meant you were being a good person. . . . You'd try to be as little manly as possible. But, you never got a positive definition of what that was.

While there was little resistance to gender equality among these Ecumenical Protestant men, the situation in their churches still left them ambivalent. Many longed for more male-specific teachings in church (across the traditionalist/egalitarian axis and the essentialist/constructivist axis), and there was a continuing undercurrent that men are different, and should be thought of differently.

There are formal men's organizations in many Ecumenical Protestant and Catholic churches. Like their Evangelical counterparts, few of our Ecumenical Protestant respondents had attended these, and the reviews were mixed. Matt Bradford had a good experience: "I got to spend a lot of time with Christian guys who were all in different walks of their Christian lives. You could talk about things that mattered as men."

Few of these men were acquainted with the neo-masculinist Evangelical literature either (with the exception of *Wild at Heart*), or for that matter with any such literature that might be more reflective of their own worldviews. Garth Johnson, an Ecumenical Protestant pastor and self-identified theological and political progressive, was an avid reader of men's literature but not that of the neo-masculinist stripe:

Some of the stuff I'm reading is specifically around male spirituality. Richard Rohr is very helpful here. James Hollis from a psychological, Jungian perspective. And Robert Johnson—he's got a book called *He-She-We*, you know, looking at [gender] differences, whether they're innate or just the way we're socialized. In the lived day-to-day in my church, it doesn't matter. This is who they are. This is where they are. I'm interested in that question of whether it's innate or not, but right now, they are who they are. This is the way they think. This is what they value. This is what they watch—ESPN. So, should I be doing a class the way they do ESPN? What does that require? So, yeah, I focus on those [types of books].

Garth was one of the few among our Ecumenical Protestant interviewees who could point to any specific religious literature or media that would be helpful for gender formation. Compared with the extensive marketplace of media available to Evangelical men, Ecumenical men found little that spoke to them from *religious* sources.

The egalitarian Ecumenical Protestant men we interviewed wanted to articulate a progressive masculinity that is aligned with feminism but is not feminine. For most, this sensibility was rooted in essentialism, in the assumption that there is elemental masculinity. But for all of them, there was a sense that religion should find a way to learn what to do with men, to help provide symbolic resources and physical spaces that would allow them to embrace feminism while coming into their own as men.

Conclusion

With few exceptions, the notion of spiritual headship was firmly entrenched among our Evangelical interviewees. They held to a kind of elementalism in their understanding of what it meant to be a man. This elementalism could be described in three words: *provision, protection,* and *purpose*. They all saw the male role to *provide* for his family, to *protect* that family, and to engage in *purposive action* oriented toward the family. The notion of headship is a way of framing gender through a divine order and channeling it through a domestic ideal, where the man's role is particular, focused, and ascendant.

This elementalism, though, must face some realities in domestic and work life. The challenge is to balance these elements and to come up with understandings of each that fit within modern life. The salient, normative symbolism of male protection, provision, and purpose is, of course, derived from earlier (even pre-industrial) times. So defining them in the modern context requires some nuance. Our Evangelical interviewees nuanced their understanding of *provision* to include both material and spiritual elements. While being the breadwinner was important, it was most important for them to exercise headship in leading their families on a godly path. *Protection* also had both a spiritual and a physical referent for them. According to many of our interviewees, the man's job is to protect his family from the dangers of the world, both symbolic and physical. As we will see in the following chapters, some of the most pressing symbolic dangers were, for them, found in the media, at the same time that media provided salient ideals of normative masculinity. These and other symbolic dangers reinforce the notion of the spiritual purpose of headship, with protection from spiritual or moral pollution seen as an important male role. Finally, it was important for them to have purpose and to see their actions in daily life as purposive. This purposiveness had two dimensions to it. First, there was the general sense that purpose is its own value. As one of our interviewees put it, "I think, you know, men, we lead by example. We share by example. We share by doing." It is in some ways enough to simply be purposive, to *do things* rather than sit back and think about them or talk about them. Second, there was the question, "Purposive about what?" For both cohorts of men, family was an unquestioned normative purpose or object of purposive action, in and of itself. One might have thought that the Biblical model of Christian purpose—"becoming fishers of men"— wherein discipleship meant leaving one's family to follow Jesus, would have carried some currency, but it was clear that it did not with any of these men (at least not in their narratives of masculinity).

In comparison to the Evangelicals, the narrative of egalitarianism among the majority of our Ecumenical Protestant interviewees was less focused and less religious. Its sources seemed to reside much more in the broader culture. These men could certainly find scriptural support of egalitarian ideas, but most did not make explicit connections to scripture. There were no Biblical proof texts for these men. Nor was there any need to navigate, discuss, or reinterpret passages about gender in the Bible. Instead, they reflexively saw their values very much in contrast to their understanding of what a more conservative view would be. They agreed that the family and the domestic sphere are the central contexts within which masculinity is most relevant. While many would agree with their Evangelical peers about provision, protection, and purpose as central elements of masculinity, they did not have a focused view, like headship, through which to particularize the male role in the domestic sphere.

A larger context of powerful social and cultural forces surrounds these domains. Cultural definitions of masculinity have shifted substantially and continue to do so. Social conditions in economics and in labor markets mean that the domestic sphere is changing as well. Longstanding understandings of gender thus face the realities of change. Ideals and symbols of masculinity must adapt. This situation is nowhere more felt than in religion. We have seen here the ways in which two contexts of religion—one more committed to conservative views of manhood, the other less so—reveal evolving symbols, conceptions, and ideas. Both contexts reveal the "ideological seams"[23] that have formed around gender struggles in American Protestantism.

We can see here evidence that these struggles actually occur on two different levels. On one level, what we might call the "normative" level, things were clearer, at least for Evangelical men. Each had a good idea of what the ideals were and of the ways questions of gender should appropriately be described. The norms differed between our Evangelical and Ecumenical men. The former looked to a normative register of meaning that was lodged in Biblical narratives and that looked more at traditional ways of being a man. The latter were less focused for their normative ideas on religious sources, looking instead at sources in the culture. Many of these Ecumenical men were more ambivalent about normative ideas of masculinity, but they were fairly unified around the normative notion that their masculinity was not conservative Evangelical masculinity (even those who were cultural traditionalists). On a different level, one we might call the "practical" level, both groups shared concern about the problems of integrating normative ideas with practical realities. This challenge was where the church and religion seemed to be particularly lacking for them. They all agreed that few, if any, clear models or teachings were available in church to help them understand their roles as men in daily life.

2

The Media That Matter

So far, we've looked at things that culture thinks of as tangible. We tend to see family, religion, and our own roles in ways that are concrete and bounded by domains of action such as home, church, and social relationships. The topic of this chapter is a domain that seems less concrete, more contested, and more open to interpretation. There are more concrete ways of thinking about media, of course, just as there are less concrete ways of thinking about religion and family. The burden of this project has been to reconsider some of these received ways of thinking. Media are rather routinely thought of in negative terms. Most of us can cite examples of negative stereotypes of men, of religion, or of family in the media. Whole curricula, both formal and extracurricular, are devoted to media impact on people's lives, arguing for "media literacies" of various kinds.

However, it is not easy to see the media in entirely negative terms, given the way people live today. Our relationship with media seems to be, at best, ambiguous, if not outright contradictory. On some level, media *are* negative. We see things we don't like. They portray important social realities in simplistic or misleading terms. We are troubled by what we see media inviting us to do, not least to spend a great deal of time and money consuming them and the things they promote and encourage. We may be even more troubled by what we see others doing with media. But the media play important roles in our lives. They are how we know about the world on a day-to-day basis. They are attractive and important centers of attention and association for us, as it is through shared media that we establish and maintain some important relationships in our lives. They are also important, even definitive, sources of shared social and cultural knowledge about roles and identities. They are, it has been claimed, today's "storytellers" through which we celebrate important ideas about social life and identity, not least in relation to gender and family.[1] We have already seen much evidence of this in this book. It was simply impossible for the men (and women) we inter-viewed to talk about masculinity without talking about media.[2] Iconic films and television roles defined the way they talked about models of manhood and masculinity.

The media are thus at the center of how we talk about masculinity, even though the men with whom we spoke wanted to stand at some dis-tance from media. We are all uneasy about our relationship to media. It is not our purpose here to explore fully or attempt to explain how and why media work in this way, but some insights are probative for the ques-tions we are considering. Our relationship to media operates through a series of frames. One determinative frame surrounds the domestic sphere, which is a central theme throughout this book. The people with whom we talked thought of home and family as a distinct and hermetic sphere of meaning and practice, and media, they claimed, threatened that sphere. Their values and their attractions ran counter to many of our respondents' normative senses of family life. This was true for our respondents across the various axes: traditionalism to egalitarianism, es-sentialism to constructivism. Media are a threat, according to most of our respondents, regardless of one's subject position regarding gender.

This view of the media is so commonplace that it is tempting to think of it as a kind of generic bourgeois idea. Indeed, a range of cultural critics and media theorists have looked at media in this way. The roots of the media theory identified with British Cultural Studies,[3] for example, are in a critique of what Raymond Williams and others saw to be a deroga-tion of the popular cultures of the working classes. Critics such as Wil-liams pointed to the need to understand and appreciate these cultural materials for their functions within lived lives. At the same time, dero-gation of popular culture could be seen to operate along certain logics of its own, preferring "high art" to "popular art" and worrying over the effects of popular culture on normative values of morality, sobriety, and industry.[4]

While cultural theorists have had much to say about the roots of media tastes and practices in social class, they have given less attention to media in relation to religion, faith, spirituality, or, even, morality. The kinds of things people in these pages have said about media are often ar-ticulated directly in relation to religious values and ideals, so it is worth considering such readings of media in their own terms. In what ways is religion uniquely active—or uniquely implicated—in a given media taste, expression, or behavior? A growing literature in the study of media and religion raises the question of whether there are particularly *religious* things about media and particular ways that religious meanings and motivations derive from media behaviors or arise in the media sphere.[5]

Thinking about the media surrounding ideals of the domestic sphere raises yet another valence of how religion might be especially involved. Taking into account the historical role of Protestantism in the American experiment suggests that the mainstream, bourgeois lenses through which we look at media derive in some unique ways from Protestantism itself.[6] The emergence of audiences for the various media that rose to prominence in the twentieth century was contingent in important ways on the readiness of Protestant culture to embrace popular print literature, then radio and film, then television. With each of these media, similar resistances emerged to the challenges these various media posed to Protestant values of industry, sobriety, discipline, and self-restraint.[7] Such values are, of course, not unique to Protestants. Whether we see them as simply consonant with broader middle-class domestic ideals, or the source of them, they nonetheless come to provide that important frame through which we—and particularly our informants here—think and talk about media.

In an earlier work[8] we suggested that media audiences describe their media practices around three such frames. The first we called "experiences *in* media." These are narratives of audiences' own media practices, including those media they like, identify with, find salient, or even consider "guilty pleasures." The second of these frames we called "interactions *about* media." These are narratives of how the media become part of the audiences' social relationships, including everything from family "appointment viewing" to "water cooler" conversations at work to casual mentions in various settings. The third frame we called "accounts *of* media." By this we meant a broader framework of public scripts about the media, generalized truisms about media use and media effects, and various concerns and anxieties about the way media might or might not be influencing the audiences' or others' families or children.[9] This last category is most intriguing in light of our inquiries here. Much of the received view of media in relation to masculinity, for example, is precisely this kind of account. At the same time, much of what we will consider in this chapter moves among these frames. To an extent, whatever ambiguities we see in people's relationships with media are both about particulars of media content and practice and about the varying ways in which each of us encounters and interacts with media.

The scholarly literature in media and masculinity reveals additional ambiguities. The majority of this work has traditionally centered on sex-role stereotypes, with the earliest studies focused on portrayals of women and girls, followed by work on male stereotypes.[10] More recent concerns of gender studies have moved the discourse in directions that broaden and deepen the way in which media scholars look at gender. Gender today is seen by scholars in more complex and nuanced terms. Scholars recognize—among other things—that rather than being singular, there are in fact "multiple masculinities" that are constructed in specific social and historical settings.[11]

How we think about the role of media in masculinity is rooted in part in whether we see masculinity as *inherent* or something that is, in fact, *constructed by* societies and cultures. Many of the men with whom we talked thought there was something we are calling "elemental" masculinity. The fundamental male characteristics of provision, protection, and purpose were felt by many to be inherent and immutable. Women, for some of these men, might share in these three characteristics also, but for the overwhelming majority of the men in this study, there was something unique about *male* provision, protection, and purpose. There is also evidence here of something that mirrors larger cultural discourses about these issues: continuing reflection about the role of the feminist movement in conditioning both everyday men's experiences and the way men are encouraged to think about masculinity and maleness. As we have noted, some voices, particularly from traditionalist and neo-masculinist directions, see feminism as largely to blame for creating whatever "crisis" there is in contemporary masculinity.[12] Equally significant voices contend that rather than a matter of a natural state of essential masculinity, what may be occurring today is the result of public representations of men and masculinity. These symbolic constructions of masculinity—so the argument goes—have displaced men's and women's attention from their concrete, everyday lives and replaced them with representations and expectations that are both misleading and unrealistic. It is a truism that critics think media are central to these issues.

Negative stereotypes of men—in this view—serve both to stigmatize them and to condition their own, and others', senses of who they are.[13]

Media scholars have substantially broadened this debate, helpfully moving it away from the persistent claim that media function only in instrumental or negative ways. To focus on media pathology alone narrows the ways in which media contribute to identities. A more "culturalist" view of media and gender instead looks at the ways in which gender identities are constructed out of available repertoires of cultural resources. Judith Butler's influential work on the constitution of gender,[14] for example, implies a role for media, as gender is understood to result from individuals' taking on symbolic resources available from a public inventory of possibilities.[15] As Mia Consalvo has put it, a large research agenda is looking into the ways media "construct masculinity in a particular time and place, and how these outlets differentiate between various forms of the masculine."[16]

Studies of such differentiations have shown a wide range of portrayals, but with two dominant themes significant to our project. First, most studies have found in many media what we might call "traditionalist" views of masculinity.[17] Second, in recent times, softer and less traditional portrayals have also begun to appear.[18] But to many observers, the dominant image of men remains traditional in such contexts as sports, dramas, and situation comedies. As one of them has put it, these media "portray men as violent and aggressive thieves, murderers, wife and girlfriend beaters, sexual abusers, molesters, perverts, irresponsible, deadbeat dads and philanderers. . . ."[19] Taken together, the available literature suggests that the media portray constructions of masculine identity that range from the patriarchal to the pathological, with a sliver of the symbolic sphere left for the progressive feminist. Still other sources suggest that a range of *receptions* of media is also possible, from those that accept to those that resist representations.[20]

In all of this scholarship, the question of whether such representations actually *construct* masculinity or merely *represent* it remains open. In important works that look at how audiences consume media, the more complex, culturalist view we introduced earlier comes to the fore. This view encouraged us to talk with people about their experiences with media and come to an understanding that it is not a matter of either construction or reflection but a complex interaction of the two.

David Gauntlett, for example, in his studies of masculinity and media,[21] draws most notably on Anthony Giddens's notion that identity today is increasingly a "reflexive project of the self," wherein individuals account for their sense of self through a sense of autonomy over its sources and meanings. Such an approach centers identity formation on the experiences, logics, and practices through which people encounter the media sphere. This reflexivity is a condition of modernity, Giddens and Gauntlett argue, that is itself an outcome of an era in which media seem to empower individuals to know more about the workings of self and society than was the case in the past. Thus, Gauntlett points outs, in order to account for the role media play in identity, we need to understand both their processes of representation and their processes of construction and to look for ways in which both are active in the lives of audience members. Gauntlett has proposed that the collection of "self-narratives" of the kind we have seen here is a powerful way of accounting for evolving identities of masculinity. He argues that this is of particular value in understanding the way media are active in gender but that this needs to be seen along a number of dimensions. First, as people work to construct "selves" today, they are objectifying and routinizing ways of life that were previously less self-conscious. Second, the "reflexivity" of which Giddens and others speak means that people are more self-conscious about social life and necessarily more calculating about their choices and actions. Third, Gauntlett points to an important *indirect* role for the media in providing a view "behind the scenes" of social and personal life, reinforcing the sense of autonomy over action even on personal levels such as in gender identity. Fourth, he sees a more direct role for the media as sources of information about lifestyle, taste, sexuality, gender, family, and domestic roles and as sources that demonstrate the reflexive engagement of the self through their narratives. Fifth, he sees a further implication that shared media consumption—like shared lifestyle choices—provides linkage to "communities of people who are 'like us'—or people who, at least, have made similar choices."[22]

The three frames for media engagement we introduced earlier ("experiences in media," "interactions about media," and "accounts of media") are active in these considerations introduced by Gauntlett. We've suggested throughout this book that the collection of narratives of the self provides a powerful perspective from which to think about disparately constituted domains of meaning and action, for example religion, media, and masculinity. While most prior work on media and gender—including Gauntlett's—does not explicitly address questions of religion or spirituality, we contemplate religion as well.

Understanding the whole project as one of narrativizing the self, we now turn to the question of media in our interviews. We expected to have collected in these narratives a range of perspectives on the way in which media seem to represent men and masculinity. It will not be a surprise to learn that many of these narratives fit into the most straightforward and traditional framework that has so dominated scholarly and lay discourse about media and men: the negative, even pathological, representations of men and masculinity that seem so common. But given what we have said about the complexities of understanding the ways in which people interact with media, we wanted to look within these narratives for differing, and even contradictory, positions, sensibilities, and purposes. And we wanted to be able to account for what we have described as the ambiguity between media and normative ideas of the domestic, of family, and of gender.

The ambiguities of individuals' relationships with media and with the domains of religion, family, and gender mean that conversations about these issues are complex. It is not easy to engage people in conversations about media, for example, that are not framed by what we have called "accounts of media." These accounts of media are suspicious of media as powerful threats to the ideals of domestic life. They also tend to agree with the media critiques of neo-traditionalists and others who have held that ideals of masculinity in media are by and large negative, counterproductive, and antisocial. The reflexivity with which people encounter media also frames their discourses with a veneer of autonomy and choice. Each of these ideas is deserving of careful reflection on its own because each conditions what we are able to know in the first instance when we engage people in conversations about media and masculinity.

Thinking about Masculinity in the Media Context

What we have learned from our conversations so far is that much of the tacit knowledge about where men construct "masculine identity" is in need of rethinking. First, there is no clear, universal sense from these interviews about the provenance of such ideas. It is not just that there is disagreement here about such sources; on a more fundamental level, there is not a clear sense that such ideas have real, direct sources in the expected places. Particularly telling to our project, most men don't attribute a great repertoire of specific ideas to their fathers. Instead, while most seem to have learned what they consider positive things from fathers, many do not want to emulate some key things about their fathers' practices. This was expressed in a common refrain, "My dad was a great dad, but . . . ." Most particularly, there is in these interviews a commonplace sense that most men want to spend more time with their own children and families than their fathers spent with them.

Thus, while most could articulate a set of core values they learned from their fathers, those values did not include much in the way of specific and direct teachings about what it meant to be a man or a father today.[23] Their relationships to these role models were more in the nature of observation or learning-by-example (sometimes negatively). And for most of the men we've heard from here, the more extensive range of things that are components of "elemental masculinity" seem to derive as much from the broader culture as they do from their family of origin.

Likewise, in most of our conversations, the role of religion or of church in making sense of what it means to be a man is rather obscure. As we noted earlier, there is a difference between Evangelicals and Ecumenical Protestants among our conversations in that while both groups had some difficulty pointing to specific ways in which religion directly shapes their sense of themselves as men, Evangelicals, at least, thought that it should. The overall sense, though, was that religion-as-a-practice, like father-as-a-teacher, had not provided enough unique, practical resources to masculine identity (at least not positively). With Evangelicals, there was a strong discourse of normative resources, for example the "theology of headship," but this discourse was made ambiguous with what we might call the "practicalities of provision" in late modernity wherein both parents in the nuclear family must engage in paid labor and where men take on broader cultural norms to provide *emotionally* for their spouses and children. For many of these Evangelicals, late modern conservative Evangelical religion either overemphasized certain aspects of provision (e.g., tenderness to the point of feminization) or failed to provide clear, practical resources with which to live out the normative ideal of headship. Like with father or sources in the "social capital" of the broader community, the broader culture seemed as much the source for normative and practical resources as religion or family of origin was.

What has emerged here is that elemental masculinity seems to be lodged in more heterogeneous and generic symbolic resources. For the men in this study, this creates fixed "zones of ambiguity."[24] The three specific elemental zones that are the consensus in our conversations—*provision, protection,* and *purpose*—are seen to be singularly important at the same time that they are both abstract and fluid. Further, while we expected religion or family to help elaborate specific realms of action that would connect these generic ideas to the practicalities of daily life, they seem not to do so in any clear way. It is clear that most Evangelical men in our sample draw on resources from religion to define these "zones" and to navigate the ambiguities therein, but even their navigation is not as direct as we might have expected.

This has two implications for what we expect of media. First, to the extent that the broader culture is the most important context in relation to these others, the media might well be important sources of that broader culture and the window through which individuals access their ideas about manhood and masculinity. Second—and perhaps more important—there may not be a reason to expect that the more "foundational" sources in home, family, and church should necessarily take precedence over other cultural sources, specifically the media. In fact, the men in our study seemed to agree with this assertion *because* media are ubiquitous and inevitable. For example, Larry Cane, an Evangelical seminary student, commented on the role of media in young American Christian lives:

Our team [on a trip in Africa] was so immersed in movies and TV shows and music. [The team from Africa] was so immersed in scripture and that sounds kind of like—I'm sure they have plenty of problems, but it was so obvious that because they didn't have all those things, they were spending a lot of time in the Word, and really knew it, and that was shameful to me and to a lot the people on our team just because it was like, well, we could recite every line from *Napoleon Dynamite* or, you know, worse movies and yet when Scripture was spoken, we'd be like, "Wow, I think

I've heard that." So it was just [that] their common language was Scripture. Our common language was movie language, was movies. And so that just—it just made me realize how powerful the media influence is on our kids and how much it's going to take to take them outside of that and see something. Because I think most of that is destructive. I mean I think that—obviously we don't want to paint media as this—there's nothing good that comes out of it because I don't think that. But within America today, most of the messages that are being portrayed through movies and TV shows are far from Biblical, if even moral, if even truthful. And so if that's what our kids are being so inundated with, it profoundly impacts their actions when, uh . . . when we're trying to present a different message. It just makes me aware of how difficult our task is and how important it is to recognize that the Holy Spirit has to play a role there because if not I don't know that we have much hope in counteracting the message that they're hearing through media.

As we see from Larry, the most common responses to media are those that see media as a threat to normative ideals, to positive senses of identity, and to the overall project of the home and domestic sphere. We also see that in American life at least, people like Larry believe the media are *the* primary arbiters of identity (at least for *other* youth). We've stressed that we need to account for this type of discourse in relation to the ambiguities of media practices. But there is also much to learn from looking at what kind of cultural "work" is being done by these types of accounts. How do the ambiguous and sometimes contradictory ways in which we think and talk about media contribute to and frame our overall sense of ourselves, particularly in interaction? To the extent that identity is something formed in relation to others (and there is much evidence to suggest that it is primarily so formed[25]), the resources and logics we use in presenting ourselves in such contexts are significant. And as we have argued, media play a central role in conversations about masculine identity. It is also clear from our conversations that to assign media only to categories of threat, portent, and danger, as Larry and many observers did, seriously limits our understanding of the ways media are thought about and used in narratives and interactions.

We have the opportunity here to focus in a broader way on the ways in which media are talked about in relation to religious identity. The large question we've wanted to address was raised by the neo-traditionalist critics we introduced earlier: that of the threat that media pose to true, normative masculinity. As we saw there, there are two valences to this threat. The first is the impact of media messages on men. The second valence raised by these critics is a kind of "displacement" effect, wherein men and families are seen to be simply spending too much time with media at the expense of other, more valuable and authentic interactions and activities. We can see both valences expressed in Larry Cane's thoughts, evidence of the ways in which many men have internalized this broader discourse.

Sex and Violence

Most of our respondents saw in media content a real threat to their authentic, spiritual, or religious masculine "selves." The larger frame of this concern is the broader societal discourse about "sex and violence" in media.[26] These two elements of media content were central concerns in our interviews but with some important differences along religious lines. For our Evangelical informants, sex in media loomed larger than violence and with some interesting texts and subtexts. The problem for these men was that they saw sexual media content as conflicting with their quest to construct authentic, spiritual, masculine "selves." They saw the kind of sexuality portrayed in most media as intervening both in their relationship with God (feeling the need for a kind of essential "purity" as a precondition to their spirituality) and in their ability to be the central, spiritual, and moral force in their households.

The concept of headship is very much at the center of this. Spiritual headship assumes moral and mental purity, and men's own consumption of sexual material in media would impede this purity, in their view, though this was not the case for viewing violent material. Both Evangelicals and Ecumenical Protestants among our conversations had the commonplace sense that media, in such areas as sexuality and violence, constitute a threat to the moral and ethical purity of the family. Keeping the essential, hermetic space of the family inviolate from such penetration by external forces, ideas, and values presented itself as an important dimension of men's sense of their essential role of protector. For Evangelicals, though, there was another, prior concern with their own purity and the impact that sexuality might have on their ability to provide moral leadership to the home.

Ecumenical Protestants among our informants differed markedly in that their concern was much more "other-centered"—that is, directed toward protecting their children. The question of how sexuality in media might affect their own identities as men was of less importance. This is interesting because it implies a different sense of autonomy with regard to media, with Ecumenical Protestants suggesting they might be personally less affected by media portrayals of sex, violence, or anything else. Concomitant with this, of course, is the notion that others—particularly children—might be more affected than they and are thus in need of protection from media. The Ecumenical Protestants here were more likely to see the problem in their own lives as one of time use or "distraction" than of actual effects of content. Garth Johnson, one of the few Ecumenical Protestant men who reflected for us on potential media impacts in his own life, said, "And I'm, myself too, I get caught because it's just, it's entertaining, um, but largely just distracting and keeping us from living lives that are—we're turning to this as a way of distracting ourselves from feeling our own pain or feeling any kind of anything real in our lives."

Garth's concern about media in his own life was centered on the media as a distraction from authentic affect. However, when Garth talked about his concerns with regard to media for his children, his primary concerns were with violence, language, and sexuality (in addition to time spent with media).

Similarly, Brandon and Louise Lane, an Ecumenical couple, provided a good example of these ambiguities as they discussed issues of sexuality in their media diets:

> BRANDON: We were huge *Friends* fans. So we have all ten seasons on DVD, and it's a funny show, pretty lighthearted. So we would watch that a lot before we would go to sleep. And we would watch it with our eight-year-old, [who was] then five- or six-year-old, daughter. And then after a while, we just started realizing that she's starting to understand this stuff, and there's not a single show that they don't have some sort of sexual innuendo. And so, I think about a year ago we said, no more because she was just—

LOUISE: We just realized that was not a very good judgment on our part.

BRANDON: We're terrible parents [*both laugh*]. So we stopped doing that.

INTERVIEWER: OK. Is the sexual innuendo in programs the biggest concern as far as what your kids can watch or not watch, or are there other things that you try to avoid?

LOUISE: Well, I think with the *Friends* show it was because there wasn't anything scary, and I think for *Twilight*, there's sexual innuendo and just suggestions, but it's also scary and pretty violent the way things turn out for some of the people in the book and in the movie because I know when that came out—she never really asked, expressed an interest because I think she knows vampires are scary or whatever, so I think we protect her, try to protect her from anything that would make her too fearful.

INTERVIEWER: Do you anticipate that changing? I mean, is *Twilight* something that will be off-limits—or anything like *Twilight*—or is there a particular time when you think she'll be able to handle that, or is it just something that you don't think she ever should watch?

LOUISE: Oh, I think—I don't know, for me I guess, just personally speaking, I was thinking, you know, maybe middle school, maybe upper middle school, kind of—

INTERVIEWER: So it is an "age appropriate" thing—

LOUISE: I think so.

Contrast this with the Southern Evangelical couple Brent and Angela Tucker, who discussed how *Friends* became appropriate after they were married, indicating that the issues of sexuality in the show were related to their own sense of purity, not the influence of sexual imagery on their children (though they would be concerned with that also).

INTERVIEWER: [*referring to a questionnaire*] You both put *Friends*.

ANGELA: It's just really funny. And neither of us liked it growing up. It's now that we're married and a little older. This is the very first time we really liked it.

BRENT: We didn't even like it when the show was on.

ANGELA: Like when we were in college, we thought it was kind of dirty, but now that we're married, I don't know.

BRENT: I guess we can listen to sex jokes now that we've had sex. I've never thought about that.

For Brent and Angela, the question of sexuality was clearly a concern for their individual lives and for their marriage. At one point in their dating life, *Friends* was inappropriate because of its sexuality. Such "dirtiness" was, we might imagine, a challenge to their sense of sexual purity. Now that they were married, this sort of sexual banter was both humorous and acceptable in their relationship. In some ways this may run counter to the stereotypical Evangelical view of sexuality, which would condemn sexuality in the media. In fact, other Evangelicals rejected *Friends* on these very terms, as we'll see below. But for Brent and Angela, their engagement with *Friends* was more nuanced. On the one hand, the Tuckers embraced a show that, in many ways, is about extramarital sex, something they would not condone. Yet, on the other hand, the sexual humor was appropriate in their relationship *because* they were allowed to have sex within the boundaries of marriage. Clearly, though, there were ambiguities and limits to their consumption of sexual content. Where *Friends* was acceptable to them, *That '70s Show* was on the very edge of acceptability (though Angela still watched it as a guilty pleasure).

ANGELA: Like *That '70s Show*, I would never watch, never watch when it was actually on, but it's on at 4 when I feed [the children], and so I turn it on and watch it. But I don't think I agree with any of the values in it.

INTERVIEWER: Do you disagree with the values in it?

ANGELA: Yeah.

INTERVIEWER: So, what's the difference in that and maybe some of the stuff that you would not watch? You didn't list [in a journal she filled out as part of our interview process] specifics on that but things too scary or too much sex or violence. Is there a threshold there *That '70s Show* doesn't cross?

ANGELA: What do you think, honey?

BRENT: I don't know if *That '70s Show* is explicit, you know?

ANGELA: Yeah.

INTERVIEWER: So more innuendo than explicit sex or violence [is appropriate]?

ANGELA: Yeah.

INTERVIEWER: So talking about sex or sexual humor is not across [your boundaries]?

ANGELA: And I really feel like it's different now that we're married?

BRENT: Yeah.

The negotiations with sexuality here are complex, even contradictory. What is central to our inquiry here, however, is that first, sexuality was a concern and negotiation for the Tuckers' individual lives much more than it was a concern for their Ecumenical Protestant counterparts and, second, engagement with sexuality was negotiated in more complicated ways *within* the Evangelical marriage relationship than many might have expected.

Brandon's and Louise's reflections also illustrate an interesting interaction between their ideas about sexuality and violence in media. They expressed heightened concern about their daughter's feeling afraid because of the violence in *Twilight*. Their concerns about sex in these films seemed to pale in comparison.

Brent and Angela also had concerns about media violence, but this concern came in third behind foul language (a concern they share with their Ecumenical Protestant peers) and sex for them:

BRENT: Language first. Because that's one of your first impressions that you get of somebody. You know, if I were to drop the F-bomb right when you came in and said, "How the 'f' are you?" That would give you somewhat of an impression.

INTERVIEWER: True.

BRENT: I would say sex probably second. It can ruin—it has a tendency to be a destructive factor until you're married and then, I don't know, violence probably after that. Same? Different [to her]?

ANGELA: Yeah, I guess similar. I kind of think violence is up there.

INTERVIEWER: On the same level with sex and language?

ANGELA: Yeah, I would say so. Like even cartoons are kind of violent. I just feel like I want to be with, which I can't be all the time, but I just really want to be with them watching TV and be involved with what they are learning, so I can know and comment on it.

BRENT: But I think it's good up to a certain age, but then I think, some movies, albeit very graphic, do expose kids to a lot of—would expose a young adult to a good perspective on life, or a healthy perspective, like historical movies.

ANGELA: *The Patriot, Gladiator*—

BRENT: Or more accurate things such as *Black Hawk Down*, along those lines. But I don't think nixing all that stuff out would be a good thing.

ANGELA: I think screening it before they watch it and watching it with them.

BRENT: Oh yeah.

Sexual innuendo was acceptable in Brent and Angela's private viewing because they were married, but in their opinion it would be unacceptable for unwed people. At the same time, explicit sexuality would be clearly inappropriate for them to view with their children, alone or as a couple. However, explicit violence, if "historical" or "accurate," could be useful, if done in the service of good moral lessons. The implication, of course, was that explicit sexuality could never be valuable in the same way.

Brandon Lane's concern with sexuality was clearly different. He was seemingly unconcerned with the question of moral purity and less concerned with sexually explicit content. Explicit sexual content, for example pornography, could be a problem, but only if it dominated time and attention:

I have a book . . . . It has to do with, um, sinful thoughts as opposed [to], you know, every man's struggle with sexuality. And impure thoughts, and thoughts about other women as opposed to your spouse. . . . Um, we had several guys in the Bible study who were addicted to pornography. And my kind of thought was, well, who isn't, you know? And then, but these guys were seriously—I realized that when they say addiction—I mean they would get on and fourteen hours later they would get off. I mean they were staying on all night just looking at porn. And I thought, "Okay, yeah, that's a different level."

The sense here is that the problem with pornography is not so much its questionable moral values as it is the question of its domination of time and will. In this way, Brandon represented a tendency that emerged from the interviews with our Ecumenical Protestant men: a desire to parse the question of sexuality in a way that was distinct from the traditional conservative moralism and looked for new ways to think about the question of sexuality in the media.

Likewise Garth, also an Ecumenical Protestant, reflecting on his responsibility as a parent to monitor or control the media his children were exposed to, addressed this question through the lens of his own fatherhood and his protection of his daughters from sexual objectification:

> It's very hard to say that it's always up to the parent—that I just have to tell my child, you just don't get to watch TV or look at magazines. And it's not [the responsibility of the media] to consider what it means to have a twelve-year-old who's got a halter top and trying to look like Britney Spears? So you can see I'm going to have to raise my daughter in this, and it's not helpful. And I'm not some damned prude that can't deal with a little, you know, sex. It's just that this isn't helping her if she starts to see herself as this sexual object when she's twelve.

Rather than frame sex in the media in relation to personal moral opprobrium, Garth saw things through the frame of the idea of "protection." His role was to protect his daughters from self-imaging as sexual objects. This turn combines the elemental role of protection with ideas rooted in feminism. Again, Evangelical families also saw this issue in terms of protection, but their concern was rooted less in feminism and more in a concern with moral purity, which tends, they thought, to connect to the notion of headship because explicit sexuality is primarily every *man's* battle, to borrow the title of a popular Evangelical self-help book about men and pornography.

This relative lack of concern among Ecumenical Protestant men with media depictions of sexual behaviors was echoed even among the most conservative among them. Mike Andrews, an Ecumenical Protestant, expressed some of the most conservative religious and social views we found among our Ecumenical Protestants. He spoke in some detail about Tony Soprano, the lead character in the long-running HBO series *The Sopranos.* Asked specifically what he considered to be negative qualities in this character, he focused on Tony's fathering skills:

> The way he would talk in front of his kids, you know, the language in front of his kids, the physical violence in front of his kids. You know, there've been times when I've been so mad at the kids or so mad at [his spouse] that I just go out to the garage and kind of get away from the situation before I let my words hurt, you know. Um, um, [*a very long pause*] I guess, come to think of it, Tony would never admit that he was wrong. I think that's a horrible quality.

Mike's view of Tony is notable in that it overlooked an extensive array of ways that the program, and Tony in particular, might be criticized for portrayals of sexuality. Tony owned a strip club and was frequently unfaithful to his wife (including casual encounters with the women in his employ). The program was sexually explicit, and nudity was common. One might have expected that a conservative parent's view of this program would focus on these areas rather than on its portrayals of parenting.

Our Evangelicals' more focused views of the threat posed by the media centered more directly on the area of sexuality. For them, this seemed to be a singular concern with how the visual representation of sex, sexuality, and nudity might affect their own personal faith. Many of our Evangelical interviewees felt that such representations might also be bad for children, but their focus on the relationship between sexuality and their own faith journeys was unique to them and important in Evangelical men's constructions of masculinity, as it related to headship.

Similar to Brent and Angela Tucker, Mark Simms expressed ideas typical of many Evangelicals, both seeing media as a threat to faith and in expressing the Evangelical view of sex and violence in media. For Mark, and for many other parents, this concern was framed by an overall sense that media have a kind of insidious role in domestic life, insinuating themselves into viewers' lives and consciousnesses: "The struggle is that we use media as entertainment when we're tired and want to relax, yet sometimes the objective of the creator is to influence, and in a sense you are not in a position to evaluate it. You're just taking it in passively. I find myself adopting attitudes."

Reflecting on the specific values contained in media, Mark made a distinction between sex and violence: "But the moral values—what people define as moral values, and in our culture that has more to do with sexuality than most things. My observation is that it's okay, it's more okay to see an R-rated violent movie than an R-rated sexual movie— that's kind of a cultural thing, I think. For me, I'm part of that culture, so I'm more comfortable with a violent movie than an overtly sexual movie."

In what may well be a change from earlier times in conservative Christian households, many of our Evangelical men and couples did, in fact, admit to viewing films with questionable sexual content. Rather than avoid high-profile and popular films, many of them took a look, but their approach to viewing was different from that of members of other households. Larry Cane agreed with the Simmses' sense that a good deal of the danger of media, particularly media sexuality, was in a kind of contagion of the mind. "Even if it's a really great, powerful story, unless there's something we feel like we need to watch for other reasons, then we can skip some parts at home. . . . Those kinds of images are the types that get burned in[to] your brain, and so there's a different level of, I don't know what the word would be, but just. . . . Those are movies I wouldn't be willing to watch."

At the same time, though, Larry articulated a central challenge that conservative Evangelicals face in today's media environment, the sense that they don't want to be left behind or isolated from the common culture:[27]

> There are some [forms of media] that we just chose not to see even though a lot of people were talking about them. Usually there's kind of those big movies that everyone's talking about; we usually want to see them just so we can be a part of the discussion, not because we—you know. But there are certain movies that we just say, "Know what? We can just opt out of this discussion." We can know a little bit about the movie, but we don't need those images to be a part of our [consciousnesses].

Larry's spouse, Linda, described their viewing method in her discussion of the film *Atonement*: "And, uh, and it was one of those movies, it was nominated for Best Picture, and everybody was talking about it, but we knew that there was some sexuality in it. I really wanted to see it, and Larry was less excited. Anyway, we ended up renting it and just skipping through the like ten-minute-long sex scene in it. And in the end we were like, 'Well, that was really not necessarily worth the dollar we paid for it.'"

Television is also a temptation of the common culture, and certain genres of television seem particularly prone to carry sexual content. Ned and Stacy Everly, an Evangelical couple from the South, identified the sitcom as such a genre. As Ned put it, "Usually just the gestures about sex. They usually go back to some sort of sex." Stacy agreed. "Sexual innuendos throughout the whole thing. That's not funny to me, although some people find it hilarious. But I personally don't think it's funny. I think it's gross, and I don't want to see it." Ned noted that they avoided the sitcom *Friends* because of its sexual innuendo. Stacy observed that this also placed them at some distance from the common culture and positioned them as outliers among some of their acquaintances and friends. "And the whole thing was about all of them living together, and they'd sleep together, which I know we get so much flack about not watching *Friends*. Everybody loves *Friends*. People have always been [shocked] thinking we're just so judgmental. But we're not judgmental [about] watching it. We just don't want to watch it. You know—everybody has their own thing, you know."

This all may be a sign of the times, as we have noted. In an earlier time, conservative Christians might well have been more comfortably segregated both from questionable media and from contexts of social pressure to participate in the common culture. Midwestern Protestant families, for example, might not have faced the challenge of participating in cultural offerings from outside their geographic or religious settings. Today, the situation is far different. As has been widely observed elsewhere,[28] children today are embedded in a media-saturated culture at school, on the playground, and in their friend relationships. Parents thus face the challenge of pervasive media and the need to address their children's (and their own) feelings of isolation and potential stigmatization if they limit media too much.

These Evangelical couples show that this is a situation they also faced. On the one hand, they saw themselves as justly distinct in their media tastes and attitudes. They were concerned that some media—particularly sexualized media—might have a negative impact on their faith (though it is clear that there was a difference of opinion among the Evangelicals about the boundaries of *acceptable* sexuality in media). They expressed personal tastes in relation to these media, tastes of which some were defiantly proud. But at the same time they were keenly aware of the ubiquity of the media of the common culture, and they were drawn to participate, at least to some extent. They didn't want to be left out. And, frankly, some like Brent and Angela Tucker clearly enjoyed sexualized media (within certain limits). This does not mean they were necessarily abandoning deeply held values. At least as they described their practices, they found ways of familiarizing themselves with and, often, enjoying these media and at the same time protecting themselves from what they perceived as the threat.

The potential influence and pull of the common culture in the media lives of our Evangelical households are significant. For example, many (but not most) of these interviewees were concerned about a specific representation of sexuality in media: the presence of gay characters and homosexuality as a theme. Clark Caldwell, an Evangelical pastor in the South, compared this with the way media treat gender stereotypes:

> They've done a lot with gender roles and trying to debunk or dispel stereotypes, which is a good thing. But on the same hand, the media portrays—I don't know how to delicately say this—alternative lifestyles as being absolutely normal. So, having a lot of homosexual influence in sitcoms and television—by and large when you have less than two percent of your population being of one persuasion, even if it's political or religious in nature, but yet in the media it's portrayed at a much higher percentage than it actually is in real life, then the value of that seems to give a whole lot more weight and credence to a particular—whether it's a political thing or whether it's an agenda to be pushed.

This was most obvious to Clark and others in two popular (and pace-setting) programs of the 2000s, *Will and Grace* and *Queer Eye for the Straight Guy*. Each of these portrayed—in the view of our interviewees—both a problematic normativity for LGBTQ "lifestyle" and a problematic image of masculinity and gender relations.

Asked for a negative example of masculinity in media, Ned Everly goes immediately to these programs:

> NED: Anytime I watch any of those homosexual-type shows where there's—I'm trying to think of that stupid one, um, I can't remember the name of it because I never watch it.
>
> INTERVIEWER: *Queer Eye for the Straight Guy?*
>
> NED: That would be a good one, but that's not the one I'm thinking of.
>
> INTERVIEWER: *Will and Grace?*
>
> NED: *Will and Grace.* That was the other one.
>
> INTERVIEWER: So that would be a representative of—is it just the homosexuality, or are there a whole bunch of other qualities that are wrapped up in that which make that a negative?
>
> NED: Both. [Will] acts like a woman about half of the time, the way he talks. He relates to his girlfriend better than he does [to] a guy friend.

Denton Calhoun saw such stereotypes in a kind of competition with positive portrayals of masculinity in media: "I mean it's all over the board because for every time you have Mel Gibson playing *The Patriot*, you have *Queer Eye for the Straight Guy*, so it's all over the board." For Denton, it was a question both of a kind of balance (or imbalance) and a sense that within the media sphere specific tropes and memes compete for ascendancy.

A much more common concern among our interviewees was a tendency for entertainment television to emasculate or feminize men, especially fathers. This "dumbing down of Dad" was by far the most common criticism of television's portrayal of masculinity we encountered. The concern with homosexuality, while notable, paled in comparison to the perceived negative portrayal of fathers.

Men and Fathers

Our conservative interviewees were (perhaps not surprisingly) more likely to point out cases of feminization or violation of traditional gender roles than were the others. Perhaps another sign of the times, these criticisms were often nuanced. For example, Denton Calhoun is here talking about gender role balance in television. Perhaps as further evidence of the appeal of the media as a kind of common culture, Denton presented a critique of some programs with which one might be surprised he was familiar:

> I was thinking about the way mass media depicts manliness. . . . I think this is probably a change from the past if you think about something you'd see on the E! network or TV Guide Channel when they are covering the red carpet thing, I would bet you that twenty or thirty years ago—that if there is a person there standing interviewing people and commenting on the way they are dressed and things like that [it would have been] a woman. And today, if it's not 50–50, then it's a lot closer to 50–50, men versus women, and that's not a very traditional idea—men talking about what she's wearing and that sort of thing. That seems to be a newer trend toward the metrosexual sort of thing and I guess the more out-of-the-closet gay. I mean it's always been people like that, but in [the] 1950s and 1960s, people who were on TV weren't like that, for the most part.

It is not surprising that for some to whom we spoke, feminization/ emasculation would be tied directly to concern about homosexuality. For many others, this was less explicitly articulated as they described an overall concern about these perceived trends in entertainment media.[29] For many of our Evangelical men, the notion of feminization/emasculation was framed within their concern for the male headship role we discussed earlier. Here is John Little, a student in a nondenominational Evangelical seminary:

> Most of the shows play down the role of men in the household. . . . Not that women can't be leaders within the household, but men are almost lacking any kind of leadership because—they're portraying the women as so dominant to men. The men are like unable or unwilling to take up their leadership role. I think that's playing into our culture. Again, I say this not to say that women can't be leaders because I think they can be, but our culture has switched to, um, such a way that women . . . [looking for words] women are . . . it—I don't even know how to say this without making it sound bad because I don't mean it bad.

As with many of our Evangelical interviewees, John struggled to articulate his ideas in relation to what he saw as the dominant gender themes of the culture:

> I think that women have equal rights with men. I'm not saying there's a hierarchical system within the household. But I do think that Biblically, men are supposed to take up the leadership role within the household as the head of the house, not that women can't be leaders as well. But, in our culture, it's—if you even suggest that notion, you'll get 1,000 phone calls or a lawsuit on you. So I think that's what the media is playing to. They're playing culturally sensitive, um, not—so they're almost going the reverse, opposite. Before it was men dominant, like all men dominant, like in the early ages. Now it's like all women dominant, and the men are in completely subservient positions, no authority, no—so it's almost flipped. So instead of doing like the equal kind of role, like equal leadership with the men—I don't think watching sitcoms can actually help me in leadership. I think they give a wrong image and a wrong perspective on what a household should be built on.

The difficulty of expressing a nuanced sense of headship in the context of contemporary gender role expectations is even clearer when John critiqued some specific television programs. Once again, the range of shows with which he was familiar may be surprising, given his expressed disdain for most of television (and sitcoms in particular) and his generally conservative attitudes about religion.

> *Everybody Loves Raymond*, that's an obvious case right there. [Raymond's] wife looks at him, and he curls up in a hole. Look at *King of Queens*, that show. These are classic examples of where the men cower down and don't actually take up the leadership role. The household dynamic, in my opinion, is messed up in these shows. I think men should be in leadership in the head of the households, but not like in a hierarchical system saying that they're above their wives. They're equal, especially in the sight of God, they're equal; they're one. But the men are like little cowards so . . . not good.

John and his wife, Katherine, had a rather wide-ranging media diet. The interviewer asked John to apply his critique about masculinity and headship to three other programs they watched regularly, *House*, *Lost*, and *The Simpsons*. Among them he found a positive example that some may find curious.

> Well, *The Simpsons*, I think, um, Homer, I think obviously he doesn't take up any kind of leadership role. I mean . . . he's not a role model to follow after, just put it that way. In 99 percent of the episodes, maybe 1 percent put him in a caring role as a father, but most of the time he's acting like his kids basically or just not a good example. Then again, *House*, there's not really like a household dynamic in that show. But um, maybe his attitude's not really a good influence—that's kind of a toss-up on that one. *Lost*, I think, actually *Lost*, you look at what's his name?
>
> KATHERINE: Jack.
>
> JOHN: Jack. He actually does take up like a head position. He actually tries to lead the people—not just the women, the men as well. So he actually does show what leadership is about, caring about others, taking care, thinking of them first before himself, um, because he does sacrifice some of his things for the people, the betterment of the people. So that show, I think, does portray leadership qualities and with the women as well.

John was eager to suggest that his view of masculinity, leadership, and headship was not sexist or anti–women's rights. However, he clearly saw the portrayal of gender roles in the culture as a zero-sum game. "You know, there's a lot of women's rights movements [and] a lot of women's liberation—I think there's a lot of those things that spawned in recent years that's brought about all these changes. A lot of these changes are good, but when it comes to the media, I think those are bad changes because it's going from one extreme to the other extreme. It's not, it's not, there's no equilibrium there. Women were saying they were oppressed, but now they're in a way, in the media, oppressing men."

The extent of this "oppression" in the media is a matter of some disagreement among our informants. Few could cite concrete examples of direct messages; instead, most saw the media as attempting to balance roles, with the effect being a kind of advocacy for women's rights, even women's ascendancy in culture and home. Most saw a kind of progression in these portrayals, from an earlier time when men were more likely to be portrayed as strong and decisive. For some, this was a function of storylines that portrayed men in careers or roles other than that of fatherhood. Characters such as Jack in *Lost*, for example, were seen as dynamic leaders who didn't contend with the challenges of headship in the domestic sphere. Further, those male roles that did contend with the domestic sphere were "so removed from what it looks like to be a strong father, and I feel like I have to look back to like *The Cosby Show*," said Larry Cane, who clearly saw a progression in role portrayals away from strong fathers toward a more troubling picture.

> It feels like there was this progression—I really feel like on *The Cosby Show*, Bill Cosby really did play, as far as I can remember at least, just kind of a strong father, a provider for his family—he was funny still, but he wasn't just this kind of idiot that got things right [only] sometimes. . . . Tim Allen on *Home Improvement* was still a good father and stuff, but it started to move toward this kind of—he was more funny, and his neighbor was kind of telling him how to fix everything. Then you move down further to *The Simpsons*, or I don't even know what all these other shows are now where—the guys don't have much to offer at all.

For Larry, and for many to whom we have spoken in both cohorts, television acted as a measure of the digression of views of men and of fatherhood. From what men like Larry saw as earlier, stronger, decisive representations of men and fathers (e.g., the 1950s television classic *Father Knows Best*, *The Andy Griffith Show*, or *Little House on the Prairie*), television was seen to have gone through an evolution wherein, first, women were shown as increasingly autonomous in society and home and, then, moved to ascendancy. The role left for fathers was portrayed, in the words of Clark Caldwell, as the "dumbing down of Dad." Even *7th Heaven*, popular with many of our Evangelical families, suffers from this tendency in the view of some of our Evangelical men and women. For example, Tim Brewer, a Southern Evangelical, spoke about the show in generally positive ways, but with qualification:

> INTERVIEWER: Is there anyone on TV or in the movies that fits your religious or spiritual beliefs?

TIM: I would definitely say *7th Heaven*. That would be my wife's favorite show. There's a lot of life lessons that are handled in a Biblical way.
INTERVIEWER: Is there a particular character?
TIM: I don't—I watch it seldom. It's usually on when I'm still at the office. So, I don't know characters' names. I don't. Obviously, the times that I've seen it, I look to the dad, who looks—in that show, even though he's the head Biblically, the wife seems to have more of the control, which is a little bit backward. Then that gets in[to] the whole issue of female pastors, and his daughter is a pastor.

The sense that contemporary television portrayals of fathers are at least problematic, if not in the main negative, was one of the things on which our Evangelical and Ecumenical Protestant informants agreed. We had nearly identical descriptions of contemporary television fathers from the two groups. The difference in narratives was that while Evangelical families couched this concern in the language of headship, Ecumenical families discussed this in nontheological terms, for example the critique that the father is inept or ignorant. While our Evangelical men tended to tie this to the progression of women's roles in these same programs, our Ecumenical men did not make the same attribution. Our Ecumenical cohort, even the more conservative men in this cohort, did not see these gender dynamics as a zero-sum game wherein the increase in women's equality came at the expense of men's roles. Instead, they tended to embrace the feminist turn in media, yet they lamented that television narratives seemed to not know what else to do with men, and especially fathers, other than to dumb them down and make them the butt of jokes.

The common concern of media portrayals of fatherhood is rooted in the central, normative place that home and family play in our respondents' senses of masculine identity. When asked directly, most informants began with critiques of the portrayals of the father, as we have seen, and many agreed with the sense that there has been a progression of portrayals from the 1950s/1960s–ideals of *Father Knows Best, Leave It to Beaver,* and *The Andy Griffith Show* through the era where *The Cosby Show*'s dad contrasted with Al Bundy on *Married . . . with Children,* and then the enigmatic and perhaps gender-balancing role played by Tim Allen in *Home Improvement* to today's seemingly confused messaging in programs such as *Two and a Half Men* and (one would assume) *Modern Family, The Middle, How I Met Your Mother,* and *Last Man Standing.* While both Evangelical and Ecumenical Protestant men saw this same landscape, they interpreted it in tellingly different ways. For the Ecumenical Protestant men, this varied landscape was simply a measure of more general social ambivalence about men and men's roles. For the Evangelical men, this situation was a bit more portentous, a kind of social-values threat.

The Ecumenical Protestant men tended to look within media portrayals for images of fatherhood that stressed relationships. Thus for them the problematic father roles in media were those where fathers walk out on families, failing to fulfill their primary role in (emotional and financial) provision. These men expressed a preference for relational men who share domestic responsibilities, who care for their children. There was ambiguity here as well, as these men attempted to interpret media through the lenses of their senses of father-selves and interpret their senses of father-selves through the portrayals in public culture. Here is an example of this ambiguity, and the way it is resolved for two Ecumenical Protestant men, concerning the classic domestic sitcom *Leave It to Beaver.* Jeremy Billings articulated a clear and focused sense of the need to rethink gender balance in the domestic sphere. He articulated a focused critique of received ideas about masculine prerogative in the home, citing *Leave It to Beaver* as an iconic example.

> I think the [gender] differences are perceived differences. I think it's expectations. I think people expect fathers to provide this certain type of support that is different than mothers'—when people see a father acting unusual or more mother-like, or a mother acting more father-like, it kind of makes people pay attention. . . . I think it's perception. You know, I can be as nurturing as [my spouse] can be for our kids—it's [the perceptions], the Beaver Cleaver stuff. You know, mom's at home making the pot roast. Dad comes home and, you know [*in a deep voice*], "What'd you do wrong today?" You know, that sort of stuff.

In contrast, Mike Andrews wished to recover some of the values of *Leave It to Beaver* in the context of a relationship that is much more gender-balanced than that portrayed in such programs. Calling *Leave*

It to Beaver a "great show" in our individual interview, Mike listed in his initial questionnaire the program as one that he felt portrayed positive family values, something that his wife, Sally, found shocking and confusing.

> INTERVIEWER: Tell me a little bit about *Leave It to Beaver* and [its] expressing your family's values.
>
> MIKE: [*sighing*] Well—
>
> SALLY: [*giggling*] You put *Leave It to Beaver*?!
>
> MIKE: Maybe I should say what I'd like it to express—it's where the, the family is a big part of the kids' lives, and um, kids don't just come home and the TV is the baby sitter, it's not that—it's always trying to teach the kids a lesson in every episode. I mean, we let our kids try to get their own bumps and bruises if we can, to a point.

Here we can see television contributing a sense of grounding with regard to gender identity but doing so by providing a kind of normative ideal that can exist in the background to be negotiated with and against. Mike longed for a simpler time when families functioned in a different way from the way they do today. While he, like Jeremy, did not wish to re-embody Ward Cleaver (the father character in *Leave It to Beaver*) as a role model for gender relations, he did wish to recover something of the traditional time and place evoked by that program. This describes well the attitudes of our Ecumenical Protestant informants regarding media and fatherhood. It is in some ways positive and in some ways negative. These men tended to favor male media roles that stress relationships and emotional connection, as opposed to the purer masculinism of the late adventurer-naturalist Steve Irwin or Mel Gibson in *Braveheart*. Other positive models mentioned by our Ecumenical Protestant men: Tom Hanks's Captain John Miller in *Saving Private Ryan* (interpreted as fighting for family); Bill Cosby[30] in *The Cosby Show*; Ned Flanders of *The Simpsons* (commended for being a caring figure); the stern but caring Rev. Maclean played by Tom Skerritt in *A River Runs Through It*; and Fred Rogers of *Mister Rogers' Neighborhood*.

For Ecumenical Protestant men, the media narrative of fatherhood was seen very much to be a set of ideas that today need to be contested directly. Barry Aaron is a typical example.

BARRY: It seems like a lot of shows have pretty defined roles in terms of husbands and wives and fathers and mothers, and there is definitely more different types of situations, but it seems over the years [media] portrayed the dad as the breadwinner, dad as the rule maker, the disciplinarian, [and] mom makes sure the house is clean and takes care of the husband and kids.

INTERVIEWER: Do you connect with any show specifically as far as fatherhood [is concerned]?

BARRY: Probably shows with fathers that take more of a role. The fathers that do cooking and cleaning and child rearing.

Or in the words of Jack Jones, an Ecumenical Protestant who was a stay-at-home father and who looked for role models more like himself in media:

I think fatherhood is not absent but not so involved that [fathers] know what is going on. It's more a physical presence than an absence of engagement. In some shows, I think there's still a sense that moms run the household. Rarely do men on TV change a diaper without making a face. Or some overreaction or I think of the *Mr. Mom* [character] with the apron and tongs and the goggles and the gloves and that's a fascinating 1980s look into the same stereotypes out there today, only more nuanced. Rarely do they portray fathers sitting down and reading or dancing on the floor like [my daughter] and I do. No physical contact like hugging or even mental contact. It's more manipulating the child for the comedy.

This is fascinating, particularly in light of what we learned earlier about the way the Evangelical cohort thought about media representations. The key distinction between the groups is not that they engaged with different programs; rather, it is that they engaged with the same programs in different ways. The problem of emasculation and challenges to headship loomed large for Evangelicals with regard to the "dumbing down of dad." For the Ecumenical men, emasculation didn't register at all. The problem for them was that men are not domestic enough, not nurturing enough. They were "dumb" because they were domestically inept, not because they failed in leadership.

That said, Evangelical and Ecumenical men here did have a lot in common. All found both positive and negative representations of men and fathers in the media. All began by assuming that the media had little positive to offer but were able to articulate positives within their own frames of reference. All lamented the "dumb dad" narrative that seemed to dominate, at least in the sitcom genre.

The television "dumb dad" was interpreted by both Evangelical and Ecumenical men with some nuance and complexity. Even some of our Evangelicals appreciated characters such as Homer Simpson or Jim Belushi's character in *According to Jim* as examples of fathers who are endearing, even sweet and caring, in spite of their foibles. But Evangelicals found these roles ultimately troubling because of the issue of headship. In their joint interview, Emory and Jessica French identified the Jim character as possessing some positive traits. Later, in his individual interview, Emory further interpreted the character played by Jim Belushi within headship's confrontation with changing women's roles:

> I think it's useful—it does show the shortcomings of fathers. But it also shows the wife and the husband coming together and resolving those things. And the husband growing, saying, "You know what, honey? I'm, I'm angry. You trusted me, and it's caused me to be a better person [*said in an acting voice*]." It's like that. But in these shows, it shows the wife as the head of the household. Now, is that inaccurate? I don't think so. I think that wives are given a huge accountability in the American home, raising the children, and, as such, do become the heads of household. And I think, you know, [in] our past as a society, the father has become the diminished figure. The father has fallen into the background.

The majority of our Evangelical informants shared this view of the relationship between the "dumb dad" and the rebalancing of gender roles. As many of our informants identified this trope as a dominant representation of fatherhood today, we can understand how it must be contended with as these men addressed the representations of men and fathers in the common culture.

Work

Our Evangelical and Ecumenical men shared a broader concern about media: that media, particularly television, constituted a challenge to men's roles as ethical, purposeful actors. Their shared concern about "dumb dads," for instance, could be seen in relation to ideals of men and fathers as autonomous and purposeful. It is both the role of father in the home and the roles of men beyond the home that constitute this sense of purpose for all of our men.

One way of thinking about media representations of work is to look at the way media portray specific professions. Among our Ecumenical Protestant informants, for example, only one (a newspaper editor) reported having seen his profession portrayed in a positive light. Others felt that their professions were the subject of negative media stereotypes.

There were also concerns about the idea of a "work ethic." A common point about media portrayals for work from our interviews was that work was portrayed as a bad thing, that a typical narrative involved men working too hard and losing their families (such as the character Jack Bauer on *24*) or seldom working at all (e.g., the male characters on *Friends*). Most of our respondents were ambivalent about media portrayals of work, though there were some specific differences of opinion. Some felt that media failed to uphold the notion of a solid work ethic, which was connected to their sense of purpose. Others disagreed, noting that some professions (law enforcement, medicine, military service) were often portrayed as normative, necessary, and purposeful. What was clear, though, was that none of these men recognized themselves in the media portrayals of work and career. They tended to attribute this lack of recognition to the commercial pressures on the media, pressures that move in the direction of the lurid or sensational. What they reported seeing were portrayals of work as trivial, comedic, or overglamorized. Where work was portrayed as a positive goal, it came with a note of danger—one can overdo it at the expense of one's family. A "golden mean" in relation to work—the sort of ideal of provision and purpose they aspired to in their own lives—was not present in the media, according to these men.

This matter is significant because men across our interviews expressed the need and desire to work hard and to work well. This need served not only the sense of provision we have discussed but also their sense of having a purposeful self. Work thus relates to the other important theme, fatherhood, not only in the concrete context of provision but also in the less concrete, more values-laden context of the need for purpose. It is important to note, though, that while all of our interviews revealed much about the way these men thought about work and all of the interviews involved sustained conversations about media, none of the men seemed to have thought much about the way media and work are related. Most had things to say; it just seemed that it was an entirely new conversation for them.[31]

That Evangelical men found the conversation about media, meaning, and work so remote was perhaps more surprising than was the case with Ecumenical Protestant men. As we have said, Evangelicalism is known for its prodigious critique of media values. What is interesting in our interviews is that—while that critique pertains strongly to issues of sexuality and gender relations, as we have seen—this critique was not as focused on questions of work and career. This is in spite of the fact that portrayals of work and vocation are at the very core of *provision* and *purpose*. In the main, Evangelicals among our interviewees largely shared the view of the Ecumenical Protestants that media representations are somewhat polarized, with work seen alternatively as a necessary evil to be avoided and as something that can be so important as to be all-encompassing. Jasper Hall, a Southern Evangelical, put it this way: "Some [television shows] sort of reinforce the notions that work, career, jobs and so forth are very important and are things that you should be highly invested in, and others sort of make fun of that and sort of assume that work is an awful, horrible thing that you just have to do, but you do it so you can get a paycheck, so you can go have fun and do the things you enjoy afterward." Any of these portrayals of work, of course, suggest dangers for the masculine elementals of provision and purpose, so our informants, overall, expressed a good deal of ambiguity about the way media deal with work and vocation.

When it comes to portrayals of work in the media, our Evangelical interviewees did not, then, apply the same moralistic frame of a judgmental "account of" media they would have applied to questions of sexuality. Not that they weren't critical. They each seemed to have an almost reflexive first response to the question that "of course" media would portray work badly. However, when they were pushed to be more specific, a more nuanced view emerged. They reported a range of media exposures and pleasures representative of many sides of this question. Brent Tucker was typical, beginning with the assessment that media would necessarily portray work badly but then reporting finding in his two favorite programs, *MacGyver* and *Grey's Anatomy*, positive examples of work, the former because MacGyver was always helping people and the latter because the workplace was portrayed as a place of sociability.

> INTERVIEWER: Do you see media teaching anything about work?
> BRENT: It's a chore. Work is a chore. You get stuck in a job, and you just have to live with it.
> INTERVIEWER: Is that even the case with a show like *Grey's Anatomy*? It seems like you might have been thinking of *Friends* when you said it was a chore.
> BRENT: Yeah, I was thinking about it. Um [*long pause*], I think *Grey's Anatomy* would partially go with that. I think for the most part most of the fun stuff happens when you're at work, most of the exciting stuff, the drama happens at work. So I think that has a more realistic view of work than a lot of shows that I've seen.

Clark Caldwell suggested that there might be a distinction rooted in television genres. He saw the negative portrayal of work as a theme more of sitcoms than of dramas:

> If you watch *The Office*, that show in particular teaches that work is always boring because those people are always dead, and they have to do something to have fun because life—work is terrible, work is bad. Sometimes work is portrayed, especially in our sitcoms, as the evil thing we have to do just to pay our rent or make our mortgage payment. But I get great satisfaction out of my job and know that I'm doing something worthwhile or hopefully productive. It's probably tainted more that way in sitcoms than other shows, I guess. If you watch a dramatic series, it seems like the police detectives or nurses and doctors, they're all real serious about their jobs. They love their jobs. As a matter of fact, they're always at their job[s]. And so it depends on whether it's a sitcom or drama how it's going to be shown out there.

Few reported having seen portrayals of their own professions in the media. Clark, however, could think of two relevant examples.

CLARK: Back a few years ago, there was this great little show [*Soul Man*] that only made it half a season. Dan Aykroyd was this Episcopalian pastor with a family and this great little associate pastor. It was just good humor, good clean kind of show, but he was a single parent trying to raise kids but also a pastor. The other one is *7th Heaven*, where you had the pastor with a family who was always trying to do the right thing but didn't always make it, but had good advice. And it showed him in a much more pastoral kind of setting where he was always trying to help people and be there and do ministry.

INTERVIEWER: Do you think media generally portray pastors in good ways?

CLARK: I think generally those are two exceptions. I think just the fact that *7th Heaven* lasted several seasons is a good indicator that people do like shows that have good quality, good values, good moral issues that they, sometimes they can't get it all to work out nicely in the end after forty-three minutes, but more often than not, you see pastors as . . . clergy or priests, maybe tainted in a little bit less than human way or less than spiritual way. Sometimes they're the buffoon or the hard-nosed, closed-minded kind of person.

Clark and Jasper Hall, also a pastor, were among the few whose professions were portrayed in media, but rarely did these men identify with those portrayals. Few others could cite positive or negative examples. In spite of this, we might have expected media to portray "purpose" through work even if media did not portray the types of professions in which our respondents found themselves. In our interviews, questions of whether media portrayals depicted work as a "calling" or a "vocation" spoke to this issue.

By and large, media did not depict work in this way, according to our respondents. When media's failure to do so did surface in our Evangelical interviews, the failure was not always conflated with religion but could stand alone as a quality that could be attributed to media portrayals more generally. Tim Brewer, a Southern Evangelical, saw this in relation to two specific programs:

Definitely a show like *7th Heaven*. And what's that show that's no longer on the air. It was on Sunday nights with the angels [*Touched by an Angel*]. Those two shows, sure. But actually, the more I'm thinking about it, something like Steve Irwin [*The Crocodile Hunter*]. I believe he feels that's what he's supposed to be doing. Jeff Corbin [*Medal of Valor*], same thing. I don't imagine them doing anything else. So, whether they believe in God or they don't, I believe they feel that's why they are here.

It is worth noting that the last two are examples of a kind of pure masculinism in addition to being about men with a sense of resolute purpose. The late Steve Irwin was an Australian whose raw energy created a complicated public persona. Jeff Corbin is a former law enforcement officer who has found a place in the reality TV genre.

As we have noted, ideas about work were a source of great ambivalence for most of our informants. Work interacted with family in interesting ways. Work was, of course, the concrete expression of "provision." It was the tacit expectation of contemporary masculinity for nearly everyone with whom we spoke. Men simply work to provide; it is not optional, in their view. This expectation was the case for all of the men in our Evangelical cohort and most of the men in our Ecumenical cohort. But work was problematic for most of them. It could be too absorbing, too involving, and it could draw them away from their more important normative role: father. It could also be seen as detracting from the time available for the private domestic sphere. Many of our respondents had seen this happen with their own fathers, and many expressed concerns that it could happen to them if they didn't strike the appropriate balance among emotional and financial provision and purpose. Media, for these men, provided a cautionary tale of men who failed to strike this balance, in one direction or another. Further, media rarely portrayed work in relation to any larger normative categories such as "vocation" or "calling," at least in the experience of these men. And when media did portray work in these normative categories, there was the danger that they would do so in a way that suggested an all-consuming neurosis *for work* that would be detrimental to family life.

Media as Productive Resources in the Construction of Masculine Selves

The media are many things in the lives of men. They are a source of values, symbols, and ideas. They tell aspirational tales. They are an imaginary through which men think about their roles and identities. At the same time, media tell cautionary tales. They are the source of messages that threaten perceived "wholesome" values. Clearly, though, these characteristics of media are not absolutely positive or absolutely negative. The same is true in media portrayals of gender, especially masculinity.

There are positive media messages about male roles and identities, according to our respondents. Media present educational values, ideas, and programs. And the time spent with positive media might be time well spent, particularly in the context of modern life, where the media stand at the center of the common culture. Many could tell of times when media contributed positively to their identities and values. Men could easily pinpoint media that expressed for them ideal characteristics of masculinity. While they framed their ideas about media through the general threats posed by media, most families and men integrated media into family life in significant ways. Media are thus layered into daily life and into narratives of daily life. While media values may be problematic, media are a fact of life and do play a positive role, according to the narratives of our respondents.

Many of the families we interviewed had favorite programs they viewed as part of "family time." Narratives of these programs provide interesting glimpses into both their values and priorities and into the way that media inevitability is negotiated in these daily lives. For many of them, media were a necessary stop in the routine of weekly life. Shane Engalls, one of our Ecumenical Protestant men, reported that media take a regular place in the Sunday routine in his family, a time when they could gather and be together. "Sunday night we tend to, you know there's church Sunday morning or Sunday evening, usually, and then— usually Sunday evening we have like family night, and we have like, you know, do an On Demand movie and get pizza, or, it's either Friday night or Sunday night, depending on which—that week, we have less going on. Um, we do try to do that once a week."

The notion of media as the center of "family night" is certainly a departure from the received scripts (that even Shane could articulate) of media threat. The pull of the media has become an important point of encounter in contemporary homes. And for Shane, and a remarkable number of our interviewees, reality shows (*American Idol* in Shane's family's case) had a particular pride of place. Shane and his wife, Andrea, described how *Idol* became a central discussion and interaction point for their family. Andrea revealed a bit of ambiguity about this, though, noting, "Really it's not the TV show as much as it is the process of just us coming together." This idea suggests that a practice that could be read as problematic instead comes to be justified by its effects on family dynamics. But the media frame is still there, creating a space and facilitating family practices and discussions that allow parents to provide for the family.

Lindsay Holloran, another of our Ecumenical Protestant respondents, described another potential dimension of media promise in relation to family viewing practice, suggesting that specific elements of content, even in reality shows, can be of benefit to families and children. "We love watching *Extreme Makeover* because our kids love watching the creation, and just helping families—'cause, you know, usually they'll either have someone that's ill, or handicapped and stuff, and our oldest one loves watching it. You know, he's almost like, 'Wow, other people have those problems.' That's actually the one show that we watch as a family."

Lindsay could not resist a standard "account of media" after offering media such praise. She followed the above remark with "We don't watch a lot," as if to say theirs was not the type of family that would let too much media lead by example in the home. Lindsay's husband, Dermott, noted that media (particularly films) can be "great bonding": "Go to the movies with your family and grab your bag of popcorn, and, you know it's different from sitting and watching at home. The big screen and the loud surround sound, and the—just, you gotta pick a good kid's movie, but . . . ."

The point here is not that these families live a contradiction, criticizing media on the one hand and watching media on the other (though nearly all do); rather, the point is to suggest the complexity of narratives about media, and the complexity of ways that the inevitable media frame is encountered by men and families today as both a means with which to provide and an evil from which to protect.

This was true for our Evangelical viewers as well. In spite of the fact that they generally articulated more vibrant and categorical critiques of media, many described regular viewing of a variety of shows. One Evangelical father reported watching *Lost* regularly with his daughter. Other shows regularly watched as "appointment television" among our Evangelical cohort were *American Idol, The Biggest Loser,* and even *What Not to Wear.*

Our interviews provide us with an opportunity to consider how the media imaginary articulates identity across our cohorts by considering which characters or celebrities in which media provide salient resources in this regard. This is a notional description, but one that we find quite enlightening.

For Ecumenical men, the characters or celebrities they loved or whom they considered to be the most valuable role models for male identity (and mentioned by more than one informant each) included the following: Bill Cosby; Tom Hanks as Captain John Miller in *Saving Private Ryan*; Russell Crowe in *Gladiator* and *Cinderella Man*; Mister Rogers; Gregory Peck as Atticus Finch in *To Kill a Mockingbird*; Jimmy Stewart as George Bailey in *It's a Wonderful Life*; Dev Patel as Jamal in *Slumdog Millionaire*; Clint Eastwood as a director; and Presidents Barack Obama and Jimmy Carter.

For Evangelical men, the list included (again, all of these were mentioned more than once): Bill Cosby; Mel Gibson[32] in *Braveheart* and *The Patriot*; Matthew Fox as Jack in *Lost*; and Michael Landon as Charles Ingalls in *Little House on the Prairie*.

There are notable findings here. These media attributions detail in a nuanced way differences in the worldviews of these two cohorts. They reveal political, social, and cultural values and articulations, and they reveal important dimensions of differing views of masculinity. We can learn even more from two other lists we've assembled: of characters that are more ambiguous or even problematic.

First, characters that our informants "hate to love": These are the guilty pleasures, the roles and images that are darker secrets revealed in our conversations. For our Ecumenicals, those who were mentioned in this way, again by more than one informant: the character Jack Bauer in the terrorism drama *24* (described, in their words, as tough, purposive, but unfortunately estranged from family); Homer Simpson (loveable but not a good role model); and *Braveheart* (with both strong positive and negative responses). For the Evangelicals, this group of common guilty pleasures included Homer Simpson, Jim Belushi, and the male characters in *Friends.*

Now a group of characters we found that some of our informants "love to hate": This means that they play a more definitive role in our informants' sense of identity, as sort of boundary markers from which to distinguish acceptability. These are the roles and images that are seen as negative but are engaged anyway as a kind of exercise in "otherness." These are attractive not for what they are but for what they represent that our informants think is negative. There is apparently pleasure in continuing to watch such characters, though. For our Ecumenical informants, this list included Al Bundy in *Married . . . with Children*; the adult characters in *Two and a Half Men*; roles played by Sylvester Stallone (though there were some who liked *Rocky*); Arnold Schwarzenegger; Jack Nicholson; Raymond in *Everybody Loves Raymond*; and Homer Simpson (note the love/hate relationship with Homer). For our Evangelicals, the following fit this category: the *Saw* films,[33] Al Bundy, *Raymond*, and shows with what they might identify as "gay" characters.

There is clear overlap here, and men within each cohort showed differences and similarities with others in their cohort and, often, contradictory expressions of characters they loved to hate and hated to love. The similarities and the differences are telling. For the Evangelicals, for example, there are no "action heroes" in the media men they "love to hate," a clear difference from the Ecumenicals. Mel Gibson's portrayal of William Wallace in *Braveheart* is listed in different places in each cohort. For the Evangelicals, the character was a positive model; for the Ecumenicals, a guilty pleasure (and, for some, a character—and a media personality—they love to hate). Homer Simpson is on several of the lists, revealing both the reach and influence of *The Simpsons* and the ambiguities of that program's representation and understanding of family life. Finally, the Ecumenicals' list of positive characters is—perhaps not surprisingly—less hypermasculine than the Evangelicals'.

We can perhaps posit a kind of composite ideal masculine media role model for Evangelical and Ecumenical Protestants, drawing on the attributions contained in our interviews. For our Evangelical informants, this ideal composite, using words from respondent interviews, might exhibit the following characteristics: a heterosexual white[34] male who exhibits great physical, emotional, mental, and moral strength. He is a leader both in home and in public. He is a man who is willing to be a warrior, to die for a cause. He is a hero in the classic sense,[35] a man who protects and cares for others, particularly the weak (including women) and does so with violence or the threat of violence. He takes initiative and solves problems. He is an adventurer and a risk-taker. He is compassionate, a servant-leader, caring and encouraging. He is dedicated to work and is other-centered. He is committed to family, honest, and (for some of our informants) self-evidently "Christian."

For our Ecumenical Protestant men, the ideal would be different in some ways and similar in others. He would be a white[36] heterosexual male who is loyal, faithful, dutiful, earnest, consistent, and responsible. He would be uncompromising, persistent, tenacious, and genuine. At the same time, though, he would have a significant streak of kindness, tenderness, and vulnerability. He is sensitive, emotional, caring, and constantly giving. There is also a kind of pacifism here (and among some Evangelical men as well). For these men, the best role models are those who are nonviolent first; however, they must be willing and able to fight for belief and for others. Thus the ideal male character is brave and courageous, but he champions mercy. He is also an intellectual—clever, even-tempered, and witty. He is a dedicated family man who relates well to his children. He is competitive, self-reliant, and driven to achieve. He is a leader of men. It is important to note that these Ecumenical Protestant men expressed a greater level of ambivalence about these role models than did the Evangelicals. While a few were wistful about the 1950s male ideal and were drawn to that ideal—as a guilty pleasure if nothing else—others rejected it. Many sought to move to a different, newer, and more pro-feminist model of masculinity, though some did not, and a large majority proposed a move to feminist models while clinging to gender essentialism.

We can see that the media play more than one role in relation to ideas about masculinity. It became clear to us in our interviews that one could not talk about masculinity without talking about media. Men and women had a hard time describing male characteristics or roles without referring to classic film or television. This fact might be attributable to the method of the study and our concern with media, but we suggest that something else is at work here. For example, *The Andy Griffith Show*, *The Cosby Show*, *Lost*, *Saving Private Ryan*, *Braveheart*, and others came up often and easily when people tried to talk about what they thought it meant to be a man (well outside our conversations about media per se). Conversely, Biblical characters rarely came up at all. On one level, this is rooted in the inevitability and ubiquity of media. As Larry Cane observed, we speak the language of movies and television in the United States. More than that, though, media articulate salient themes, symbols, and ideas in the culture. These expressions of the culture work precisely because they make sense in the culture and to its participants. They are part of the "common culture," the broad marketplace of consensual ideas and resources that become its "imaginary," the common touch points of cultural conversations and interactions. In short, media culture is the water in which we swim.

We should not forget that the role of media is also rooted in pleasure. The media provide pleasure, and a good deal of people's reaction to media and use of media are best explained in this way.[37] In spite of their complex of ideas, identities, claims, and affordances, media are at the most basic level pleasurable, and their consumption involves ranges of pleasures, not all of which follow in a straightforward way from the claims and values ostensibly at their core. We can see this in our interviews. Not all male media roles are important or pleasurable because they are agreed with. Some are contested, others negotiated. There is attraction and pleasure in each of these approaches.

This means that the process of decoding how media relate to something like masculinity involves a more complex process than simply assessing media content through some objective means (counting various stereotypes, for instance) and then evaluating whether viewers understand that objective content. What is needed is more like what we have done here, an attempt to evaluate the various frameworks through which our informants engage media and working with their own responses, motivations, and derived meanings from those texts and tropes.

How the Media Matter

Doing this kind of analysis reveals, in the first instance, that one of the provocations with which we began this study deserves rethinking. We

have noted that many critiques of contemporary fatherhood and observations about the so-called crisis of masculinity carry in them an explicit
critique of the media. In the voices of some of these critics, media are
categorically suspect or even "bad" in these regards. What we have
learned here is that the situation is more complex. In fact, as we have
seen, respondents who were the most committed to the goals of the
conservative critics, for example, engaged secular mainstream media in
their daily lives in ways that actually reinforced neo-masculinist ideas
about men, fathers, and families rather than contradict them. The same
could be said for our more progressive or egalitarian men. They were
also in the thrall of fairly traditional ideas about masculinity, expressed
to some extent in their media diets. None of these informants appeared
to be "dupes" of the media. In fact, they seemed to be well aware of the
widely circulated criticisms of media and the impact of media on family
life, values, and behaviors. Further, many agreed with those criticisms.
Those criticisms formed a large part of their initial framing of their
"accounts of media."

But what we have found differs from the ideas of critics who stop
the conversation there. It is not simply a matter of relatively critical and
conscious men and families choosing or rejecting straightforward media
messages of gender, masculinity, fatherhood, or family life. Instead, it
is a much more complex negotiation with meaningful and pleasurable media. We can see men from a variety of perspectives interpreting
media genres, characters, roles, plots, and messages in ways that interacted with their own views of what it meant to be men and fathers. Far
from being a categorically negative force in these regards, media instead
provided important touch points in the cultural landscape for these men
as they navigated their understanding of provision, protection, and purpose. Media at the same time provided positive and normative ideals
and values and more troubling and contested symbols and values.

Taken together, though, these men's media lives reveal a role for
media that relates in a rather fundamental way to our evolving analysis
of how men's ideas of themselves are derived from, or rooted in, their
religious and media lives. We have talked about two "registers" of masculinity: the "normative" and the "practical." We've suggested that the
men we've interviewed have found religion in general and churches in
particular wanting in addressing both of these registers. We saw earlier

that many of our informants articulated ambivalence in the ways that religious or spiritual contexts provided resources to their senses of masculinity or male-ness. We further saw that, to the extent that religion did serve this purpose, it did so primarily for our Evangelical men, and then primarily on the "normative" as opposed to the "practical" register. The normative register, it will be remembered, is that in which the essential characteristics of masculinity (the symbolic tropes of *provision*, *protection*, and *purpose*, in the terms of our narrative here) are most active. The difference between our two interview cohorts tended to be that, while the Evangelical men expected religion to provide more help, the other group did not. In fact, for many of our Ecumenical Protestant men, religion tended to posit a patriarchal norm that these men longed to reject. Yet even for the Evangelical men, the "normative" symbolic resources with which to discuss masculine headship were nonetheless rather unsatisfying (because they sounded sexist), and the "practical" messages about masculinity were largely confusing and contradictory.

From what we have seen here in relation to media, the situation is somewhat different. It seems that for both cohorts, media are far more connected with their senses of themselves as gendered beings, or, at least, men could more easily express narratives of gender *through* media than they could through religion (either its texts or structures). We found in our interviews many examples of the ways in which media provided powerful and salient normative models. Both groups of men derived a great deal of meaning from their negotiations with the range of normative images of masculinity present in the media.

On the level of the "practical" register, though, things got complicated. It is clear that for both groups, media provided more salient, more meaningful, and (on some level) "truer" representations of the practical register than did their religious lives. In interview after interview, with individuals and couples as well, media representations of the struggles, strains, gestures, and challenges of shifting gender roles, expectations, and dynamics were discussed with great familiarity and even passion. Not all of them found answers in the "practical" register, of course, and many of the representations in media were contested or negotiated, but it was clear from these interviews that the media played an important and salient (and even pleasurable) role as a common context and common language for understanding these important and challenging issues and dynamics. At this point we might say it appears that, to the extent there is a "contest" between "religion" (writ large) and "media" (writ large) to claim the central ground in helping contemporary men and couples grapple with the shifting sands of gender relations, the media seem to be winning, though not in the "feminizing" and "corrupting" ways that the neo-masculinist critics suggest.

3

Elemental Masculinity, the Domestic Ideal, and Everyday Life

During the 2012 U.S. presidential campaign, there was a moment when both candidates, Mitt Romney and Barack Obama, agreed about one thing. They agreed that Romney's newly announced running mate was a good and decent man because he was a family man. "Paul Ryan is a decent man; he is a family man," said the president.[1] Romney stressed the point in his acceptance speech at the Republican National Convention, linking his own and Ryan's commitments to their families directly to their character and fitness for office.

Throughout the conversations here, we have seen family centered as an ideal. The men and women with whom we have spoken concentrated their energies and ideals on family. The domestic sphere was the definitive space for their identities. Their ideas of family were thus entirely consistent with what seem to be the dominant ideals in the broader culture today. The way they articulated this in relation to media and religion—the other themes of this book—is not exactly what we expected when we began. We thought the situation would be closer to that suggested by the conservative, neo-traditionalist social critiques and commentaries we pointed to earlier. We thought we'd find that their ideas of masculinity would result more or less directly from resources and influences in the culture and in the family.

After these conversations, we are still not entirely sure where masculinity comes from. We can say that it comes from culture (consistent with our own intellectual commitments to constructivism and interpretivism), but beyond that, we can say little else definitively. We can say that the men and women with whom we've spoken wouldn't have described it as coming directly or solely from any of those expected sources, except in a kind of combination or interaction, where ideas and values from one context achieve new meanings when they interact (in their experience) with things from another. Perhaps we should have expected a lurking essentialism in our respondents' ideas, that they might resist the idea that gender could be rooted in cultural sources because it comes from somewhere else outside of culture, essential to our being. We nevertheless expected at the outset that these men and women would be able to articulate for us fairly clear and unequivocal accounts—at least for themselves—of what masculinity is or what it means. We thought the masculinity compartments in what Anne Swidler calls their "cultural tool kits"[2] would be well organized and well labeled.

Instead, things are muddled. We do think that politicians who identify "family" as a central marker of values are correct. Our interviews reveal that "family" *is* the central normative test for individual worth today in dominant American culture and is the generative location of masculine identity. Thus, those things we might discuss under the heading of "gender" or "masculinity" are seen primarily in relation to the domestic (even for single men in our conversations). The central context is not their family of origin, as we've seen here, and it is not church or religion, as we've also seen. It is not either the broader culture, whether we mean by that media culture or other contexts. The central context of the family is in all of these other areas—in a complex constellation of symbolic resources from which people construct gender identity.

The central meaning of masculinity was in flux for these men. There were some normative ideals and aspirations, but these were more conflicted and less settled as may have been the case in the past.[3] Also, the central meaning of masculinity was for them clearly influenced by the women's movement, the feminist critique, and a generalized contemporary social preference for egalitarian rather than traditionalist gender relations. Yet in many cases there was a clear and sustained backlash to the feminist critique, even as patriarchy "softened" in a number of ways.

The central meaning of masculinity was clearly influenced by realities "on the ground"—in relationships, home, and family. These constituted an interconnected set of realities, beliefs, and commitments that did not fit smoothly into either traditional or postmodern definitions. By and large, our respondents' spouses were not comfortable with fully "traditionalist" roles and gender relationships. Some of these women worked outside the home, either by choice, by shared choice, or by family necessity. Even those women who identified primarily as homemakers described this identity as a *choice* they had made while fully cognizant of broader social discourses about women's rights and women's roles. Further, many Evangelical women had made the *choice* to embrace headship and to actively encourage their husbands to take up the spiritual leadership of them and their home.[4] At the same time, men also didn't wish to limit their own daughters' life and career prospects.

Also, most of these men regularly found themselves in professional and social contexts that were mixed-gender, where traditional gender definition was breaking down. They were also self-conscious and explicit about how these realities were new for them and for their generation, and they were clear about how the traditional lessons of masculinity no longer hold sway. They were even critical of their own homes of origin and their own fathers' styles of parenting and approaches to masculinity. There was a clear sense from them that things have changed and things continue to change. They didn't categorically resist this change, but they searched for models.

So it is not surprising that these men struggled to find definitive descriptions of what it means to be a man today. These men and women were concerned with finding models that work for them. And that does seem to be the most important consideration: what works. Against the model that we have been implicitly testing—that of relatively fixed and structural sources of received norms and models providing influences and insights in a nearly pedagogical way—things were more layered. The traditional sources and ideas of masculinity did not exactly work for them anymore. They looked for models and sources in home, family, church, and the broader culture as they crafted accounts of themselves.

So are there no normative models of masculinity or maleness anymore? If the traditional models are no longer persuasive, have they not been replaced with something else? What we have seen is not so much that the traditional models have been replaced but that they have been negotiated and brought into a kind of dialectic relationship with other values and with lived experience. We should emphasize again that the difference is a difference in kind. It is not just that the content of masculinity had changed for these men (and women). The very idea of masculinity and its sources had also changed. These men were—consistent with the ideas of Anthony Giddens about the characteristics of identity in modern life[5]—reflexive and creative in their meaning-making about masculinity. They thought of masculinity as something whose sources were within themselves and within their own experience (even as they continued to look for models and definitions outside of themselves).

This does not mean that the ideas of masculinity we see here are entirely solipsistic or self-referential, which is how they might look if we analyzed them entirely from a perspective of social structure. Instead, there is a systematic logic to them, and a remarkable consistency can be seen. There is a way in which they "make sense" in broad social and cultural terms. Because the central project is perfecting the self and the self's sense of its gender meanings, the relationship to other sources then is different from what we might have expected. Instead of a kind of instrumental relationship between the putative sources we've looked at— home, father, church, media, and the broader culture—it instead seems that these other sources or centers of potential meaning and insight are described as revolving around the central project of the self. They are resources *to* that project, not the direct sources *of* it. We have described this as a *negotiation*, which is a term of art in media audience studies, and that turns out to be apt. As we have seen, these men very much viewed themselves as being in negotiation with history, tradition, received ideas, and with the range of on-the-ground issues and contexts where they located themselves.

That this was a negotiation for them did not make it incoherent. Instead, there is a remarkable consistency in our interviews concerning a definition of masculinity today in three dimensions: provision, protection, and purpose. One way of thinking about these is that they do, indeed, bear a family resemblance to traditional descriptions of masculinity and male roles. However, whereas in the past men might have identified with a set of more refined and specific characteristics,[6] the men with whom we spoke rejected those specifics. Presented, for example, with a model list of "male role norms," we found them choosing among the list, rejecting some, accepting others, qualifying others. Provision, protection, and purpose were a kind of compendium of what remained when these men had thought about and negotiated the received ideas of the culture and of society. To reiterate a term from the previous chapter, these are "zones of ambiguity" that men inhabit—bounded zones but also unsettled zones with room for movement, negotiation, and change. Provision, protection, and purpose are the elements of what it means to be a man that made the most sense to them. These elements are influenced by other contexts but not created by them, so it would seem to the men in our study. These elements are a kind of a streamlined sense of what it means to be a man. These ideas may be, as we suggested earlier, the residual that remains when traditional senses of male-ness are contested and eroded through social change. Or they may be a particularly flexible and functional set of ideas—fitted to the postmodern moment—that work well as these men continue to define who they are. That, in a way, awaits further study and historical experience. There is some evidence here of how an elemental masculinity composed of provision, protection, and purpose works, and it looks as though it is an open question, particularly when the larger needs of society for effective and active citizenry are taken into consideration.

We must note again how grounded in the domestic sphere this definition of masculinity is. Masculinity for these Christian men is all about their relationship to home and family. Even though, as Clark Caldwell put it, men might fantasize about fighting for a "greater cause" that is "bigger" than the family, their narratives of protection, provision, and purpose were centered on their families. Always. The "greater causes" were part of their gendered, mediated imaginations that were reinterpreted not toward "the public" or "the civic" but toward the home—the place where they performed what many called their greatest calling: being husbands and fathers. The domestic ideal was thus the definitive ideal and definitive space for these men as they thought about their masculinity. The other normative contexts—family of origin, church, community, media—all revolve around this ideal. The two we've been most interested in—religion and media—function on several levels in relation to this domesticated idea of "elemental masculinity." Religion and media are, on the one hand, sources—symbolic repertoires and accounts that position these men and women culturally and socially—and, on the other hand, things to "think with": contexts of exploration through which the ideas of provision, protection, and purpose have been refined.

It is at the boundary between the domestic and broader contexts of life that all of this finds force in broader culture, both for these men and for the broader cultural contexts through which they defined themselves. It is important to be well thought of, to be the kind of family man Paul Ryan was said to be during the 2012 presidential campaign. This implies that masculinity is not about itself alone, that it must also be about some larger purpose. This is at the center of the contemporary neo-masculinist discourses we've discussed. Those voices agree that it is not enough for men to be focused entirely on themselves, or entirely on their families as objects of affection and relationship. Fatherhood is about the next generation and about providing good and positive models outside one's own home. It is about what many call "civic engagement," the set of sensibilities and actions that place us in broader relationships of purpose and action. This lack of male purpose in the civic sphere is one of the central anxieties of the so-called crisis of masculinity. Men simply don't know what their role is in those broader contexts. This includes the devoted Christian men in these pages, not just the secularized men who bear the brunt of the neo-masculinist critique. And, as we've noted, religion seems to feed the crisis as much as or more than it resolves it.

Civic engagement involves a range of actions, including direct involvement in social organizations, community affairs, and politics. Much of that language has been influenced by Robert Putnam's notion of "social capital," which holds that individuals locate themselves in networks of relationship outside their bounded domestic ones.[7] So, to what extent do men step outside of the domestic sphere and for what purposes? These are important questions. We need to recognize, though, an inherent contradiction or tension here. Diffuse and unspecific as the notions of "provision," "protection," and "purpose" seem to be, they nonetheless evoke some fairly specific—and potentially problematic—ideas about the relationship between the contemporary domestic sphere and spheres beyond the domestic. That men are primarily devoted to "protection" of their families is particularly problematic. Is this to be read metaphorically only, or do men on some level hold in reserve the option of rather more direct—and potentially violent—means of protecting their families? As we've seen, many of the most often mentioned "masculine" media are precisely about this register of "protection." This notion of protection is also one of the things that have been thought to be most socially challenging about masculinity as traditionally conceived, with the implication of male violence also being one of the dimensions of masculinity most derogated in contemporary gender discourse. And, there is, of course, ample evidence that men think of protection quite nonmetaphorically.[8] This is all very much up in the air, indefinite, negotiated on the traditional end, of course—of contemporary "gender trouble."

For all of the putative egalitarianism of contemporary social and media discourse about men, traditionalism persists. Many of our interviewees found messages in entertainment media that supported the notion of male elementalism with regard to provision, protection, and purpose. That was one of the places where media had been the most powerful and probative for them. Potential tensions between those ideals and the lived domestic were all around them, some explicit in their experience, some implicit in their accounts and descriptions. The ideals, though, were everywhere in media and in mediated public discourse.

One area where this tension is most profound is in recent discussions of violence, and particularly gun violence. The 2012 election was followed by a horrific shooting at the Sandy Hook Elementary School in Newtown, Connecticut, that again raised the public profile of questions of protection. For some, this was a chance to talk about traditional ideas of male protection and masculine violence. Writing about the 2012 Newtown massacre in *National Review Online*, Charlotte Allen evoked the whole range of issues—from reaction against the feminization of culture to the so-called "crisis of masculinity"—wrapped in an argument for a very specific kind of elementalism:

> There was not a single adult male on the school premises when the shooting occurred. In this school of 450 students, a sizeable number of whom were undoubtedly 11- and 12-year-old boys (it was a K–6 school), all the personnel—the teachers, the principal, the assistant principal, the school psychologist, the "reading specialist"—were female. There didn't even seem to be a male janitor to heave his bucket at Adam Lanza's knees. Women and small children are sitting ducks for mass-murderers. The principal, Dawn Hochsprung, seemed to have performed bravely. According to reports, she activated the school's public-address system and also lunged at Lanza, before he shot her to death. Some of the teachers managed to save all or some of their charges by rushing them into closets or bathrooms. But in general, a feminized setting is a setting in which helpless passivity is the norm. Male aggression can be a good thing, as in protecting the weak—but it has been forced out of the culture of elementary schools and the education schools that train their personnel.

> Think of what Sandy Hook might have been like if a couple of male teachers who had played high-school football, or even some of the huskier 12-year-old boys, had converged on Lanza.[9]

Coupled with this type of elementalist, masculinist response was a related response that connected Sandy Hook to the essentialism of the domestic sphere. Following the Sandy Hook event, James Dobson claimed that the massacre was caused, in part, by the "redefinition" of the "institution of marriage."[10] Dobson's response was specifically aimed at current debates about same-sex marriage, but anxieties about masculinity and the domestic ideal are clearly embedded in those debates, especially for Dobson, who claims homosexuality is a disorder caused primarily by father troubles.[11]

A similar surge in discourse about elementalism followed the May 2014 shootings in Isla Vista, California, near the campus of the University of California, Santa Barbara. In this case, the shooter was a young man who left a number of digital documents, detailing his intentions and motivations, which were steeped in a certain kind of arch masculinity. He described himself as a victim of women's rejection, and he threatened retaliation against women as a result. Perhaps it was a function of the times, or of the generation involved (the perpetrator and victims were all in their twenties) or of the fact that so much material from and about the shooter was available online, but the Isla Vista events unleashed an unprecedented discourse in social media.

The precise history of this discourse itself became a subject of controversy, but it revolved around two contested reactions, primarily on Twitter but also extending to other media platforms. The first reaction was a defense of men, attempting to separate this particular shooter and men like him from men in general.[12] The Twitter hashtag #NotAllMen became the emblem of this argument. This was quickly met by a second discourse, following the hashtag #YesAllWomen. The latter argued, in the words of one tweet, "Sure #NotAllMen are misogynists and rapists. That's not the point. The point is that #YesAllWomen live in fear of the ones that are."[13] A wide range of social media discourse then ensued, becoming a vibrant review of contemporary norms and expectations concerning gender, focused on the demographic category where questions of power in gender are perhaps most pointed and critical. Many different voices weighed in, from pro-feminist, to anti-feminist, to a number that revealed how disturbingly unsettled these matters are. Voices from the world of religion were also heard, with some of these providing additional insight into the questions and issues under consideration. Religion got involved as it was directly confronted in some of the discourse, including in the hashtag #YesAllBiblicalWomen, which focused on experiences of oppression of women in religion.

We would assume that most of the Evangelical men we interviewed here would focus on this tragedy in a certain way. They would, we think, condemn the violence and would likely engage in some reflection on what this incident means about masculinity in general and masculine violence in particular. We know that many of them would be critical of the broader "hookup" culture that circulated around this incident, focusing on its sexual impurity and threat to disciplined and Godly masculine behavior. Given what they told us, they likely would also identify with a particular stream of religion-based commentary on Isla Vista that attempted to shift the focus away from the larger, structural themes found in most of the feminist and feminism-inspired commentary and back toward sin. Their response would have focused on what they perceived as the individual sin of the shooter, as well as the broader collective sin of culture that is chipping away at the elementals of masculinity and the essentials of the domestic sphere, echoing comments made by Ken Blackwell, senior fellow at the Family Research Council, who connected the shootings to "the crumbling of the moral foundation of the country" and "the attack on natural marriage and the family."[14]

Our informants might have been motivated to respond to this tragedy because religion was referenced in the various discourses as a contributing factor in the construction of traditional American masculinity.[15] Gene Robinson, the first openly gay bishop in the Anglican Communion, put this criticism in the voice of the Ecumenical side of the divide we've been pondering.[16] Like several of our Ecumenical Protestant informants, Robinson conveyed a criticism of traditional church teachings about gender relations. He noted that Christian scripture is part of the problem. St. Paul's admonitions to women's submission constitute "a view that has been interpreted to mean that the only proper role for a wife is subservience, the only rightful 'head of the household' and decision-maker is the husband, and the only appropriate response to a

husband's desires/commands is 'yes, sir, whatever you say.' At its most
extreme, it is used in the husband's or boyfriend's mind to justify domestic abuse ('she had it coming'), violence and death."[17]

Robinson's critique was unflinching: "[R]eligion is not solely responsible for the bias and violence against women, but we need to be a part
of this conversation, acknowledging that our religious views and systems
contribute to a world that in large part threatens, intimidates and endan-
gers women."[18]

His solution was to take the feminist structural critique that circulates
in the wider culture and turn that critique on religion and the churches.
Religious people, in his view, needed to lead in a self-critique and a
larger discussion "rather than [bring] up the rear." Robinson's statement
echoes the comments of the egalitarian men in this study who longed for
a pro-feminist discussion in their churches.

A contrasting view, one that directly confronted Robinson and one
more consistent with the views of the Evangelical men and women we
present here, was articulated by Chelsen Vicari, a spokesperson for the
conservative (and virulently anti–Ecumenical Protestant) Institute on
Religion and Democracy (IRD). Writing for the website of the Southern
Baptist Convention's Ethics and Religious Liberty Commission, Vicari
noted that the social media stream following the Isla Vista shootings
had included some material directly critical of religion and the churches.
Focusing on arguments such as Robinson's, she responded, "[H]arm
against women is real. But resolution will never be found in hasty pre-
conceived notions and finger pointing at men in the church." She pro-
ceeded to inscribe a bright line between the conservative/Evangelical
and liberal/Ecumenical sides of this debate: "Contrary to what some
religious feminists or liberal Christians will tell you, the Bible does not
prescribe violence against women."[19]

Writing on the IRD's own blog, Vicari put the case in a way that again
contrasts a feminist structural critique with one more familiar to conservative Protestants: "Gender inequality is not the crux of this heartbreak-
ing tragedy that led to the death of four men, two women, and wounding
of 13 others. The problem is larger than sexism, it is human sinful nature perpetuating the harming of human beings by other human beings. . . . Sin lurks in the depths of us all[,] stirring feelings of control,
self-gratification, anger, bitterness and hatred. As Christian women, we

know that the eradication of sin does not come in the form of feminist slogans nor [sic] man-hating retaliation."[20]

Many of our Evangelical informants would likely support Vicari's and Blackwell's views. The connection between sexuality, sin, and violence in the Isla Vista incident would have them focusing again on the individual's accountability in gender relations rather than on larger, more societal or structural attributes, with the notable exception of the institutional structure of heterosexual, headship-oriented marriage, which they see as crumbling and, thus, weakening the moral foundation of the country. In a similar way, many of our Ecumenical Protestant informants would probably identify with Robinson's critique of the church and of religion as places where gender equality is yet to be achieved and would identify with his positioning of the situation in a way that stands outside religion, with religion having a particular responsibility to be responsive to the larger societal issues involved. The negotiations over the meaning of masculinity and of gender, and the layering of the place of religion in those negotiations, emerge into public in incidents like those in Newtown and Isla Vista. They reveal in a telling way how the negotiations we've been looking at in these pages are in some ways what the construction of gender identities is all about. These constructions exist, as we've said, somewhere between structures, meanings, values, and truth claims.

Thus very stark ideas of gender, "gender trouble," and elementalism can seem always to lurk beneath the surface of public discourse, mirroring and informing the reality in private and individual spheres. Other, less searing examples of public elementalism abound. The Obama administration has been interpreted in relation to gender, race, and class very much through the lens of putative elemental male values. Obama himself has been likened to a "metrosexual,"[21] and his administration's positions on a range of topics have been critiqued for their alleged bias in favor of progressive and feminist values over against traditional (read: elementalist-male) values. The 2009 racially charged incident wherein Harvard Professor Henry Louis Gates, Jr., ran afoul of a Cambridge, Massachusetts, police officer was addressed by President Obama in a very "male" way, with the three guys gathering for a "Beer Summit."[22]

Even in the United Kingdom these struggles over elementalism and societal aspirations for "new men" persist. In the fall of 2012, Nick Clegg,

Deputy Prime Minister of the UK's governing coalition, made a public statement of apology for his party's role in several unpopular coalition policies. The British press interpreted this act very much in gender terms, as a sign of weakness, a loss of Clegg's "manhood." This coverage came at a time when gendered discourse about politics had suddenly resurfaced, something that a number of (particularly) female opinion leaders noted with some disquiet.[23] It was surprising to them how quickly this essentialism entered the discourse, as though these ideas had always lurked just below the surface.

Public discussion of gender reveals much about how broader cultural contexts express masculinity and the domestic sphere, about the extent to which elementalist ideas can come to the fore. Our interviews here reflect the fact that the pull of "the domestic" in relation to normative ideals of masculinity has much currency in this broader public discourse. It is a fundamental dimension of the construction of masculine gender today. Its instability in relation to other values, ideals, and directions is perhaps at the root of its momentum and force at this point in history. And, as it is commonly resolved, the norm of domestic commitments is the definitive norm.

This is a core underlying narrative in popular Evangelical literatures. Eldredge's *Wild at Heart*, for example, calls men to the "wilderness," objectifying and articulating an implicit tension between such purpose and the responsibilities of "the domestic." (Of course, Eldredge resolves this tension by creating a world in which men's being "wild" will lead to better domestic relations.) Perhaps more metaphorically, Evangelical and traditionalist discourses about the dangers of pornography or other vices carry within them a kind of moral panic about this same tension.

But it is the very taken-for-grantedness of the domestic and its commitments and concerns as definitive that is so interesting here. It is perhaps a measure of the *zeitgeist* that we can think of the concerns of individuals, of affectionate relationships, and of bounded and inward-oriented spaces of home and family as unquestionably prior in moral terms. This, of course, makes sense. The lessons of the gender revolution have been very much about the need for men and women to refocus energies on righting the relations in the domestic sphere. But that is the point. In broad terms of social values and normative relations, Western culture today says that men should think of the domestic as central, and for a variety of reasons, many men (including most we have talked with here) see that space as both the most important, and the most satisfying, object of their energies.

This means that the focus of male purpose today is largely in the domestic and that we have experienced a collapse toward the domestic in relation to broader goals or objectives or needs of civic engagement. One implication of this is that one assumption of the "crisis of masculinity" critique—that there is a kind of seamless contiguity between the domestic and the public spheres, with men and their children acting as "little platoons" of normative action—has been turned at least inward, if not on its head. Men today are encouraged—by their own experiences in the private sphere, by their religious contexts, by the broader contexts of discourse in which they find themselves, by broader cultural messages and tropes, and by a public discourse that values the domestic at the same time that it extols elementalist views of men that do not find real purchase in the actual facts of men's lives—to hold two potentially contradictory values in mind. On the one hand is the value of their commitments to the affectional needs of the domestic sphere, particularly of their children, and on the other hand is a rather diffuse set of residual values of traditional masculinity, values we call "elemental masculinity" (captured best in Clark Caldwell's comments[24] about *Braveheart*'s embodiment of a greater purpose to protect and provide for his country).

Indeed, it is within the domain of the domestic where masculinity finds its greatest purpose in American life. The domestic ideal becomes a locus of identity, around which provision, protection, and purpose revolve. This is why changes to the domestic and men's roles in it are so often perceived as threats or crises.

In this chapter, we return to Denton Calhoun, an Evangelical from the American South, and his Evangelical contemporary Larry Cane, from the American West, to explore the ways in which what we call the "domestic ideal" comes to dominate American masculinity, as not only the "real life" of American Protestant fathers but also as the idyllic aspirations of fatherless men, even as they chase their "wild hearts." We will juxtapose these two Evangelical men with Ecumenical men, exploring nuances, similarities, and differences. In most cases, provision, protection, and purpose can be cloaked in different rhetorical and performative strategies, but they are still essential to a "normal" masculine sense of self. We will also talk again with Ricky McDonald, something of an outlier who nonetheless provides some valuable insights into the extents and limits of these conceptions in making meaningful senses of masculinity. He represents the minority of our respondents for whom elementalism was problematic, yet he still found it inescapable. Like many younger men on the progressive wings of Evangelical and Ecumenical Protestantism, Ricky struggled to reconcile some of his commitments with an enduring sense that there are, still, things that are typical of men. Finally, we will consider how the domestic ideal influences "the public," whether the foundation for "decent" life or the launching pad for a successful political career, as in the case of Paul Ryan. It is the former—decency—that concerns us mostly here because the domestic ideal as a launching pad for political life is primarily the privilege of the elite. For our men—men in the pews, men within different layers of the middle class—the "domestic ideal" is not a launching pad but a powerful lens through which the "public" is seen. In important ways, this lens creates dissonance necessitated by the desire to be present with family yet also have a desire to be purposeful through work and vocation.

Elementalism in Context

We have said that elemental masculinity, with all its sources, meanings, and nuances, must be understood in relation to the home. It makes most sense in this way, and its logics are clearly derived from the more fundamental commitment that most of the men with whom we've spoken have made to home, to family, and to fatherhood. Every man we interviewed who held the status of husband or father pointed to his location in the domestic sphere as the central location for explaining who men are. Typically, we'd ask, "What are the important roles that men play?" We might have thought that a wide range of such roles would occur. We at least might have expected that some balance of roles between the domestic and broader civic sphere would be meaningful. That is, after all, what traditionalist critics have suggested, that the role of men as husbands and fathers needs somehow to be linked to broader needs and concerns of community and society.

Rarely did we find men who expressed such a clear and untroubled linkage between the domestic ideal and the public. What we found is a more complex picture of men wrestling with their senses of public/private in relation to the pressures of everyday life. Some men subsumed the public under the domestic ideal. Other men expressed a link between the domestic ideal and public life (mainly in terms of paid labor), but this public/private link is better understood as a rupture. That is, their "calling" to public life (to the extent they acknowledged such a calling at all) was in constant tension with their "calling" to the domestic ideal. These men were constantly seeking *balance* because they were torn between dueling purposes. For each man, though, the domestic ideal was the pivot point.

Denton Calhoun is an exemplar for men whose primary focus is on the domestic ideal. Denton loves his work, and he has ambitions related to his work. But work was necessary to fulfill his role of husband and father, provider, and protector.

DENTON: Some of the roles I play in my life? Husband, father, employee, supervisor, friend.

INTERVIEWER: Which of those would you say—you don't have to put them in order—but what is your most important role?

DENTON: Definitely husband and father are right there together.

INTERVIEWER: And all the others you do for those two?

DENTON: Yeah, more or less. . . . So, there's been a little more than a year now growing into that role of thinking that when I'm on my way home from work that I'm coming home to my other job that is a lot more important than the job that I just got done doing. I mean that's true when you're married as well, but even more so when you have a kid, you know, because [my spouse] is not necessarily waiting to wrestle with me or something like that [when I get home]. But [my son] is, and, you know, [my spouse] is looking to dump him to some degree by the time I get here.

Denton expressed in personal terms a tendency that has been broadly observed by scholars of the domestic sphere. We've pointed to the work of Anthony Giddens on the contemporary "project of the self" as in part explaining these trends. Against a modern condition that is seen as increasingly risky, individuals today turn inward, framing their senses of self and identities in the context of meaning projects that they can themselves define.

Contemporary studies of men[25] show that this orientation toward self and identity carries with it an orientation to the spaces and spheres that are nearest to the self, those that can most readily be the locations of effective practice. Thus the preponderance of attention to "the domestic" in our interviews is indicative of the general picture. This research finds that, where men might once have identified themselves with work and career, today the home and the family are the normative core of practice. Denton was rather explicit about his sense of the relationship between his roles inside the home and outside the home, especially in the workplace. The job at home "is a lot more important," he noted, than his paid position, even though he also noted that he had more work aspirations than his father had. Denton also introduced a dimension to all of this that points to a major point of negotiation and determination in his domestic relations. The way he talked about expectations of him at home, that his wife may well need some relief of the burden of child care, is significant. That he was conscious of domestic relations as a negotiation both evinces some consciousness of ongoing gender dynamics in the culture *and* embeds him clearly and self-consciously in the home in a rather concrete and visceral way. No more the abstract and remote status in the home of the men of the past (the era portrayed in television programs such as *Mad Men*, for example). Today men like Denton experience—and accept—a situation that positions them as active participants in the worklife of the home. In fact, for men like Denton, this active participation has greater purpose than anything else they can do. But there is tension here related to his interpretation of his own father and his life as a worker and father.

As we've observed widely among our interviewees, Denton framed this self-consciousness very specifically and directly in relation to his own father and the model of parenthood he represented.

> DENTON: I don't think that for my dad [work] was a large part of his identity. He worked for himself, and [so] he wasn't an ambitious businessperson trying to impress the boss or climb up the ladder or anything like that. . . . And I think, for myself, I'm probably a little more ambitious than he is. And I struggle with that a little bit because I want to balance my life where work is not the most important thing in my life. So, I don't want to treat it like that, but

also I'm probably more ambitious to go further, or if I even have my own business someday to make, to treat it more like a small business and see it grow and that sort of thing. So, it would probably be a little more of my identity in some ways, but I mean I also want to be cautious and guarding that from becoming too much of my identity.

Denton's self-awareness here reveals more about the contemporary situation in which he finds himself. Men today—at least like the ones we have spoken with here—seek to be and to be understood as professionally ambitious. The culture expects them to think about career and career growth—the Horatio Alger myth is alive and well—but in the contemporary mind, this aspiration is tinged with concern about the potential danger it poses to domestic responsibilities. Rarely do men express the connection between the domestic and the public as something that is naturally seamless. Rather, this connection is tense with the potential for rupture and the need for "balance."[26] And balance for these men is weighted toward their domestic responsibilities.

Men today can be ambitious, but this ambition is always understood to be potentially at the expense of something else. This may well be new and the significant marker of the age. That Denton was a conservative Evangelical makes this position interesting on a couple of fronts. First, all of these men had on some level taken onboard the feminist critique of traditional gender roles. They understood the injustices and limitations of the old ways of gender roles. Denton certainly saw things in this way. However, we can also see Denton's view as potentially significant in another way. It allows men like him to claim a feminist value—that of egalitarian involvement—as normative not because it is just but because it is just "good fathering," and fathering that is better than that carried out by their own fathers, from whom they want to be distinct in this way. Of course, it is also notable that Denton (like many Evangelicals) couched this feminist value in the anti-feminist notion of headship. Feminism has "softened" patriarchy, not replaced it.

Larry Cane, another Evangelical Christian, expressed the relationship between the domestic ideal and public life in different terms that are closer to the imagined ideal of conservative and neo-traditional critics:

I think the reason I'm doing what I'm doing, working in this ministry, especially, specifically now with youth[,] is because I feel like it's been a clear calling from God that it's what He has for me and it's what He's really called me to do. And so that shapes our family in large part. There are a lot of great things about being involved in youth ministry, but there are a lot of things that would be easier if I [weren't] involved in youth ministry. And there are a lot of things that were easier when I was just working in the business world. But I think when God calls you to something, not only is it a strong calling that it's best for us to follow, but it's also a fulfilling calling. While the road can be really hard at times, there's a fulfillment that's reached when you're doing something that you're called to do that can't be met any other way, I don't think. And I think that has shaped the reason why Linda is staying home with the girls. I mean it would be a lot easier if she [were] doing something, I mean working, income-wise at least. But, we feel so clearly that she has been called to be a mom and that is the greatest calling; the greatest thing that she could be doing right now is being a mom to the two girls. That doesn't mean that at some point down the road she might not do something else as well. But right now that is the greatest calling that she has, and we believe wholeheartedly in that, which has led to a lot of sacrifices in terms of things that we have. But we would never change that because we feel so clearly that that's what God has for us. It's such a great and secure place to be when you feel that you're within His calling because the struggles that you go through or the difficulties that you face are not ones that you're facing on your own. Instead they're things that you're facing together with God's help because you know that you're where He wants you to be.

Larry's "calling" and purpose were to be a good father and husband, which required that he follow God's call in his work life. This pulled him away from the family and into the more public life of ministry. There were clear tensions here in terms of provision (something we'll return to), but Larry reconciled this tension because it was God's will. Thus, the loss, in terms of time at home and material comforts, was mitigated by the "fulfillment that's reached when you're doing something that you're called to do." Larry also expressed this relationship as one of struggle, but there is a clear sense also that "doing God's will" yields provision and protection (i.e. "a secure place").

Larry and Denton are bookends of an Evangelical spectrum. Men who were involved in ministry or other "caring" industries like education or health care tended to express narratives similar to Larry's. Others leaned toward Denton's narrative. For each, the domestic ideal was paramount. For each, there was a certain amount of tension between the domestic ideal and public life. Even for Larry, the discussion about "doing God's will" was in conversation with the potential consequences of his responding to his calling to his family, which were mitigated, of course, by his having a spouse called to motherhood. It is also notable that the tension here was always between domestic life and work life, not between the domestic and other forms of public engagement.

For Ecumenicals, the story is more ambiguous. As we've noted, the range of Ecumenical voices in this study was broad. The questions we've been talking about—how men connect their religious lives, their senses of self and identity and gender, and their senses of purpose—reveal some real differences between these two cohorts. Evangelicals like Denton and Larry must contend with a range of taken-for-granted and tacit discourses, of which the idea of headship is central. For Evangelicals, these questions are far from determined or straightforward. Instead, they are contentious, yet their conversation is in a sense "on the same page": These men tend to have a more articulated discourse about provision, protection, and purpose.

Our Ecumenical Protestants did not. This is not to say that Ecumenicals lacked any clarity about provision, protection, or purpose, but it is to say that they did not contend with the received discourses in any clear way. For example, Mike Andrews—the most conservative Ecumenical Protestant in our cohort—expressed purpose in similar ways to Denton's (purpose as providing for his family), but he did not use the idea of headship at all. Ricky and Jennifer McDonald, who constructed an identity narrative contrary to Evangelical narratives of headship, shared an almost Evangelical embrace of "calling," but this calling had nothing particularly to do with the domestic ideal.

RICKY: I think everyone has a calling, I don't think there's one answer to what that calling is for every person. Like, you could have a calling to be a social critic and that could look a lot of different ways. Or you could have a calling to teach; that could look a lot of different ways.

You could have a calling to be compassionate; that could look a lot of different ways.

JENNIFER: Well, the guy who's—I wish I could remember the people who say things—like, your calling is when your deepest joy and the world's deepest hunger meet. And so, for me, there is that, like, is what I'm doing important enough? Um, but then Mother Teresa said that it's not about doing great things but doing small things with great love. And so, like sometimes I think, rather than going, "Why am I not in Iraq helping orphans?" I should be thinking, "Why am I not reaching out to my neighbors?" And maybe there will be a point at which I am in Iraq. Meanwhile, like, instead of thinking, "I can't do that, so I won't do anything," what can I be doing that's reaching out to people, I guess.

Ricky's and Jennifer's domestic responsibilities and expectations seemed to force them to scale down their expectations for calling and purpose. In some important ways, the domestic did not help them achieve their sense of calling, even though they both saw their family as central to their purpose. The types of contradictions and tensions expressed by the McDonalds and the Andrewses are typical of our respondents along the spectrums of traditionalism/egalitarianism and elementalist/constructivist.

We see similar tensions and contradictions in Evangelical discourses as well, but it is notable in this study that Ecumenicals lack the focused articulations of gender in their broader symbolic universe that Evangelicals have. To the extent that Ecumenicals have a focused discourse, it is a polemical discourse that is explicit about not being Evangelical.

All of this is evidence of the extent to which questions of male purpose and male identity are today diffuse and in flux. We've thought much about how this is and why this might be. It is a combination of issues and contexts. What has resulted is a situation wherein there is a great deal in contention and much in play. What we have seen so far is the range of ways in which questions of masculine identity resolve themselves. The outlines of our analysis turn out to be in some measure the differing ways in which these various individuals and groups contend with the same issues. For some of them, clear attributions and symbolic resources are available to meaning-making, and they make more or less satisfying sense using them. For more of them, though, the resources of meaning-making remain ambiguous and in flux. The actual outlines of action are hard to express in concrete terms. Instead, notional and aspirational claims and ideas hold sway, claims that are clearly rooted in traditional senses of masculinity, manhood, and gender. These have evolved into generic senses that the elements of masculinity must be somewhere in these categories of provision, protection, and purpose *and* located in the domestic sphere.

Thinking about Provision in the Domestic Ideal

Provision of the material sort appears throughout our interviews. Men said again and again that it is men's fundamental responsibility to "bring home the bacon." Denton Calhoun and others, though, introduced another meaning of provision as well: that men should ideally provide emotional and spiritual resources in the home to go along with the material resources they provide from outside it. He addressed this rather directly in response to a question about the career aspirations he has for his own son.

INTERVIEWER: Let me give you a hypothetical situation. Would it be a problem when he gets older if he were in a position where he was a stay-at-home dad and his spouse was the primary breadwinner? Would that be a problem, and if so, why?

DENTON: As far as we're concerned?

INTERVIEWER: Yeah.

DENTON: I don't think so, but it probably would be for my parents.

INTERVIEWER: Continuing the hypothetical. If that were the case, how would the idea of headship or leadership play out? Would it be different at all?

DENTON: I don't think so ... and if it [were] different, then I would be saying that staying at home would demote him in leadership, and I would be saying that staying at home is less important than going out and working, and we don't treat it that way here. I tell [my spouse] all the time that what she's doing by far—I mean talking about priorities—the number one priority isn't work and making money, but doing the family and having a relationship with God, and she's

actually spending her time everyday on something a lot more important than what I spend my time on every day. If I didn't have to pay
the bills and stuff like that, I would spend my time where it was more
important too. I have fun making advertisements or whatever it is we
are doing, but at the end of the day, if I'm not making that website or
advertisement or whatever, the world's going to keep spinning, and
it's not that big of a deal. It's not that important.

Larry Cane also stressed a more affective relationship with his family
wherein emotional provision is central to his role as a father. For Larry,
this was not simply a matter of quantity—that is, spending more time
with family—it was a qualitative matter as well. According to Larry, one
must be affectively present (again perhaps a veiled critique of the traditionalist, remote parenting style of his own father).

There are some things that were incredibly positive. Um, my dad worked
a ton when I was a kid, and so I think that there is impact there in terms
of [his] not being around a lot although he wasn't absent from our life.
Because he was still, I mean he was a soccer coach for me, I mean he
was like an assistant coach, so he was really intentional about still being
involved in my life in places that mattered, which is a lot different from
a lot of fathers that I get to see now where it's that they work a lot and
they're checked out from their kids' lives and so—it wasn't that he was absent. He did Boy Scouts with us some, but he did work a ton, and so that
meant that Mom was the one that really set the boundaries. Mom was the
one that we really talked to about everything. And so there is a piece of
that where I think that negatively I was [affected] in the way that I didn't
have to go to him to deal with conflict even. Even if there was something
going on that, you know—especially as I got older sometimes he did a
lot of handyman stuff, and so sometimes I'd help him out around the
house. And you—sometimes I just would feel like I didn't want to work
anymore and I'd just go inside, but I'd just talk to my mom about it. And
he wouldn't ever really confront me on those things unless it was maybe
blowing up or something at some point. But I think that it modeled to me
at least a home where Mom's the one that really sets the standard. Mom's
the one that really, even by faith—I mean my dad used to just come to
church on Christmas and Easter. Not until I was in late high school, early

college did he start coming to church all the time, which was really neat. I mean he was totally supportive, but he worked so much that Sunday was the day he slept in, you know. So faith wasn't a huge part of his life, and so I think some of those things were some of the things that I missed from a father. What does it look like to pass on your faith to your kids? What does it look like to be a leader in the family? What does it look like to, you know, help set boundaries and to really, um, speak life into your kids? The flip side of that is he was always around and wasn't disengaged from our lives and sacrificed a lot for us. I mean it wasn't a selfish pursuing his own career, I don't think, ever. I mean he was always providing for our family. So I think I learned a lot about what does it mean to really sacrifice for your family from my dad. What it means to work hard. As much as I bailed on him a lot, it still rubbed off on me, which I am so grateful for because I just think that you know, the work ethic that I have now is so much characterized by my dad. You know we'd work on cars sometimes together, and he would be up until 4 in the morning if he needed to fix our car. I'd stay out with him until about 2 or something, and then I would just be like, "I just can't do this anymore." So I think I learned a lot about commitment from my dad. About sacrifice from him. And even, just, I think that he loved me deeply, and so I think that that rubbed off even though it's so easy to look and see that these are places I want to be different in the way I'm a father.

This long excerpt introduces a range of possible definitions and meanings of provision, suggesting that financial provision must not trump emotional provision or, for Evangelicals, spiritual provision. Practically speaking, for Larry—and for the overwhelming majority of men here—financial provision was important because they were in the position of primary wage earner. But, at the same time, financial provision competed with emotional and spiritual provision. This competition may have been primarily a symbolic or narrative one, but it was nonetheless important and definitive. The point here is not so much that these particular ideas exist as possibilities but that they are in circulation and negotiation. They appear in Larry's and Denton's and others' accounts of self as a set of values that must be honored and accounted for. Further, the values themselves, and the aspirations of these men to articulate them with one another, suggests a broadening and deepening of domestic roles and identities. The discourses carry in them markers of the sources of this deepening and broadening: in feminism, in changes in labor markets and the meaning of work life, and in changing aspirations with regard to class.

These ideas are not unique to our Evangelical men, however. In broad terms, the same ideas about shifting responsibilities and about the role, place, and meaning of provision appear in our conversations with Ecumenical men. Mike Andrews, for example, felt strongly that provision is the most important role for men, one that trumps other values and commitments in life. Provision for family was his primary responsibility. In response to questions about his notion of "calling" in relation to work, he shifted the focus back to the domestic and family sphere.

> MIKE: Yeah, I mean, I—I'd—I wouldn't hesitate to walk away from sales if something else is my calling. Um, I kind of look at this stage in life, though, as, you know, the sales is providing the financial, uh, means to be able to provide for the family well during these younger years. You know, I like to think that and when the kids are out of the house, and, you know, we don't have such high financial commitments, I could do something else.
>
> INTERVIEWER: OK. Do you see provision as being particularly your role?
>
> MIKE: For the most part because [my spouse] stays at home.
>
> INTERVIEWER: Do you think that's general for men, or is that just your situation?
>
> MIKE: You know, I think anymore, you know, it's more rare to see a, a, a single-parent breadwinner. You know, mostly it's both the mother and father who are working. Um, you know, growing up, that was my goal—to be able to be the breadwinner, have my wife stay home.

Like Larry and Denton, Mike felt that provision must be seen to include material, affective, and spiritual components.

> You know, since I started the first Bible study and the whole theme is always the parental-child view. You know, God and his Israelites, His children, and, you know, everything always goes back to the parent-child.

You know, correcting once you've gone off the beaten path. You know, constantly forgiving and guiding. You know, because there's so often that I'll see my kids doing something and saying something, and I'll think, man, that's just like the Israelites. God warned them and warned them and warned them and warned them and warned them. And as mad as God got at the Israelites, you know, He didn't destroy them. You know, He always forgave them and brought them back, and I'm thinking there's been so many times that I've had to leave the room because my kids made me so angry. But then, you know, at the end of the day, you're hugging them and thinking, yep, that's just part of growing up. So, I think part of being a man is, you know, realizing when we've done something stupid in front of our kids, knowing that we're the role model, being able to then tell the kids when we messed up. And, encouraging the kids as well as reprimanding them. Boy, you know, I look at that, that's like, *I look at that as the role of the mother too* [emphasis added]. You know, it's a similar thing.

We can read through Mike's discussion of a fathering God his sense of the various dimensions of affective and spiritual provision assigned to men. There is a loving, affectionate father as well as a reprimanding father. The tension between the two reveals his normative commitment to the affectionate side and his sense that that is—or should be—his role in his own home and family.

You know, before I got into the Bible study, you would have never heard me talking about God. Or maybe the extent of it is that I went to church and heard a great sermon, but that's it. But I think getting past that stigma that it's, it's, not uncool to talk about Jesus. Um, and, you know, not uncool to say, you know, "Thank you, Lord" instead of "Oh, what a coincidence that was." And, um, I think showing the kids that you can be a man and say the word *love* too. And constantly telling our kids, "I love you. I love you. And, we love so and so." And I think kind of taking that macho-ness out of being a man. You know, I remember growing up, with my dad, we had really no relationship whatsoever. And we still don't to this day, you know. And never have I—I can't ever remember hearing him say, "I love you." So, it's like, you know what? That's not going to be the case with my kids.

Mike is a model of what W. Bradford Wilcox has called, in his studies of religious masculinity,[27] a "new man." Like other Ecumenical men, including those in Wilcox's study, Mike self-consciously contended with a full range of affective roles and meanings for manhood, many of them rooted in ongoing cultural discourses of gender. Mike wished to explore and emphasize men's abilities and responsibilities in nontraditional valences of parenting and of family life. He consciously linked this to a softer and more affective sense of his faith and spirituality as well, speaking in Evangelical terms about his relationship with Jesus.

But Mike was quite distinct from the Evangelicals here in that he did not place this sense of his role within the confines of the notion of headship. He shared with Evangelicals the basic theological need for a personal relationship with Jesus. His turn to religion in talking about manhood was rooted in the notion that there is something essential that men must provide as their particular gift. But he did not use the Evangelical language of headship. Mike's religious commitment was more about moral leadership (shared with his spouse) than about spiritual hierarchy. This is not to say that Evangelical men are not interested in moral leadership or in the language of love and affection; rather, it is to say that for the Evangelical men with whom we talked here, conversations about love and morality were couched in the language of headship. For Ecumenical men—even for Mike, the most "Evangelical" of our Ecumenical men—headship was not an important metaphor or idea at all. Instead, Mike represents the model of "new men" sensibilities (to use Wilcox's term once again), providing financially, but also—and importantly—emotionally and morally. Further, his was an emotional provision that sought to drain masculinity of its "machoness," a sensibility that put him at odds with many of his Evangelical peers.

The difference between Evangelical and Ecumenical men with regard to the question of provision may not be that significant. Both groups seemed to hold the same commitment to provision in material terms, as well as beyond that in affective, moral, or spiritual terms. At least men from each group could articulate such ideas and chose to frame the situation of contemporary masculinity or manhood in these terms. What was different between the two groups was the importance, for the Evangelicals, of coding this commitment in terms of authority (even while "softening" this with egalitarian language). While something softer might be implied by the notion that *affective* provision is among men's roles, Evangelicals balanced this with a strong sense of the framing of their role in the notion of headship.[28]

As we've already suggested, whatever rethinking of the notion of "provision" might be taking place among these men seems to have its roots in the contexts of contemporary culture and its evolving values of gender. It is within the lived conditions of domestic life and its shifting demands, in the conflict between a very traditionalist sense of "provision" (such as the anachronistic model of the male hunter-gatherer) and in the actual conditions of modern life and its structural and historical demands that all of this plays out. Simply put, it is no longer the case that most men must provide in the way that we imagine was the case before the Industrial Revolution. Today, provision occurs through institutional and structured workplace and career locations, where the provision is of financial resources and other securities that modern industrial and post-industrial life expects and demands. In all of these ways the traditional and traditionalist idea of "provision" must necessarily be negotiated. Thus, while material provision is certainly important to these men, provision takes on new and more symbolic valences in modern life.[29]

Still, with all of the disembedding of contemporary life from roots in traditional cultural contexts, many men today retain a sense of elementalism and traditionalism. They have not discarded prior ideas about what it means to be a man in the face of shifting realities of modern life. They have not completely rejected traditional manhood and its aspirations in the face of advances in egalitarian gender relations. Instead, they negotiate these other factors against a persistent sense that, all other things being equal, it is up to them as men to provide for their families. This notion of provision itself carries the markers of contemporary cultural negotiations and meanings, however. In the era of risk culture,[30] and in a time when we focus increasingly on the emotional and affective as the central areas of normative value in life and identity, these men articulated these values with their sense of elemental provision. A fascinating feat.

Protection in the Domestic Ideal

The second dimension of elemental masculinity that surfaces in these interviews is the male responsibility for protection. In the traditional framing of masculinity, this is rooted in archaic responsibilities for the safety of the family group and tribe. It is significant to our explorations that this particular area has been the central theme of so much oral history, folklore, fiction, and artistic portrayals. Narratives of male protection are, simply, a rich source of creative ideas for writers, television producers, filmmakers, and game designers.

It is thus not surprising that protection would persist as a theme in our conversations. For example, the character of William Wallace, portrayed by Mel Gibson in his film *Braveheart*, was the most often mentioned filmic portrayal of protective masculinity in our interviews. Some men (in the Ecumenical cohort) also pointed to Tom Hanks's character Captain John Miller in *Saving Private Ryan*. Clearly, the plot of *Braveheart* portrays the ideal of "protection" a bit more directly (of family and then country), but the men who talked about these films suggested that it was their portrayals of the male *capacity* for protection that was important.

The implication of violence that resides at the center of the notion of protection is at its core problematic in contemporary life—and in our conversations. Some we've heard from, such as Garth Johnson, found the embrace of characters like *Braveheart* or the generic "John Wayne role" problematic because of the valorization of violence. Also, among several of our Ecumenical men, there was a general reluctance to embrace the "warrior hero" (aside perhaps from Hanks's Captain Miller, who seemed more reluctant or measured to them than Gibson's Wallace). But all men did idealize aspects of these characters and idealized their portrayal of the capacity for masculine protection. The filmic repertoire of images of masculinity, along with the ambiguities of identifying with the implicit capacity for violence in the midst of civilized modernity, provided the central language through which masculinity was discussed. We clearly found this in our interviews and focus groups (and we saw it in the public discourses surrounding the Newtown shooting, noted above).

There is further evidence of the centrality of this filmic repertoire in both popular and scholarly literatures. John Eldredge's influential

Wild at Heart book and its sequels center the conversation very much on symbolic claims about masculinity in the culture. Those symbols are almost entirely filmic symbols. The same can be found in a range of the scholarly literature[31] and the critical commentary both feminist[32] and anti-feminist.[33] It is simply not possible in contemporary American culture to talk about this "essential" masculine characteristic without talking about films (and media generally).

And it is not just that these are salient symbols; they invite us to think about these relations in a specific way, at least as evidenced by our conversations and by some of these literatures. The perspective articulated by Eldredge—and echoed by many of the men with whom we've spoken—is that late modern American life poses a challenge to the elemental capacity that men have for protection (as well as purpose). Culture has become "domesticated" in important ways. The project of the settlement of the frontier with all of its implications and its imaginaries in the popular mind has been accomplished.[34] This means that men today have nothing to fight, and nothing to protect their loved ones *from*. These voices clearly search, then, for alternative ways of articulating and performing protection. Some choose metaphoric protections of various kinds; some redefine protection rather fundamentally. Still others focus on the fact that physical danger does still exist, even in modern life and, particularly in "new media" life, for example the concern with online predators.[35]

We do wish to acknowledge that men who worry about real physical dangers have some evidence—primarily media evidence[36]—on which to base this concern. The wide availability of guns and what seems to be a continuing series of gun-related events, including mass shootings and school shootings, do constitute a real threat. Thus, that these men hold out the real possibility of needing at some point to exercise violence in order to protect their families has some basis in reality. So the model of a William Wallace or man on the frontier continues to be salient on some level. But the fact remains that all of the men interviewed for this book live today in a settled domestic space where civil authorities bear the responsibility for maintenance of order and where private citizens are expected to defer to those authorities except in exceptional circumstances. Thus the ideal of masculinity in modernity is one that is to hold the possibility of violence largely in abeyance, a potential or imagined capacity more than something that is realized. For the men in these pages, actual physical threats will likely remain potential threats.

For many we've interviewed, though, there was another "enemy" in their midst, another perceived war to be fought. For a number of men, there was an ongoing "cultural war" underway, largely borne by the media. The media are part of a larger cultural onslaught against the values of home, faith, and family, so this argument goes. They are also a direct penetration of the sanctity of the sacred boundaries of the home and the domestic sphere. Many of the accounts of masculine selves we see here embraced this narrative of an ongoing culture war and connected this narrative with their ideals of domestic life, making the role of protection one that could be directed at the dangers of this broader culture and its media. Even Ecumenical men like Ricky McDonald, who would otherwise be critical of conservative views of the situation, saw media as a key site of struggle in maintaining the moral culture of the family.

On the most basic level, the media become a kind of common enemy from which families and particularly children should be protected.[37] Time and again, men combined conversations about the sources of masculine ideals in media and film with articulations about media as a source of danger. Many agreed with Denton Calhoun that media culture evinces a deeper decline in the broader culture. In a discussion centered on the situation comedy *Friends*, which Denton and his wife watched regularly in syndication, he suggested a narrative of cultural decline and described his concern for the impact of such media on his son.

> You kind of feel in some ways that the world or culture is going to pot, and you just get more on the TV and radio—I guess this is really pertinent to what we're talking about here—you know, when we were kids it was *Full House* and *Cosby Show* and Nick at Nite and stuff that you would watch and there's so much on TV now that really if you pay attention to [*Friends*] what they're talking about it's, you know, they're sleeping around and that sort of thing. So it definitely scares me just from the influences he'll have from all sorts of mass media.

As is commonplace across audience research such as ours, Denton was rather un-self-conscious about his own complicity in *Friends'* popularity. It is often the case that people have well-developed criticisms of the media they watch, and they express anxieties about those media in relation to their own families. This is often, but not exclusively, in the case of sexuality in media, something that is of more concern to Evangelicals like Denton than it is to Ecumenicals. We saw examples of this earlier.

In addition to concerns about sexuality, there was the sense from many of our men that media are the key threat to moral living in general. Larry Cane put it this way: "I just think that goes back to a little bit what Linda was talking about, even in the TV shows that she likes the way the family's portrayed or the father's portrayed as strong or whatever, but just the messages that come across in almost all movies nowadays with few exceptions are messages that are a completely different worldview than our own."

It is thus not just the specific messages in these media; rather, it is that media convey the completely different way of looking at the world. The media seem something "other" to men like Larry. Many Ecumenical men shared this view as well. For example, Mike and Sally Andrews expressed this sense of differentiation between their ideals and media ideals in a discussion of their favorite or important media. We reproduce here a section of their interview we excerpted earlier. Looking over lists they'd made of television programs that express ideals of which they approve, Sally noted one of Mike's selections.

SALLY: Haha, you put *Leave It to Beaver*?!
INTERVIEWER: Yeah, he did!
MIKE: Maybe I should say what I'd like it to express—
SALLY: I was going to say [*inaudible*].
INTERVIEWER: Oh, okay, hahaha. It's an ideal—
MIKE: It's an ideal. It's where the, the family is a big part of the kids' lives, and, um, kids don't just come home and the TV is the baby sitter, it's not that—it's always trying to teach the kids a lesson in every episode. So that, that kinda—I mean, we let our kids try to get their own bumps and bruises if we can, to a point.
MIKE: Well, it's too bad that *Two and a Half Men*, we stopped watching that—
SALLY: Yeah, we used to really like that one, but it's not—

MIKE:—but they've really gone over the edge now, with the language and the—um, well, a lot of times we'll start watching something and the language will come out—oops: inappropriate, turn it off! But if *The Simpsons* comes on—*vrrmmph*, inappropriate.

SALLY: Like *The Simpsons*, and *Family Guy*—

MIKE: Yeah, *Family Guy* is another one, gosh.

SALLY:—are two that I would say are absolute.

MIKE: But the kids have gotten to where if they're flipping through [the channels] they're like, "Oh, inappropriate, keep going!"

INTERVIEWER: Yeah. Is it mainly the language that's the issue in those shows?

SALLY: To me it's not the language as much as it is usually the topic that the language just filters into.

MIKE: Well, and even with *Survivor* lately they're not bleeping out a lot of the words. I mean, it's become acceptable to say some of these things.

It is clear that for Mike and Sally—as with the Evangelical cohort in our interviews—sex and sexuality remained a concern for the family, though not a primary one for Mike personally, as is evidenced by some of his earlier comments about *The Sopranos*, which he watched regularly. For Mike, and for most Ecumenicals, concern about sexuality was almost entirely focused on the needs and interests of children. For Evangelical men, as we noted earlier, sexuality in media was a kind of challenge because its moral effects redound to them and their character through the effect this has on their preparation to be the upright, moral center of the family. For Ecumenical men, the conversation about sexuality was primarily about children. And, tellingly, it was about the influence on children. Further, as we saw earlier, Ecumenical men's concern about sexuality was often couched in feminist terms, suggesting that sexuality in media is of concern because it exploits and degrades women, not because it is a temptation to men.

Whether concerned with sexuality, violence, or the amount of screen time spent by the family or its children,[38] Evangelical and Ecumenical men note that media culture remains an important battleground. This led the McDonald family to remove television from their home.

For them, the battle was not about sex, or even violence, but rampant commercialism.

> RICKY: There was some concern about advertising, mainly, right? What's the impact of advertising, especially after Sophia was born. How does that, kind of—that and time-use, right? We could be doing other things with the time.
>
> JENNIFER: Two or three years we didn't have a TV before Sophia was born, and then we haven't had a TV since. I think that there's a lot that people don't realize about how much even just commercials affect them.

But the media still remained in most of these homes. They were still watched. They still became the stuff of family and broader conversation. They were ever-present, ubiquitous and inevitable, and ever necessary (as media theory would suggest) for the accrual of cultural capital. Our respondents weren't, though, simply resigned to the ubiquitous and pervasive media. Teaching their children about media became a central part of their calling as Christian parents. This teaching became an expression of the masculine function of protection.[39] We have talked elsewhere[40] about the moral valuation implied by such education in media households. Parents today seek to raise conscious, intelligent, discerning, autonomous children. Training in discernment of media becomes important to that task. For the Evangelicals we interviewed, there was an additional valence to this, that such properly conscious children could also become "salt and light" to a culture sorely in need of their influence. Larry Cane and his wife, Linda, were typical of this.

> LARRY: We don't want them watching those things because they're so malleable and shaped by that without even realizing it, so there's that side of us that, I think, is more willing to shut out media in our girls' lives as much as possible while not wanting them to be completely irrelevant to the culture because they can't speak the language.
>
> LINDA: So that's an important thing to, that now at this age and up to a certain age—I don't know what that age is going to be, we'll know at the time—but now it's shutting out until they're old enough and then

it will start to be, "OK, let's include this." It's a different worldview, and let's watch it together, and let's talk about it. But that's—we're not there yet. We're still at just shutting out, and we'll be at that for a while, I mean through this early formative age. But that change will come like later elementary school, starting middle school maybe watching some of those things that really do differ from our stuff.

This echoes Mike's proud account earlier of how his children learned to police their own media diets. Parents simply want to think of themselves and their children as sentient, autonomous moral beings who can make good decisions about their lives. This sense of pride is also—for many—tinged with a fear of being (or of one's child's being) an "outsider," an outcast, or culturally irrelevant. Jennifer McDonald, reflecting further on these questions in relation to commercials, used the ubiquity of the media as a way to discuss how she has taught her daughter how to navigate a dangerous media world. "And, sometimes people are like, 'How will Sophia ever learn how to discern about commercials?' And I'm like, she still sees ads every day. We don't, like, stay in our house— well, we do sometimes. You know, like, we see billboards, and she sees ads in magazines, and she hears ads on the radio sometimes—and in the bus, you know?"

The ambiguity of the media in these conversations—on the one hand a ubiquitous challenge and inevitably something that we must learn to negotiate with, yet, on the other hand, something that is a vibrant and attractive source of cultural information and pleasure—vexed most of these men and couples and families. This is one of the fascinating complexities we've encountered in our explorations. On the one hand, they could not think about or talk about masculinity without talking about the media. On the other hand, the media, and the broader common culture the media represent, carry messages, symbols, and values that they found problematic and threatening to their ideal sense of masculinity and normative domestic values. The media, writ large, played two contradictory roles for them. One was as this cultural challenge or threat and something over which they must exercise authority. The other was as arguably the most influential and consensual source of what it means to be a man. This speaks to the range of symbols available to them in mediated culture. Further, as we've noted elsewhere,[41] perceived "negative media" are constructive in these men's senses of self. This applies here also. "Media as threat" works constructively in identity formation by providing men a practical way to embody the normative ideal of protection and to do so in the domestic space itself.

But this protection was of a peculiar sort. Rather than cordon off their families or themselves from these media, they allowed media to continue in their homes and their lives. They were experts about many of the programs that concerned them. They watched many such shows as "guilty pleasures" and watched others simply so that they would not be left out of the broader cultural conversation. They tolerated their children watching certain programs and certain commercials because they didn't want them to be "left out" of the culture either.

Our informants recognized that media are ubiquitous, and the media are the primary way that we participate in the broader culture. Further, the media have their own inherent saliencies. They work because they are attractive, pleasurable, meaningful, and culturally relevant. So these men and women found themselves embracing media at the same time that they thought of media diets as an important arena for their goals of protection. Thus, their protection was through careful inoculation, not prophylaxis. This was, by and large, an approach that "worked" for them and that allowed them to distance themselves from their (either overly protective or absent) parents. This was particularly the case with Evangelical families that sought to stay connected and relevant to culture through media in an effort to be "in but not of" the world, as they might have put it.

What results is a negotiation with media. In these accounts we can see the ways in which the notion of authority and protection is redefined in subtle and unsubtle ways, for example reestablishing domestic authority *while also* inculcating autonomy in children. This is one of the rhetorical "accounts of media" strategies people use today to define themselves in relation to media. We all know and speak a set of "cultural scripts" about media, about which media are "good" and "bad," and about who should consume which media and where they should do so. But these "accounts of media" are more than just strategies for life and for parenting. In important ways, they are rhetorics of values and of class and of moral culture. Which media one consumes and which media one thinks of as appropriate are important markers of class and culture (and of religious subcultures). Thus the negotiations we see here are about more than just their potential efficacy in relation to the lived culture of the home. They are also about positioning these men and these households in relation to larger cultural "maps."

The notion of "protection" in these regards, then, functions in a very different way, one that makes the situation seem less contradictory and ambiguous. We can see protection functioning not only to place these families as families but also to place these men as men. This notion of protection—or, more precisely, the aspiration to be seen to be articulating protection in relation to media—is one that articulates with, rather than contests, media. Further, it solves a fundamental problem we've identified here. It gives these men and these households a way to inhabit an identity of protector, but to do so in a way that is relevant to the conditions of modern life. Real physical threats to home and family are dealt with in other, more socially responsible, ways than with the violence of the past (though violence is still an option, if necessary). But, real, tangible, knowable, and identifiable threats to family and family values can be identified in the culture and the culture's media. That the response is ambiguous actually fits the age as well, providing these men with a way of being protectors, but protectors of a "modern" kind, fitted to the challenges and threats of today and to the child-rearing practices that are acceptable and normative today.

Masculine Purpose and the Domestic Ideal

The notions of "provision" and "protection" seem to flow rather directly from traditional senses of the masculine. Further, each of these terms points to rather concrete spheres of action in both traditional and modern settings. That each of them is made problematic by modernity's demands, both moral and practical, does not detract from their effectiveness in describing two tacit and taken-for-granted functions of what it might mean to be a man. Even men and women who doubt the continuing efficacy of such elementalism nonetheless can understand what *provision* and *protection* traditionally meant. These same discourses can also conjure the idea that provision and protection necessarily collide with modern life, where more domestic and routinized modes of social practice are the norm. Men today—at least the type of men in this study—provide by being organization men, not by being hunter-gatherers. Men today protect by finding ways of protecting—and things to protect from (as we have seen)—that do not carry within them the implication of violence. These facts on the ground introduce a certain measure of uncertainty that must be articulated with the sense of the self. For many of the men with whom we spoke, this articulation has been accomplished by their finding ways to provide and protect more symbolically and metaphorically, instead of directly and physically.

If we can understand provision and protection, even with some ambiguity or complexity, it is harder to define what is meant by our third elemental characteristic: purpose. This idea came up clearly and decisively in our interviews, but *purpose* is less of an "action verb" than the other two. It is a quality of life, a state of mind, a moral claim, more than it is something that can be tangibly demonstrated (except for those in ministry, health care, or education professions). But it remains important to these men and important to traditional conceptions of what it means to be men.

In his book *Manliness*,[42] Harvey Mansfield attempted an argument for masculine essentialism without appearing essentialist. As an intellectual historian and classicist, Mansfield searched for essentialism in the deep roots of Western civilization. In ancient Greece and Rome, he found what he considered to be the essentially masculine or "manly." And it was, indeed, not provision or protection (each of which would actually have been beneath the dignity of someone like Odysseus) but *purpose* that he found. In Mansfield's telling, what made ancient Greek, Spartan, and Roman men—well, *men*—was their sense of *purpose*. It mattered not so much which particular values were in play; what mattered was what he called "philosophical courage," seemingly that men should act in a way that shows that their commitments and their actions matter. This is the sensibility that we get from the men we've interviewed—that there is something elementally masculine about the need to organize one's life around a sense of purpose.

The idea of purpose, of course, dovetails with provision and protection. And to an extent these are elements that can be purposive, but these voices mean something more by "purpose," something more akin to Mansfield's ideas. While they value a conventionalized sense of purpose, such as in the notion of "calling," this is not quite what they mean.

There is a sense of calling in Denton Calhoun's life, for example, a purpose in serving others, but this sense of calling takes a back seat to his sense of purpose in relation to his family. And again, this sense of purpose is not exhausted by provision and protection. There is a surplus of elemental meaning, something undefined beyond.

> INTERVIEWER: Do you see calling as something outside of paid employment?
>
> DENTON: Yeah, absolutely. I think theoretically now when it comes time to pay my bills, it wouldn't last very long if I put my theory into practice there.
>
> INTERVIEWER: Well, it could include that, but do you think it's beyond work?
>
> DENTON: Oh yeah, absolutely.
>
> INTERVIEWER: So, in your case then, or generally, what could that include for people, just anything?
>
> DENTON: At this stage in my life, I certainly see a large part of my calling as being a father and a husband. Ultimately that's much more important than a calling to work at an ad agency.

It should be noted, however, that many men among our interviewees who work in service industries like teaching, health care, or pastoral care expressed a sense of purpose that extended beyond the family. For Larry Cane, for example, his sense of Christian call extended into what we might call a "culture warrior"—a purpose that served others and God by trying to change culture.

> I would think that all Christians would have a calling of some sort. You know, maybe, I just feel like that can probably be broad to narrow and so you know, if we want to speak really narrowly, maybe I'd be less sure that every Christian has a specific call to be involved in an exact ministry at an exact church. But I do think that God has put a—I mean broadly He's put a pretty clear calling on all Christians' lives. I think to love Him and to serve Him and to love others. I think that broadly, that exists. But I think somewhere in between there, I really believe that as a Christian, God does have a purpose for our lives and that there is a calling that goes along with that. You know for some that's a real specific call for ministry. But

I just think, as I said before, there's a real clear call for Christians to love God wholeheartedly and to love others. And with that there's a leading that comes from that and that leading may be toward anything. It doesn't have to be ministry. It could be any profession or any job. I just think if more Christians really were to seek that out it would transform the way our culture looked a little bit.

Yet, even with Larry, this sense of call worked its way back to the family. In the earlier quotation when he discussed his call to ministry and his wife's call to motherhood, he noted how this call required sacrifice, which was an important lesson he could provide—a lesson of dependence on God. For Larry and Linda, then, following God's calling dovetailed with domestic purpose. This sense of purpose allowed Larry to stay "in step" with God's plan, which was essential to his call to provide for and protect his family because it put them under God's "protection." In this way, Larry articulated a sense of purpose that is something beyond that articulated by Denton Calhoun. Purpose was important for both, but each had his own interpretation of the scope of that purpose. Denton's was somewhat narrower (and inward); Larry's was broader and more global. Both versions were common among our interviewees, but the sense of purpose—however articulated—was shared across them as an important masculine trait. There is a telling difference in nuance between Larry and Denton, however, that circulated around each man's work life.

Larry and Linda described trading off financial "provision" for "purpose." They had made financial sacrifices to follow Larry's sense of purpose. Denton did not and would not sacrifice financial provision, and he reconciled his more acquisitive sense of provision as enabling him to pursue purpose and calling *through* that provision. Many men talked with us about this tradeoff, and many described themselves as making the same decision as Denton. For all of them, the model described by Larry, that of purpose conflicting with modulating provision, created an implicit challenge—a challenge to sacrifice financially for the sake of greater purpose. And, for many men, like many among our interviewees in service professions (pastors, teachers, a chiropractor, doctors), a sense of purpose transcends the family and commitment to family provision or protection. The notion of "vocation" or "calling" is, of course, commonplace in discourses about work and career. In a way, men who see themselves as having a vocation or a calling are seen as saying that their vocation satisfies a sense of purpose in their lives. We find in our conversations with men two dimensions of this that nuance and complicate this commonplace. First, for all men, "calling" or "vocation" made sense not just because of a moral or value commitment to service of some kind; it also satisfied the expectation that to be a man is to have purpose. Second (and in a way more interesting), men who did not see their work or vocational activities as satisfying this normative sense of purpose reinterpreted their domestic roles in this larger way.

To the extent that purpose can be about something beyond the domestic, it has its own logics, saliencies, and resonances in the culture. The dominant, traditional model of purpose that is beyond the home is the normative model, one that is clearly meaningful on its own terms. It also articulates with larger cultural narratives of masculinity as expressed in such contexts as narrative fiction and film. Clark Caldwell, whom we met earlier, demonstrated this in his discussion of masculinity, coded by a popular filmic representation.

> But then just to use Mel Gibson again, you go to *Braveheart*, and you see a man who has a cause. He has a passion; he has something he is willing to die for. And I think that's probably—if you're going to say what's the core difference between a man and a woman, a woman by and large will be protecting her children, and she may be willing to die to save her children. But she's going to try to do everything she can to protect her family. Whereas a man, he may be willing to die for a cause that he just firmly believes in, and that's kind of the *Braveheart* mentality. You go out. You believe something strongly. You're willing to stand up and paint your face blue and do whatever it takes because injustice needs to know that it's wrong. So sometimes men seem to need to stand up and fight for a cause.

This is a fascinating argument, and one that worked well for many of the men with whom we spoke. The idea of purpose, so well articulated here, is seen as central to masculinity. Implicit is the notion that this purpose has within it a potential conflict with provision or protection. Perhaps this is the core attraction of Gibson's reading of William Wallace in *Braveheart*. He portrays the narrative as a domestic drama—a conflict over the competing elements of masculinity. We see this best in Wallace's relationship with Isabella, which he must ultimately forsake for the freedom of his people, the greater cause Clark referred to earlier. The tension, and how he chooses to resolve it, becomes the central point of the narrative. This can be a metaphor for contemporary men's own sense of identity, their resolution in their own lives of the sense of purpose over domestic responsibilities, which again, has been the dominant model of masculine purpose for centuries. For Christian men, following pure "purpose" (e.g., rejecting family to follow Jesus[43]) can have dire consequences. Some men make those sacrifices; most do not. None in this study had done so, and given the strength of their commitment to the moral center of the family, we can't imagine that they would. For most men, there is another option—recasting provision and protection *as* purpose. They can read William Wallace in a different way—the principled, reluctant warrior. Wallace took up "the call" and the sword only after his family was destroyed. In the beginning, all he wanted was a quiet, peaceful life with his wife—the rural domestic ideal. Providing and protecting were his purpose. Until tragedy struck, there was no higher purpose, no greater cause. He had little interest in freeing Scotland. He simply desired peace and the domestic ideal.

The idea of some greater purpose is embedded in the work of men in "caring" professions. Not unlike Gibson's Wallace, they are confronted with a choice between dueling purposes. Unlike works of fiction, the reality of the everyday lives of men makes this a choice of competing goods. But to forsake the domestic for some greater good is not acceptable. The traditionalist ideal of purpose has given way to a symbolic environment wherein "the public" is eclipsed by "the domestic" in men's lives. This forces them to negotiate and "balance" purpose at work with the dueling purpose embedded in the domestic ideal. For men who are not in these tacitly purposive professions, other contexts for purpose must be found. For men like Denton Calhoun and Mike Andrews, the primary context *is* the domestic sphere, and the primary purpose *is* being good fathers and not being distant fathers as their own fathers were to them. This is significant "purpose" in and of itself. In fact, for Denton and Mike, it was *the* greatest purpose of all.

We should not, though, dismiss the normative or even practical value of the idea of purpose, even for men who on the surface seem to have negotiated it into something that could be perceived as thin or weak in dominant, masculinist culture. The traditional norm may be changing, but it has considerable residual power, even among those who negotiate it or reject it. The way cultural narratives work is that they provide valuable and orienting resources, symbols, and models. That these men can all point to common symbols of masculinity such as this idea of "purpose" binds them in common senses of what it means to be a man. That these symbols can provide powerful, focused senses of what *purpose* might mean, and what its costs might be, makes it even more valuable as a resource to identity. Just because it must be negotiated or nuanced does not detract from its value as a culturally meaningful symbolic possibility. Further, the fact that men today—from conservative Evangelicals to liberal Ecumenical Protestants—can recast purpose in different ways speaks to the possibilities and challenges inherent in the late modern project of the self. And the media role here is central. Normative models of masculinity, clearly articulated and visualized, find their place at the center of understandings of gender. These models or symbols are thus quite naturally in tension with one another. That is how these things should work. This negotiation—among the fissures in career, vocation, fatherhood, and calling—actually *defines* identity work in complex social contexts in the industrialized West. And cultural values, articulated so effectively by media and art, provide the models and symbols that give this negotiation its "poles," its *orthodoxy* and, in a minority of negotiations, *heterodoxy*.

In our Conclusion, we will consider some implications of this negotiation for public and domestic life, and we will consider the implications of continued negotiation with the authority of religious communities and media cultures in the ongoing project of the masculine self. We will, of course, come back to the questions that prompted this study in the first place: how it is that contemporary masculinities find their footing in competing spheres of public life, private life, and religious and media cultures.

Conclusion

Does God Make the Man?

A kind of conceptual and linguistic instability is at the root of the con-versations we've seen here. What many of the men with whom we spoke expressed as a "crisis" of masculinity seemed to be simply a lament over the loss of a social compact under which male prerogatives of various kinds were given tacit support in the culture. This echoed the larger public and media narrative of this "crisis" we introduced earlier. This lament is widespread and salient for many cultural voices, and one does not have to look far to hear it. It was put particularly succinctly by *Fox News* correspondent Brit Hume in a discussion program on that chan-nel focused on the nature of contemporary politics and the specific experience of one politician, the governor of New Jersey, Chris Christie. Hume observed that traditional "hardball" politics—explicitly defined as masculine—is on the wane, the result of a "feminization" of American culture,

> [b]y which I mean that men today have learned the lesson the hard way that if you act like a kind of an old fashioned guy's guy, you're in constant danger of slipping out and saying something that's going to get you in trouble and make you look like a sexist or make you look like you seem thuggish or whatever. That's the atmosphere in which [Christie] operates. This guy is very much an old fashioned masculine, muscular guy, and there are political risks associated with that. Maybe it shouldn't be, but that's how it is.[1]

This is a particularly striking statement of the condition many of the men we've spoken with feel they find themselves in today. To this way of thinking, what has been lost is the ability to say what one is thinking, defying the consequences. But beneath this are assumptions about the dynamics of gender prerogatives and priorities. What has been lost is the ability of men to make judgments about others, to express their ideas without fear of contradiction or nuance. What is also central here is the implication that this important social space—politics—is normatively a *male* space. For Hume, the loss of the ability of men *to be men* in this space is a loss of great moment and great implication.

The crisis of masculinity—as expressed in these spaces and in some of our interviews—is thus revealed as a discursive crisis. This is not meant to trivialize it, to say that it is nothing but a "language game." We know that words, languages, and discourses have important constructive power, and the fact that these men see this linguistic turf shifting and falling away could be portentous. In a way, the neo-traditionalist discourse with which we began this book is an attempt to shore up these shifting sands, to find languages and symbols that can reinvigorate a more familiar version of masculinity in service of a larger goal of firming up social spaces that seem to be spinning out of control. "The media" are a natural *bête noire* of this discursive drama. And as a symbolic core of tradition and received categories of value and action, religion is an obvious counterbalance. There remains a residual belief that, against all the structural vicissitudes of contemporary social spaces and against all the cultural changes that have riven American life since the mid-twentieth century, a return to certain basic values, symbols, and ideas can correct the drift.

To return to the question in the title of this book, many of the men with whom we spoke here did believe that God does make the man. But this belief is far from the kind of consensus we might have expected to see among men who are, by and large, firmly grounded in American Protestantism. The ways in which men discern who they are in relation to their faith traditions is far more diffuse and layered than we might have expected. This begins with the very nature of what it means to be a man and how that meaning is achieved. Among our conversations were those that revealed a kind of constructivist view, reminiscent of Butler's and others' gender constructivism. For them, it was possible to describe specific cultural sources of these ideas. But that kind of articulation about the sources of masculinity was not common among the voices we've heard from here. Instead, most of the men in this study could be said to hew to a sense that there is *just something about being a man*. That "something" was not hard to describe. In fact, as we've noted, it can be described rather simply and firmly. Masculinity, most of these men agree, is about *provision, protection*, and *purpose*.

What is most striking here, though, is that if we move behind the superficial received bromide that God *does* make the man, we find that American Protestantism has a far more ambiguous role in the construction of contemporary masculinity than that claim would suggest, even among faithful American Protestant men. There is a prodigious and extensive discourse of masculinity in Evangelicalism, to be sure. Evangelical publishing and the structure of Evangelical churches (where women's pastoral leadership is still seen as problematic) undergird a rather consistent view of what men should be, at least in the context of the home. The idea of headship, which we explored in chapter 1, stands as a kind of consensual marker of the persistent idea that, all things being equal, men in their homes should be more powerful than others. White, heterosexual, married Evangelical fathers were the intended subject of our inquiries because, as we have said, they represented the context where things—in the form of traditionalist ideas about gender, religion, and media—ought to be working. They were our "test case," and we intended the comparison with Ecumenical men to provide more insight into the extents and limits of the possibilities of gender discourse in contemporary American Protestantism.

Evangelical Men

As we have seen, nearly all the Evangelical men we interviewed used the language of headship to describe their roles, aspirations, struggles, and identities as men. Yet, their descriptions of *how* headship works were conflicted and contradictory. Even those who seemed most confident in their ideas struggled for language to describe how headship played out in their everyday lives. And they were explicit that neither published resources, the pulpit, nor their faith community provided enough help to them in this.

This contradiction—in a way a struggle for the language to describe the situation—moved in two directions in our interviews. First, some men seemed to be self-conscious about the obvious conclusion that a notion like headship could be read as sexist to outsiders. Thus, they qualified their narratives for us. Some depended on conversational devices such as "I don't want to sound sexist, but . . . ." Others, like respondent Mark Simms, used humor. These men were clearly both aware of the broader egalitarian cultural discourse that is common today, and they were sensitive to that discourse—a measure of the success of feminism in reaching even these territories in the cultural landscape. Second, for others the conversations revealed less of a rhetorical project and more of an actual struggle to come to terms with what headship should look like in their everyday lives. This latter effort manifested along the lines of redefining the meaning of provision, protection, and purpose in the present day.

The contemporary American labor market has irreversibly changed the relationship of gender and breadwinning. Women are today more and more involved in work outside the home, a situation that is now largely perceived to be the norm in everyday America. Most of the Evangelical men we interviewed were the primary breadwinners in their households, and yet all seemed to accept the notion that work and career should be an option for women, even for their wives and daughters. There was another challenge to the norm of "provision" for them, though—the struggle to balance the need to provide financially with the responsibility (as they saw it) to provide emotionally and spiritually for their families. They clearly saw these two types of provision to be in tension. This tension also pervaded their thinking about the norm of "purpose," where they also struggled to balance their career ambitions with their desire to provide, protect, and have domestic purpose in the home and family. For most of them, career and the domestic ideal constituted mutually exclusive values, which existed in a zero-sum relationship. Investing in one necessarily would disadvantage the other. This made the achievement of balance between them an ideal loaded with expectation and anxiety.

Where provision and purpose were all about ambiguity and conceptual struggle, protection was, for these men, the simplest and most unproblematic essential. Men seemed most confident here. And for many, protection was where the media entered. On the one hand, media seemed to be pleasurable and to add value to the quality of domestic life. On the other hand, media can be threatening, with potential to penetrate the sacred space of the domestic sphere with unhealthy or dangerous influences on belief and behavior. As with other issues, men spoke of the need for "balance" in protection in relation to media. All discussed with ease the perils and pleasures of media, and their discernment and aspirations to action in addressing media provided them the clearest and most focused example of "protection" at hand. Thus, while men would describe themselves as constantly vigilant and prepared for the need for physical protection of the family, the media were the most persistent and salient threat most of them faced.

This complex and layered picture of the construction of masculinity in these contexts goes a long way toward addressing some of the questions with which we began. If we are to somehow judge how men make sense of masculinity today, it is important for us to see some of the significant experiences and contexts within which these men make those connections. This discourse of ambiguity and struggle seemed to define the whole project of the masculine self today. The question of what role religion should or might play also revealed important ambiguities.

The Evangelical men we interviewed, the cohort we expected to articulate the clearest accounts of how religion fed into their senses of their masculine selves, revealed instead a great deal of ambiguity. They had difficulty recalling specific messages from the pulpit about masculinity and manhood. They also struggled to recall specific church resources, teachings from Christian schools, or para-church resources that had offered much support or insight they found relevant. They were aware of things but had rarely availed themselves of them, they reported. Ironically, they seemed to regard church-provided resources in the same way they thought about other things—that taking time to be more involved in men's groups or other such activities would take precious time away from their roles in their families. Most of the Evangelical men with whom we spoke simply assumed that their faith communities believed in headship just as they themselves did. And what was the source of this assumption? Most seemed to believe that some vague notion of "Biblical teaching" and patriarchal church structures were both somehow emblematic of a deeper, underlying commitment to the idea of male prerogative in the home as well. Thus, as it was experienced and articulated by these men as a context for learning and influence over their lives, the notion of headship in their faith communities was largely tacit rather than explicit and pedagogical. Rather than a "structure of feeling" (with a nod to Raymond Williams here)—practices emerging that are not yet articulated—these men seemed to have "feelings of structure,"[2] a vague, diffuse sensibility of meaning structures that are so embedded and entrenched they are difficult even to discuss.

The profile of the notion of headship as a feeling of structure is not as firm and predictive as Bourdieu's notion of doxa (which we discussed in chapter 1). Headship is spoken, written, and performed in a number of obvious ways in Evangelical communities and social networks. But this articulation seemed more obvious to outside observers than to the men we interviewed. For all but two of the Evangelical men with whom we spoke, headship was largely settled as a normative issue. At the same time, these men were well aware of the growing conversation about gender roles being expressed in contemporary cultural discourses. While headship—as vague a notion as it is in practice—was settled for them, they found themselves facing a cultural challenge to make an account of themselves as men and of their ideas about headship within the larger "culture war." They seemed to be experiencing a moment when gender doxa needed to be articulated as public orthodoxy (or, to borrow from Peaslee, a moment when feelings of headship needed more specific articulation and practical application), and they found this to be a conceptual and rhetorical challenge. However, while this need to make an account was important to them, it was not the most pressing issue in their daily lives.

At the same time, they did seem to feel that their faith communities were failing to provide them the concepts and language necessary to weave these two registers together. They found themselves challenged to navigate traditional notions of headship in contemporary life in ways that did not seem to violate contemporary egalitarian gender norms and that took on some elements of the feminist critique in their quest to be more *nurturing* husbands and fathers. Neo-traditionalist voices are therefore right in one sense. For these men, churches have not done or are not doing enough to provide teachings, spaces, and symbolic resources for men to become the men "that God intended." But it is too easy to confuse whether this is a *practical* or a *normative* issue. The failures of the churches seem, for these men, to be in the *practical* register, while the neo-traditionalist discourse is almost exclusively in the *normative* register. While the churches seem not to have provided much in the way of either normative or practical input, it is the latter area—the practical—where the men with whom we spoke seemed to be most disappointed. This is, perhaps, part of the reason that the countless books, materials, and experiences provided by the Evangelical marketplace do not resonate for them. These resources focus on gender as a normative issue, which is settled for most of these Evangelical men, not on practical applications of the diffuse notion of "headship." Further, for those few Evangelical men for whom the normative questions are as yet unsettled, the traditionalist message was not resonant. Instead, the normative discourse that attracted them was far more egalitarian, more influenced by feminism than by neo-traditionalism.

Prominent Evangelical pastors such as Mark Driscoll and David Murrow have taken up the call to address directly what they perceive to be a crisis of masculinity in the churches. Reminiscent of the "muscular Christianity" discourse at the turn of the twentieth century in the United States, these voices have been joined by para-church movements such as "GodMen," stressing a more masculinist, even pugnacious approach to faith. These men and groups seek to *masculinize* church, to reorder and restructure gender roles *within* Christian churches and homes. This is rooted in two related trends, in their view. First, the perceived ongoing feminization of American Christianity (wherein the commonplace conventions of Christian community life stress cooperation, compromise, and caring) is seemingly antithetical to men's natural impulses. Second, this situation—again, according to this view—has led to more and more men leaving the church.

While we did find among our informants men who would articulate versions of this critique, such as the voices from an emerging church focus group we introduced in chapter 2, this hypermasculine rhetoric did not resonate for most of the Evangelical husbands and fathers we interviewed. The majority of Evangelical men were not looking for a "Mixed Martial Arts Jesus." Certainly, there was a normative attraction to a tougher, more classically masculine version of Christianity (as evidenced by such things as their attraction to *Braveheart* but not, as mentioned, Gibson's production of Jesus in *The Passion of the Christ*). But their chief concerns actually focused on navigating the pressures and struggles of provision, protection, and purpose in the context of modern life. They were looking for *practical* models of how to be committed to work and home in an everyday struggle over limited time and resources. They were looking for guidance on how to navigate the financial realities of dual-income households within the frame of headship. They were looking for insights into emotional and spiritual headship, how to be nurturers and servants as well as "warriors." Finally, they were looking for resources to help them express narratives of headship that could be "plausible accounts of the self" in the shared common culture. That means accounts that do not appear sexist to the broader community—or to their spouses.

A few of the men with whom we spoke might have been feeling disconnected from their churches because of this lack of practical guidance, but the majority was well settled in faith communities. They had become used to, and, we must suppose, satisfied with, the vague, rarely spoken patriarchy of their churches. They were content with the *normative* ideals they experience there (to the extent they do), the loose conglomeration we have called headship. For many of these men, the Mixed-Martial-Arts Jesus might be fun for a weekend with the boys, but it didn't give them much insight into living their lives.

Evangelical masculinity is thus not a theological problem. For most of these men, the values of the normative register of masculinity are firm. The notion of headship is clearly entrenched. The men we've heard from—who have not left the church and in the main express values of headship—were not compelled by rhetoric such as Mark Driscoll's or other masculinist voices in Evangelicalism (save, perhaps, Eldredge's form of masculinism). Instead, they were looking for help in the practical register, a way of *experiencing and expressing* what they would call Biblical masculinity in a way that incorporates elemental notions of masculinity yet does not at the same time diminish women. Most of them expressed values that might be more aptly described as "complementarianism,"[3] a term that none explicitly used but that many expressed. In their view, men and women complement each other. They are equal but have different roles. The man's role is to lead, to be the "head."

There is, of course, gender trouble within Evangelicalism at the *normative* level. There are those who seek to embrace the central Evangelical project while also embracing feminist[4] or even queer[5] ideas about gender. For these voices, gender is a theological and ecclesiological problem. Among our conversations, gender egalitarianism, and these emergent modalities of gender, were more of an issue for Ecumenical men. But perhaps as a sign of emergent change in Evangelicalism itself, these were also issues for two of our Evangelical men. Gender heterodoxy in Evangelicalism is not new, and it appears that Evangelical feminism is experiencing a revival today. Survey data indicate growing support among Evangelicals for same-sex marriage,[6] which may point to a growing broader support for changing gender roles, notions of family, and sexual politics. Evangelical feminist authors such as Rachel Held Evans have begun to find an audience in Evangelical circles (even if banned from some of the major Christian bookstores[7]). Another measure of this trend is the "pushback" Evangelical feminism is receiving from Evangelical pulpits, blogs, and books, indicating that this counterdiscourse is a big enough "problem" with which to engage in Evangelical communities.

Yet we need not overstate the influence of this counterdiscourse among our respondents. For a small number of our Evangelical respondents, complementarianism was not enough. For these two, egalitarianism was the Biblical and moral imperative. For them, "softer" versions of patriarchy were still patriarchy that inflicts unnecessary, even immoral, symbolic violence on women and members of the LGBTQ community. But for the overwhelming majority of our Evangelical men, a struggle between this feminist change and retrenchment in the church was not on their radar.

The crisis of masculinity for the majority of Evangelical men in our study was of a different, more practical sort. For them, the central complementarian notion—the idea that men and women are separate but equal in the domestic sphere and beyond—seemed persuasive. Most of them, however, would reject the abrasive rhetorical tactics of complementarians like Mark Driscoll and seek a "softer" expression that would articulate gender essentialism, expressed as headship, with practical ideas of how to live headship in more caring, domestic-centered ways.

To a small number of the men with whom we spoke, the problem of the so-called feminization of the church was an important issue, but they still failed to find in the broader discourse voices that articulate this in satisfying ways, again with the possible exception of John Eldredge, to whom we will return shortly. Some men felt that church emasculated them, but they didn't seem eager to embrace the steroid- and testosterone-driven rhetoric of Mixed-Martial-Arts Jesus, either. Thus the Evangelical marketplace, as extensive as it is, seemed to offer them very little in terms of *how to be a man*. They might agree that "God has made them men," but religion has been of little help in navigating what they believe God has intended in twenty-first-century American cultural life.

Ecumenical Protestant Men

One of the striking learnings from our inquiries was that Evangelical and Ecumenical men do, in fact, think differently from each other about gender. In a way, this should not be too surprising, while from another perspective—more outside the world of Protestantism in general—there might have been some surprise at this. After all, all of them are Protestant, and the men we interviewed on the two sides of that boundary were demographically comparable. What distinguished them, though, was their affiliation with either the Evangelical or Ecumenical end of the Protestant spectrum.

As we discussed in chapter 1, the Ecumenical Protestants among our interviewees differed in that they lack the Evangelicals' rhetorical scaffolding around the concept of headship. In fact, in their own terms, what distinguished them from Evangelicals was something more in the realm of religious politics, or polemics, as we've noted. They were emphatic that their identities as Protestants depended to a degree on their *not being Evangelical*. In the less political terms of their actual ideas about gender, they were more similar to their Evangelical cohorts than we might have predicted—the important concept of headship aside. In Ecumenical Protestantism, there is a wider and less contentious discourse about gender and about women's roles in the home and the church. Many of the Ecumenical men in our interviews, for example, had attended churches with female senior pastors. For them, this was normal and unproblematic, even for the more conservative and traditionalist among them.[8]

For these men, religion had little to offer them at *either* the normative or the practical level. Many noted—and some lamented—that their faith communities had little to say on the topic, that the question of gender had become a kind of void in the discourses that defined their church experience. For the more constructivist-feminist among them, this was not necessarily a problem. For the more gender essentialist among them, who moved between a kind of cultural traditionalism and egalitarianism (men whose experience here looked more like the negotiations we saw among the Evangelicals), there was a longing for religion to more actively engage gender in more meaningful ways.

Joseph Gelfer[9] has suggested how complex a challenge this might be for men and churches that would wish to achieve a truly progressive masculinist spirituality. Such spirituality, he suggests, "should complement feminine spirituality and provide a framework in which the different experiences of men and women—of different people—can be expressed and honoured within a spiritual context."[10] Instead, such views as complementarianism, which attempt to address the genders as classes, will inevitably verge toward patriarchy, in Gelfer's analysis. Any essentialisms, he argues, will move in the same direction, resulting in the subjugation of women and of subordinate masculinities. But our interviews suggest that any attempt to move more in the direction of a progressive masculinist-feminist articulation of gender within religion will run up against a barrier, even among Ecumenical men: the barrier of implicit and explicit essentialisms. So long as men are convinced that there are things that are essentially masculine—things that many articulate under the banners of provision, protection, and purpose—it seems unlikely that true progress toward an ideal of egalitarian comity can be achieved. To do so would require men (and women) to move beyond the easy assumption that there are simply some things that men and women do, and that those differences can be ascribed to the genders as structured classes and then prescriptions and proscriptions inferred and applied. The difference between the Evangelical and Ecumenical contexts, it seems, is their readiness to address this question. While there are certainly many elementalists among the Ecumenicals, their experience of church is one where there is at least a self-conscious appreciation of the need for men's and women's roles to be brought front and center and addressed as part of a collective process of articulation. Further, more than half of them expressed egalitarianism and nearly a third of them expressed constructivism. Finally, of the Ecumenical traditionalists and essentialists, none of them registered on the "strong" end of the spectrum, using definitive religious sources as proof of their essentialism or traditionalism. However, for Ecumenical Protestantism as well, there is still quite a distance between aspiration and practical egalitarianism, and an even greater distance for an egalitarianism rooted in gender constructivism.

The Media

We noted earlier that it is simply impossible in American society today to talk about masculine gender without also talking about media. Thus the media are at the center of the discourse about men and masculinity, though the exact nature of their role is complex. They play a central role in the formation of religious masculine identities, to be sure, but they also reflect and represent those ideas whether or not they can be said to "cause" them in some instrumental sense. The media in question may be *religious* media, of course, but the *secular* media are far more prominent. As we've seen, men (and women) use media to talk about what it means to be a man. Less than 10 percent of our informants offered Kings David or Solomon, the Apostle Paul, Simon Peter, or any other Biblical character as a role model of masculinity, including Jesus himself. In fact, the only dialogue about Jesus was met with a sort of confused ambivalence about Jesus as a *male* role model, as if this were a new (and perhaps troubling) idea. Instead, men more easily and facilely pointed to and interpreted characters from secular media—Jack Bauer from *24*, Jack from *Lost*, William Wallace from *Braveheart*, Captain Miller from *Saving Private Ryan*, Andy Taylor, Mister Rogers, or Cliff Huxtable.

In this respect, the neo-traditionalist argument against media is on to something. Secular media appear to be at the center of the articulation of masculinity today, and in much more salient ways than religion or even family of origin. To put it another way, media symbols seem to provide a much stronger and more meaningful imaginary of the masculine with which to talk about masculinity and to construct plausible and aspirational narratives of the self. Whether this actually "makes" men is an open question. But from some perspectives—including our own symbolic interactionist perspective wherein such "plausible narratives of the self" would be seen as actually generative of identity—such talk about masculinity would, in fact, *make* men.

The neo-traditionalist critique, though, misses a central point about media. Men (and women, and families) are selective and negotiate the media sphere in interesting and generative ways. Thus, rather than a culture war waged between Hollywood and Christianity, what we've seen here is a more complementary relationship between the two. As a range of studies have shown, Hollywood, in fact, offers more resources supportive of patriarchy and essentialism than it offers progressive feminist or progressive masculinist resources for the self. This is, of course, nothing new. A robust and extensive feminist scholarship has been addressing the white, patriarchal, monomythic ideal in American media for at least four decades.[11] If there is a culture war over gender being waged between Hollywood and "religion," it is actually with progressive religious feminists, not with traditionalist masculine Christianity.

Nonetheless, conservative religious critics can find much to lament about mainstream media production. This also has a long history.[12] But it is notable that among the men with whom we spoke here, the ones who had the most difficulty finding resources for their kind of masculine identity in media were the egalitarian, pro-feminist ones. These men typically noted (and celebrated) progress toward more egalitarianism in popular media but at the same time lamented the common media trope that portrays men and fathers as alienated or inept. The media icon of the "dumb dad" irritated all of our men, but for the progressive feminists among them, it was additionally troubling as it seemed to represent a misguided attempt to balance things. At the same time, these men found it difficult to relate to the hypermasculine images of Jack Bauer and William Wallace embraced by conservative voices and Evangelical men in the pews.

While we would not deny that there is a culture war over gender that waxes and wanes and that it is felt as real and is central to some conservatives' sense of anxiety and crisis, it does seem that men "in the pews" are less anxious about this than are the neo-traditionalist commentators. This goes along with—and may be related to—the fact that these men can engage in media culture and its symbolic resources in ways that can help reinforce normative, essentialist ideas about manhood and that give them accessible language and symbols with which to talk about their masculinity. The critique that we set out to investigate—the commonplace notion that "religion" and "media" are somehow on opposite poles of what should be God-centered masculinity—is challenged by what we've heard from our respondents. Instead, the evidence suggests that much of mainstream screen production (film and television) actually supports the commonplace ideological scaffold of headship rather neatly, though in a secular rather than a religious language. What has been lost in these media over the years has not been ideas of essentialism or patriarchy. Instead, what has been lost for neo-traditionalist masculinity—and this loomed large in our conversations—is the *religio-moral sensibility* that should accompany the normative ideal of headship, a sensibility most keenly felt with regard to issues of sexual morality and particularly sexual purity.

Patriarchy is still the norm in American domestic dramas, sitcoms, and reality shows, but it is a more promiscuous (and, thus, a less moral-religious) patriarchy than in the past. The positive portrayals of men in situation comedies remained problematic for many of our conservative informants because the portrayals lacked either the commitment to settled fatherhood or the commitment to "pure" (hetero)sexuality. On the one hand, there was *Friends*, beloved yet problematic because of its perceived promiscuous sexual content. On the other hand, there was *According to Jim*, problematic because of its reliance on the "dumb dad" narrative. Thus the televisual discourse—that is, the domestic sitcom, whose setting and content could be closest to the actual, practical experience of the men we interviewed—was incomplete and partial for them. Other media, especially films, provided more complete, complex, and compelling versions of masculinity, rife with tropes of provision, protection, and purpose, but few of these approached the practical context of the home and family life. *Braveheart*, *Saving Private Ryan*, or even *Lost* may have provided the masculine "essentials," but they are situated in fantasy (and, loosely, historical) contexts removed from the everyday experiences of these men.

On the larger question of how these various media relate to the questions of masculinity, the picture thus seems complex and even contradictory. Some media articulate senses of masculinity that are positive and normative; others portray versions of the masculine that are problematic for these men. There is, then, no singular "media" which might be blamed for the situation with contemporary masculinity. This reveals a much larger theoretical issue for media scholars: the question of how media work. Both the Evangelical and Ecumenical men with whom we spoke were attuned to secular media as both positive and problematic resources for identity formation. At the same time, there was the confusing finding that the Evangelical men had at the same time rejected or were simply uninterested in the extensive media production (books, DVDs, online resources, films, etc.) available in the Evangelical cultural marketplace. Why would these men, otherwise connected with Evangelical communities, not engage with the Evangelical media sphere? Why do secular "mainstream" media, which, in the first instance, most of the men in our study claim to reject under a "culture war" rubric, have so much more resonance with their gender narratives than the media produced within Evangelicalism?

It might be, of course, that these men simply chose not to tell us about religious media, even though we specifically asked them about this. Perhaps some "social conformism" mechanism had them hesitating to talk about religious media. This seems unlikely. They showed little reluctance to talk about their faith, their faith histories, or their faith narratives, so it seems unlikely they would be shy in speaking their minds about religious media.

We think there is a better explanation, one that takes as a given that they were providing us accurate accounts of their relationship to the various media in their lives. As is the case with most other media audiences, media behaviors here are driven more by pleasure than by faith. Simply, these men, along with many others, derived pleasure from secular mainstream media. This is not a simple matter of what they *get out of media* in any cognitive sense.[13] Instead, it is better to think about what their media lives *do for them* in the sense of generating salient, meaningful, and, most important, pleasurable experiences. From this perspective, there would be no particular reason to expect that a subculture such as that of Evangelical men would demonstrate media behaviors that were largely at odds with others in their demographic cohorts.

Brian Ott[14] has argued that media generate pleasure. We consume media because the structure of narrative, poetics, and aesthetics—the *sensations* of media—draws us in. Media engage desire and the satisfaction of desire—the desire to look, to be a voyeur in screen media, and the desire to engage in cultural conversations within larger communities. Hoover[15] has elsewhere argued that religiously defined media audiences are drawn to so-called secular media because of this draw of the broader cultural discourse. There is a powerful pull to a "common culture." This double pleasure—the presenting satisfactions with the nature of the media experience and the broader satisfaction of articulating those satisfactions in the context of a "community of shared interpretation"[16]—constitutes the sense in which media experience constructs cultural experience.

Even though we engage in media simply for such pleasures, pleasure is not a simple matter. Ott draws on Barthes's two notions of pleasure—*jouissance* and *plaisir*—each of which can be applied to the media experiences we report here. They provide deepened insight into the categories we introduced in chapter 2: the media men love, the media men love to hate, and the media men hate to love.

Plaisir, as interpreted by Ott, is "the pleasure of identifying with, and submitting to, a text's socially-accepted (dominant) meanings."[17] *Plaisir* is about comfort and the familiar, being washed in the messages of the media. The so-called media men love we discussed in chapter 2 fit most neatly into this category. For Evangelicals, these included Mel Gibson in *Braveheart*, Andy Griffith, Bill Cosby, Kiefer Sutherland in the 24 franchise, and Matthew Fox in *Lost*. For the "Ecumenical" Protestants, the list was similar except for a notable ambivalence about Mel Gibson.[18]

These media resonate with these men because they are fans of these media texts. They know them well. They watch them. They see them remediated in contexts such as the book *Wild at Heart* and other accounts of contemporary culture. Evangelicals see them re-mediated and reinforced from the pulpit. In the case of *Braveheart*, in particular, the film has itself become iconic in Evangelical circles, a kind of quasi-sacred text used to invoke the symbolism of the masculine spiritual warrior.[19] That *Braveheart* was not produced to *be* a quasi-sacred text (even though it does contain a great deal of religion) is beside the point. It is now read that way in specific contexts. And this is the case with most of the media from which these men derive comforting pleasure and in which they find positive symbols for masculine identity. Their reading of Jack in *Lost* or William Wallace in *Braveheart* is not a "secular" reading; it is a religious one, and one that articulates comfortably with culturally—and, more important, *religiously*—based values of patriarchy. Thus where the pleasure *is* is also the place where the culture and religion coincide in relation to generic ideas of what it means to be a man. A specifically religious text articulating the same thing is unnecessary and redundant and lacks the pleasurable surround of the broader cultural conversation.

Our other two categories—media men love to hate and media they hate to love—are more complicated. We were intentional in the construction "love to hate." The accounts of experiences with this category of media are not simply marketplace selections, the choice to watch or not watch. Rather, there is specific pleasure in rejecting these shows and hating these characters. The pleasure may not be rooted in the text itself (that would be a "guilty pleasure," which we will get to shortly). Rather, the pleasure is derived from engaging in a subcultural conversation—a "meta-discourse"—*about* these shows and these characters. They become markers, foils that can mark identity boundaries, thus confirming the identity boundaries of the men engaging in the discourse. As we noted in chapter 2, these media gave these men bright lines for identity boundaries. The media in this category were not an actual threat to their identities as men; rather, they reinforced masculine identity for them through the pleasurable practice of isolating and critiquing such media. The men with whom we spoke did often describe these media as threats in their "accounts of media," their meta-discourses. But rather than consider them an actual threat, they could use their perception of threat to derive the pleasure of discursively protecting themselves, their communities, and their families. Such media might be a threat, but only as they would fit into our third category, the "guilty pleasures" of media they "hate to love."

The guilty pleasures of religious men are (presumably) the media category of greatest concern to the neo-traditionalist critics (as well as to other critics such as Bill Cosby and Barack Obama) and of most interest to us here. As Brian Ott points out in his assessment of the way critical cultural studies has looked at practices of reception, this concern is based on an assumption that a guilty pleasure must necessarily be a kind of comforting *plaisir*. For the cultural studies critique, the concern has been that pleasurable experience would open the door for corrosive influence—influence of the ideology of capitalism, patriarchy, and so on. For the neo-conservative critic, the concern would be that such comforting pleasure of media would open the door for corrosive influence but from a different ideological direction—that religious men would be "washed" by feminist or alternative sexualities–friendly ideologies that would challenge religion's "fundamental" values. Men would watch guilty pleasure media and come under their influence, in spite of their judgment that these media are something they *should* be guilty about—that is, something "bad."

But media reception does not necessarily work that way. Ott points out that consumers of media could derive great pleasure "from being able to make their own set of connections."[20] We suggest that a similar experience is possible for the "guilty pleasures" of the men with whom we spoke. Certainly, such pleasures could be comforting, as in the first category of media men love. But in that case, there would be no reason for them to express reservations, to be "guilty" about their consumption. The "guilt" experienced was connected to a sense of duty and to moral purity (to a great extent), yet these men still derived pleasure from such contradictory media. And we could see them using this pleasure constructively, making connections to the text through their religious and moral sensibilities. Thus, the love–hate relationship with Homer Simpson, for example, is not necessarily evidence of a lapse in their own certainties but rather a marker of those certainties, expressed and re-celebrated through their discursive positioning in contrast to what Homer represents.

In this kind of engagement with media, these men might have been experiencing the second of Barthes's categories as invoked by Brian Ott, *jouissance*—a form of pleasure that is immediate, that changes the rules of engagement, that drifts from established norms. Referring to Victor Turner, such experience is *liminoid*, "an interval, however brief . . . when the past is momentarily negated, suspended, or abrogated, and the future has not yet begun, an instant of pure potentiality of everything, as it were, trembles in the balance."[21] In fact, it may be such indefinition and liminality that actually concerns conservative critics about media. If the messages are not negative, then at least they open up possibilities for viewers, something that might go in unexpected or undesired directions. But the experience of media does not end in such a liminal space. The power of the liminal in ritual is not only in its ability to suspend structure and open possibility but also in its power to ultimately use such suspense to reinforce structure. In the case of the guilty pleasure of media, as the men we heard from reflected on the *jouissance* of these texts, they also found comfort (a kind of *plaisir*) as well in this feeling of "guilt" (i.e., these shows still registered as "bad," in spite of their providing a pleasurable experience). Thus the ultimate act of engagement with the text was not for them a drift away from structures or received religious values. Rather, it was experiencing, interpreting, and internalizing the media experience through common and commonplace religious and cultural lenses.

This is one way to account for men who readily (and guiltily) engage in what they know to be negative media yet continue to police the moral boundaries those media supposedly violate. There was little evidence in our conversations that men who consumed guilty media pleasures of a specific sort—those that expressed progressive, feminist, or egalitarian values—were being influenced by those values to any great degree. Their commitment to patriarchal, complementarian, and essentialist values did not seem to be undermined at a normative level. There is, as we have noted, evidence of a "softening of patriarchy" among conservative men, but perhaps such softening is less a challenge to the idea of patriarchy than it is a *renegotiation* of it.[22]

Most certainly there are moments where guilty pleasures might hold the potential for rupture rather than for renegotiation. But for most of the men with whom we spoke about media that fit in the category of "guilty pleasure," whatever dissonance or contradiction they experienced had soon passed. They found comfort in a sense that their moral universe remained intact *because* the pleasure remained guilty and *in spite of* their fandom of such questionable media. These negotiations allowed them to weave into their narratives of identity a fandom about which they could feel guilty and to derive satisfaction from both the fandom and the guilt (or rather from the moral framing that led to the "guilt"). The moral order was reinforced, not undermined.

When the men here engaged media—at the end of the day when the work day was over and the kids were in bed—they were looking for pleasure, not for an engagement with the claims of Evangelical thinkers such as Mark Driscoll or Rachel Held Evans. Instead, they were seeking pleasure, readily available through the normative framings of the "common culture" of the mainstream media sphere. This is, of course, something we've long known about media reception. Academic researchers, educators, and moral and religious leaders may frame media as a kind of cognitive engagement, effective both on their own terms and symbolic of broader issues of value and meaning in the culture, but media are consumed in less cognitive and iterative ways than that. They "work" because they are salient on a number of levels, and their consumption can be seen as symbolic of certain kinds of personal politics and negotiations of identity. In the cases here, this involved media these men loved to hate and hated to love, and those positions became part of the material out of which they constructed their own narratives of masculine identity.

Religious media, which in relation to gender are largely an Evangelical marketplace, simply did not seem to be pleasurable in the same way for most of the men in our study, notably for the Evangelicals among them for whom it should have been the most appropriate fit. The only examples about gender that came up consistently in our interviews were John Eldredge's mega-blockbuster *Wild at Heart*, and the most widely read religious-masculinity response to the so-called pornography crisis, Steven Arterburn and Fred Stoeker's *Every Man's Battle*. Each of these was in a way inevitably in discussion because of its prominence and attention in the market. No other titles about gender surfaced in our discussions. *Wild at Heart* could almost be read to make the same case we make here.[23] It has a subtext of essentialist male pleasure reinforced by extensive references to secular media portrayals of masculinity that Evangelical men should love, such as *Braveheart*.

No broader range of material from the Evangelical media marketplace resonated in the same way. To the extent that such sources did come up, they were met with wariness (e.g., one respondent's cautious treatment of Rick Warren's *The Purpose Driven Life*) or even ridiculed for not being up to the quality standards of mainstream media (e.g., another respondent's mocking response to the *Left Behind* films). To put it simply, "Christian fiction," film, and music just did not work as well for these men as the secular media did. This suggests that taste cultures and their aesthetics have less to do with the prerogatives of religion (and with the results of religious production) and more to do with broader cultural norms of humor, narrative, and production values. It should not surprise us that media pleasures are cultural constructions. It is notable that for this Evangelical subculture within a larger context, that larger context seems to be the standard by which media are judged, and it is more influential in establishing taste and pleasure.

We are arguing, then, that we should be looking for media resonance through pleasure rather than through other avenues, such as moral or religious framings. It was the pleasure of watching Jack work through the latest plot twist on the island in *Lost* that drew John Little to Jack, not just that Jack exhibited some normative characteristics of masculine leadership. But the fact that Jack could be said to exhibit such characteristics allowed the character to resonate with John's identity narrative through the pleasurable experience of this character. John's engagement with *The Simpsons* did not derive from a kind of masochistic annoyance with Homer's negative role model. Rather, the aesthetic range of *The Simpsons* as a cultural statement (its humor, color, plot, etc.) resonated for John as it does for its wider audience. This did not cultivate tolerance for Homer's model of the "bad dad." Instead, *The Simpsons* could be put to positive use as John filtered Homer through his own religious ideals, allowing him to critique Homer, reconcile the guilt of his own pleasure, and love *The Simpsons* simultaneously and without much dissonance.

Even though the men in this study tended to eschew (and to skewer) "Christian" media, we cannot argue that religious media are entirely meaningless to broader Christian or Evangelical ideas about masculinity. As we've seen throughout these conversations, religion still offers a powerful frame through which men engage media. If religion did not play such a role, then the religious articulation of the idea of headship might not be so firmly entrenched. Nor would men be at least vaguely aware of the central idea behind the Promise Keepers movement or of books about men that they claim not to have read. Nor would they be at least vaguely aware of the conservative theological response to the feminist movement. Nor would they filter mainstream media through the religious lens. Clearly, religious ideas are distilled into these masculine identity narratives—even on some level religious mediations of masculinity that are not in and of themselves pleasurable in the same way mainstream media are.

Pleasure is thus not the only principal dimension of resonance, though we should not assume that religious media are not pleasurable for some audiences. Our point is that the men with whom we spoke did not find pleasure in those religious media intended to address them as men about the meaning of contemporary masculinity. Or, at least, they did not express such pleasure when given the opportunity to do so. The

Evangelical media marketplace exists because it finds enough audiences that we should assume derive pleasure from these media. If we were to push the men here, we imagine that they might have accounts of having enjoyed some religious media at some point, such as in Sunday School or through community rituals in youth groups or from Fellowship of Christian Athletes meetings or from Contemporary Christian Music. That they did not express these sources as salient in the interviews is notable for their lives today, but this should not be taken to suggest that they have never derived pleasure from religious media.

It must also be true that symbolic resources need not be only pleasurable to resonate. We suggest that the men here—and American culture more generally—also connect and learn through media in less pleasurable ways: out of duty, responsibility, or information-seeking. These men were not hedonists. Rather, they found value in learning and developing religious lives and felt called to do so. Thus the religious mediations of their faith communities also distilled into their sense of gendered being and became powerful lenses through which to engage other media that they found pleasurable. The success of *Every Man's Battle*, specifically targeted at the experiences of male sexual pleasure through pornography, might be instructive here. The moral pull of sexual purity is a powerful counterweight to carnal pleasure, and a call to purity attached to the idea of headship ought to make such a book powerful and meaningful to some men.

We are arguing that religious men have a complex engagement with the media sphere—one that creates pleasure, tension, and contradiction. Media, rather than competing with religion, exist in a larger symbolic universe *with* religion. Both are symbolic. Both figure powerfully in men's identity narratives. It is not a matter of one's being more powerful than the other, but it does seem clear from our interviews with religious men and from many other voices as well that American men cannot talk about values without talking about media. The media provide the language through which we think about masculinity. This language, however, is filtered through powerful religious-moral lenses. At the same time, much of the language of media (such as films and television) aligns rather easily with our interviewees' senses of masculinity and with particularly essentialist and patriarchal registers at that. Thus, while some of the conservative and neo-traditionalist critics are right that media have become powerful storytellers, perhaps more powerful in some ways than religion, those critics misunderstand how men engage media, and those critics overstate the contradictions between "media" and the traditionalist and essentialist values they espouse.

Thinking with Braveheart

That *Braveheart* can serve to articulate senses of purpose and protection and can be read so facilely through the lens of contemporary experience, as Clark Caldwell did, makes this film worth exploring further as we think about how media work. Gibson's 1995 role as William Wallace (Gibson also directed the film) turned out to be one of the most-mentioned examples of normative masculinity from the media in our interviews, as we have noted. This was somewhat surprising, not least because we might have expected a more recent Gibson film, *The Passion of the Christ* (2004), to provide normative masculine symbols in our interviews, and yet it came up only one time, unsolicited.[24]

So why *Braveheart*? As we began discussing our interviews in various contexts, we came to learn that it is not only in our interviews that this film and this character loom large. Many Evangelical churches continue to show the film, either in its entirety or as excerpts, almost two decades after its original release. A cursory scan of the World Wide Web supports the view that in this religious context, *Braveheart* continues to ring true.[25]

As we have seen, our interviews provide some insight into why this would be. First, the character portrayed by Gibson in the film unequivocally instantiates masculinism. He is a hard, decisive warrior, evocative of the fundamental tropes of masculinity that are of positive value for our Evangelical informants and a guilty pleasure for at least some of our Ecumenicals. He is unequivocal and clearly articulates a sense of righteousness and justice. He embodies all three of the essential characteristics we've been discussing: provision, protection, and purpose.

But Clark Caldwell's reading of *Braveheart* as a domestic drama as much as it is a military drama is a subtler—and in a way far more profound—reading that appears in many of our interviews. It is about domestic values, ideals, and—most important—responsibilities. But it is also layered and nuanced in the way it lodges Wallace's struggles in a larger context that can be fitted to the contemporary age. Gibson's Wallace, according to many of the men with whom we spoke, is a valuable model because he is seen to struggle over these various responsibilities. He is a "conflicted—if not a reluctant—warrior."

The following conversation, from one of our focus groups of younger, mostly single men in an urban "emerging church," demonstrates the extent to which, for this and other reasons, *Braveheart* has achieved such currency[26] in Evangelical circles:

INTERVIEWER: So how about this one [*shows an image of Gibson as William Wallace in "Braveheart"*]?

FRANCIS: I've watched it like ten times.

GREG: Oh yeah.

INTERVIEWER: Positive?

[*general murmur: "definitely"*]

COLIN: Let me just say that like for ten to fifteen years, [*names a lead pastor*]—that was his most-referenced movie.

FRANCIS: Especially in Christian circles too.

INTERVIEWER: Really?

FRANCIS: Yeah, I was in Campus Crusade in college and whenever we had like men's time, [it was] always mentioned. Like there was even one time when we like painted our faces blue and tore off like a piece of tape, like—

INTERVIEWER: Like this [*shows image from the film of Gibson with blue face*]?

FRANCIS: Yeah. A really random thing, but—a little over the top.

BOBBY: So, behind it, like right at the beginning when they asked him to fight? And he says, no, didn't I just stand up for it, didn't I just prove it? And then later he does fight because it's for his family, for his values, sticking up for his country, and not just trying to kill somebody to show his manliness.

INTERVIEWER: So a reluctant hero—is that what resonates with men?

GREG: Not with me. Reluctant—

COLIN: I don't think he was reluctant.

ELLIOT: I think he was principled, so when it came to the point where fighting was his choice, then he fought. But up until then, fighting wasn't a necessity.

DAVIS: He was able to control his emotions and use them for the greater good.

ELLIOT: Yeah. And tapped into them when need be.

INTERVIEWER: Any other things about William Wallace and why he is a good example—or Mel Gibson as William Wallace?

GREG: The idea of [his] standing up for what he believes in and willing to sacrifice so much for that. I think that's kind of what I picture a man doing.

Gibson represents William Wallace as a simple family man who wanted only to get on with his life—to raise his family and tend his flocks. Instead, his domestic space was violated by dark and impersonal forces from the outside. His family (or, rather, his intended) was quite literally violated, and thus his actions, no matter how futile (he is martyred in the end) were thus justified on this more powerful and normative level. As opposed to the reading of the film in Scotland,[27] the reading in our interviews is that *Braveheart* was the ideal of the family man, expressing concretely what all family men of the normative ideal should know that they have the potential to express. That he fails is beside the point. He did what men and fathers have to do. And in so doing he represented for many of our informants (and apparently has done so for many others) a normative ideal. That it may seem archaic is, in fact, another meaningful dimension of the filmic trope and its influence. As we've seen again and again in our interviews, "essential" or "elemental" characteristics of masculinity are described as old, time-honored, received. They may be under assault today, but they have stood the test of time.

Braveheart thus is both iconic—a unique statement for many men—and at the same time a more generic model of what we have learned about the culturally generative potential of media in relation to men and masculinity. The media imaginary functions powerfully to articulate things that are hard to see or to describe in the context of daily life but that our informants continued to feel were foundational and essential. Media are very good, as we've said, at presenting the complexities of the shifting dynamics of gender as experienced in the *practical register* in daily life and in the home. But the media are even better at portraying the large and salient and "time honored" *normative* themes. This should not be a surprise, of course. What might be a surprise, and might be the challenge that the media pose to traditional social and cultural authorities of the meaning of gender, is that the media are the inevitable and central location of the articulation of these things, and that even our most conservative interviewees happily engaged with these representations. They are part of the common conversation that the media provide, and these men saw the media as a place where their values and ideals and struggles can be understood and represented (though they are not, of course, universally satisfied with what they see there). The relationship between media, masculinity, and religion is thus much more complex when we look in depth at the ways in which specific media— such as *Braveheart*—are involved in gender and in religion. In chapter 2, we articulated this as a situation wherein powerful or influential media statements are most relevant on a normative rather than on a practical register of action. Bringing things to the practical level is one of the challenges and, as we have seen, is also one of the frustrations expressed in these pages. This is the case with each of the dimensions of "elemental masculinity" we have been discussing. Films such as *Braveheart* provide attractive and compelling articulations of these elements, often in faux-historic or other contexts where they are more or less hermetic. They are viewed by men and women who live in another context, that of their modern urban and suburban daily lives. Thus, some of what they experience is the contradiction between the normative elementalism of films and the practical needs and challenges where they are. The normative resources and models of the broader culture, including its media, are thus in the background as they work out the meaning of things such as "purpose" for themselves. In short, these men long for Claymores (William Wallace's iconic sword), but they're armed with smartphones. They long for wild terrains, but they live in tract houses with rugged daily commutes.

A media sphere that stresses purpose as an important masculine characteristic does not provide practical and grounded senses of what that purpose might mean in contemporary life. The moral culture tinged with religion that has been pointed to by many as the important predicate of positive moral action by men seems instead to offer these men opportunities to negotiate their senses of provision, protection, and purpose in a way that makes the private and domestic sphere the whole point and that lets them imagine that it can be the *potential* for some of these things that is the important thing.

Domestic "Purpose" and the Challenge of Civic Engagement

Senses of purpose and of potentially greater purpose than that which might be focused solely in the private sphere is a concern of much public and scholarly discourse. There is widespread concern about the privatization of contemporary life and about the reticence of many people to engage socially beyond the home and private life. In sociology and political science, much concern has been expressed about the decline of "social capital" expressed through out-of-home commitments, social activities, and service activities.[28] More important to our project here, the neo-traditionalist critique of the crisis of masculinity has at its center, as we have said, the sense that men must increasingly focus their attention and resources of time on the needs of the broader society for a stronger moral culture. Thus both of these discourses are fundamentally interested in the negotiation of provision, protection, and purpose.

That the negotiations concerning purpose—presumably the masculine value of most importance to civic and political engagement—can be nuanced in the ways we've seen here will not be reassuring to these discourses. In fact, as we've noted, the orientation to the domestic that we see here nearly across the board of our interviews has men and families thinking in a private and inward direction, even as they contemplate the meaning of purpose today. Further, those who express more outward notions of purpose express a feeling of tension, contradiction, and rupture with what they see as their purpose as husbands and fathers. The media symbols of purpose, playing the social role of providing symbolic resources to masculine identities without necessarily grounding those symbols in contemporary life and life pressures, do not point toward the sorts of things that proponents of increased civic engagement are concerned about.

For people like Denton Calhoun, the meaning of citizenship and public engagement is entirely wrapped up in the domestic and the domestic ideal. Public life, or publicly oriented life, is family life, where the role of the father is to get things right at home. For Larry Cane, family becomes the example for the world, a social actor as a model. The "little platoons of the family," the commonplace found at the center of the neo-traditionalist critique we presented in the Introduction, are then a valuable point of concentration and focus. The collapse toward the domestic sphere that we see in these interviews seems objectively to run counter to ideals of active citizenship and civic engagement. Is this really what Don Eberly or Barack Obama has in mind when calling for more active and engaged husbands and fathers? We doubt it.

Rethinking "the Crisis"

Our conversations here have elaborated upon and nuanced the problem of the crisis of masculinity and its relationship to religion and media both through the specific questions of how religion and media differentially provide resources to the quest for masculine identity and through a broader set of insights into the way in which contemporary life complicates the picture. Most versions of "the crisis" rest on an explicit or implicit essentialism about men and masculinity. Most also assume that men operate within a field of action that must somehow incorporate work, family life, marital relationships, beliefs and values, and broader responsibilities to family and community. Most discussions assume that these other fields of action are straightforward and stable things. Our discussions here have shown that this is not the case. Instead, these other dimensions are in flux, and major transformations of them are underway.

From our conversations it seems obvious that two related trends, each of them actually encouraged by the Protestant faiths represented here, effectively condition the possibilities for the imagination and expression of masculinity today. The first is the turn toward the self and identity. Anthony Giddens's now-classic reading of this situation[29] demonstrated how contemporary life is experienced as a pattern of risks on the outside that must be met with cultural work for the individual on the inside. Most important, people today arrogate to themselves the responsibility for seeking the necessary resources and constructing out of those resources an ideal "self" that is able to withstand the vicissitudes of modern life. This is, of course, rooted in Protestant individualism, but it tacks away from structure and—specifically—from authority. The second significant trend, then, is that we are encouraged today to be our own authorities—social, cultural, and religious—and to take responsibility because no one else will.[30]

This project of the self was so much the common mode of practice among our interviewees that it was nearly unremarkable. All of them assumed that this whole project, including the project of establishing and narrating a sense of the masculine self (armed with but three "essentials"), was up to them. This might explain, in part, their approach to the sources that might have been thought to be important—the pulpit, the media, their own families of origin, and so on. It was not so much that they expressed great disillusionment that they got no help from such places (none were leaving their churches, after all); it was more of a disappointment that their task of making these connections for themselves might have been made easier if more valuable insights had been on offer from these places.

For the majority of the men here, this project of the self was inextricably connected to a larger and, in a way, more remarkable piece of the puzzle—its connection to family and to the domestic sphere. For them, the church or the community was not the primary referent for identity—the family was. The domestic sphere was the central context of meaning and action and the one toward which all purpose must be focused. A sort of "crisis of the domestic" that has been the subject of an emerging literature in sociology and family studies as well as in popular settings[31] is clearly on display in our interviews. The men with whom we spoke wished nearly universally to differentiate their style of fathering from what they themselves had experienced as children. They wanted to spend more time with their children, to be much more involved in domestic life. Their narratives articulated what has become a central concern of contemporary observers of the family—that we may, in fact, be loading too many expectations on the domestic sphere. We may be expecting both the possibility of perfection there, and the possibilities of personal satisfaction there, that are beyond its means to be able to deliver.[32]

It is clear that our men expect and invest much in the domestic sphere. For most of them, work took a distant second place to family and children as a locus of identity. In a way, it is clear from our conversations how complex the contemporary domestic sphere has become. New ideas about gender roles and the evolution of the American labor market have made far more obvious and pressing the need to define an essentialist masculinity that can ascribe to values of provision and protection but do so while accommodating the potential claims of women and partners to occupy the same turf. Thus, there was a motivation to a greater sense of concentration on the domestic sphere brought about by these men's self-consciousness of the challenge. At the same time, there was a sense in which the feminist critique had presented to men an obvious—and sympathetic—way of addressing egalitarianism and the need for a renewed sense of self-conscious and positive masculinity by turning toward—and being more involved in—the home. This kind of logic can be seen throughout our interviews with both our Evangelical and Ecumenical men.

Thus, the crisis of the domestic in these interviews is articulated in more than one register. There is a widespread sense of anxiety and risk in relation to the home and the family. There are more and more dangers all the time, and more and more potential forces that threaten to penetrate the sphere of the home. Some of these are physical and some cultural, and all are the challenge that essentialized "protection" must now rise to meet. The cultural ones, of course, include "bad media," and we've seen how the impulse to protection was commonly invoked among our respondents in relation to media in the home. Another valence is the challenge to shape an ideal domestic sphere, one that differs in positive ways from the past and from the remembered fathering of these men's own experience. There is the project of negotiating a sense of essential masculinity that serves these various levels and these challenges. This means that the domestic and family lives of most of the men we have heard from here demanded a great deal of time, effort, and work. Their professional lives were seen in relation to the provision they could make for the domestic sphere and were seen as a potential threat in that they could draw time and attention away from the primary task of fathering. This tension—fulfilling an "essential" role on the one hand, yet creating a "threat" on the other—was further exacerbated when men considered their professional lives as part of their *purpose* outside of its value to their domestic lives.

It is important to note again that the purpose of our conversations was to focus on masculinity and on men's ideas and articulations of masculinity. This concentration on the domestic sphere and the work associated with perfecting and policing it therefore could be significant primarily on the level of identity. Even so, it is significant how dominant "the domestic" was in these interviews. Further, here is much evidence that a kind of "collapse toward the domestic" was both discursive *and* *material* in the families represented here. This was evident when we attempted to explore the matter we introduced earlier in this Conclusion, articulated by one of the neo-traditionalist critics, Don Eberly, in the Introduction—that one of the consequences of a revitalization of fatherhood would be a broader service to society through "the little platoons of the family." In this calculus, ideal fatherhood produces ideal families that are ideal foundations for broader social spaces—for civic engagement. As we have seen here, there are reasons why received notions of civic engagement were contradicted by the actual experience of the lives we have described.

One of the most striking things about our interviews here is the paucity of examples of—or even concern about—how fathers and families *should* be civically engaged. Our respondents struggled to produce narratives or memories of these families' being involved in more than the most trivial ways outside the home. Certainly, children today are encouraged to engage in school, church, and other activities outside the home. And many such activities are service projects. But the focus of many of these is on the children and on their individual cultivation as students. As Robert Putnam and the stream of thought he initiated with *Bowling Alone*[33] have argued, a broader social project is being neglected today, and voices such as Eberly's have claimed that proper, God-centered masculinity should be at the center of a process of revitalized civic engagement and that the family should be engaged in this on its own terms. We saw little or no evidence of this in these interviews. The turn toward "better fathering" in these interviews constitutes a concentration on the domestic sphere as the normative object, and one of the casualties of this turn is a broader involvement by these men as individuals or a broader engagement by their families with a sense of civic purpose. We don't mean to argue that the family is the only or even the best medium for a revitalized civic sphere. It may be. What we are saying is that the assumption at the center of the crisis of masculinity seems not to be borne out in the lives of the men we interviewed. In fact, the project at the center of the neo-masculinist critique seems to be counterproductive. Rather than cultivate a domestic sphere (with men at the center) *for the larger purpose* of civic engagement, the turn toward the domestic focuses on the domestic sphere and stops there.

What We Can Say and Not Say

What we have done here, as we've said, is a kind of "critical test." We began with a commonplace critique rooted in a neo-traditionalist worldview concerning elementalist masculinity. These voices say that there is something particular and specific about being a man, and that "something" involves both characteristics and responsibilities. They further say that certain normative ideals of masculinity need somehow to be reinvigorated today, to be brought into a common project of addressing important social ills by means of a new concentration of masculine energy on the project of fatherhood and on the needs of the domestic sphere. The most vibrant of these voices have been ones that have been rooted in traditionalist and conservative religion. These voices have suggested that the moral core of this project should rightly be in religion and that a certain religious worldview—one that is most consistent with the important neo-Evangelical turn in the past century—should come to assume its place at the center of ideas of normative fatherhood. At the same time, many of these critics, religiously conservative and beyond, have identified "the media" as a major challenge to the normative sources of idealized masculinity.

Thus, the "test" we devised was to go where this all ought to be working. We would go to the white, heteronormative, nuclear, and religiously identified households that presumably have the capacity at least to come closest to this ideal, and we would see how this all works out there. While we have interviewed a broader constellation of families in the course of our research, the one comparison group we have included here consisted of men who were otherwise similar but who differed on the "religion variable." That is, we compared men who identify with the conservative side of American Protestantism, whom we've labeled conditionally and conventionally as "Evangelical," with men on the more liberal, or "Ecumenical," side of the Protestant spectrum. This has given us some interesting insights into both groups and into the challenges both face that condition and limit the range of thought and action—the "moving parts"—with regard to the problem of domestic masculinity today.

We do not, then, include here interviews with men or families of color; with gay, bisexual, or transgender men; or with single fathers, single mothers, or gay parents. Such interviews would and will all be interesting and intriguing further explorations. It is worth noting here that the whole question of difference of these kinds did come into play in our interviews. Many of the men with whom we spoke did feel a kind of crisis over the meaning of masculinity. For some, this was clearly articulated as a kind of zero-sum game between the gains of feminism and egalitarianism against the losses of the traditionally masculine. For others, the rise in the perceived prominence of nonheteronormative sexualities was also seen as a loss.

The echoes here, among some of our conservative men, of the broader crisis of masculinity discourse are articulated by voices such as those of *Fox News* personalities Bill O'Reilly and Brit Hume. It is not the full-throated lament of the loss of traditional male privilege heard there, but it is nonetheless similar in tone. Alternative gender expectations, growing social consensus favoring egalitarian rather than patriarchal social and economic relations, the emergence of different sexualities and patterns of family structure and relationship—all can be seen as a threat from the perspective of men who lack the contexts, or discursive or language resources, to think about masculinity outside of essentialist registers. At the same time, these are men of some privilege and residual social capital. They are white and heterosexual, and most are successfully negotiating the challenges of contemporary American life. What anxieties they express are internal more than they are external. It is hard to see, either in their own accounts, or in the larger social and cultural landscapes within which they reside, actual threats to their lives or their prospects posed by the evolving nature of gender relations today.

An obvious next task would be to look outside the boundaries of this study to men of color, gay and bisexual men, and men of different nationalities, religious backgrounds, and social classes. Would the dimensions of the situation we've seen here—the ways in which values and beliefs are integrated into narratives of the self through a process of negotiation among religion, nation, community, and the larger "common culture"—be similarly constituted in the lives of these men? Would the contrasts, in modern life, between firmly held and received ideas of masculinity and the actually existing realities of daily work and home be as keenly felt and negotiated in the same way? Would the larger cultural marketplace—represented in our conversations here and revealed across American culture today in "the media"—be resonant in similar ways as with these men, or would there be important differences? Would these men also have found various essentialisms as the most salient ways of expressing what it means to be a man? Could we put the same question to these other men that we've expressed in the title of the book: Does God make these men, too?

These are fascinating questions, well worth a careful look.

In a way, it is hard to think of what we've seen here as a "crisis." The men to whom we've spoken seemed clearly to have reached accommodations with the shifting sands of gender meaning and gender dynamics. They had figured out ways to articulate their religious senses of self with the larger culture of which they are a part. They had taken onboard, to an extent, the shifting definitions of masculinity and of feminism, and they expressed evolved understandings of their roles and their prerogatives. They seemed not to desire to return to an archly patriarchal past. They thought about their wives and daughters and their prospects for satisfying home and work lives. They understood that they must be self-conscious in ways that were not possible in the past. They tacked between the winds and currents of a broader culture that carries contradictory messages about all of this—its media reinforcing conservative and patriarchal ideas about gender as commonly as they convey alternatives at the same time that public discourse seems to be moving inexorably toward normative egalitarianism—and personal faith histories that provided, at best, ambiguous languages to account for all of this.

If there is a "crisis" here, it is in another place. For these men, there was a "crisis" of the domestic sphere, a set of challenges to an ideal and hermetic image of home and family. They had felt this crisis in their own history, as they almost universally expressed dissatisfaction with the level of commitment of their own fathers to the home. They also keenly felt the diffuse sense of risk and dread that seems widespread today, anxiety about a world that is growing more complex, dangerous, and challenging all the time. This had moved them to action in the form of an identity as men and ultimately as fathers for whom the domestic sphere and the home should and will be their primary concern. The broad social and cultural consensus that homes and families should be the central normative index through which all personal action and public policy should be judged was realized in their narratives of their lives. What was lost was a sense that the domestic sphere should be about something larger than itself in social terms. The collapse toward the domestic sphere seems nearly complete and absolute in these pages. Any larger project in civic space seems not to be part of the equation, and thus the idea that the family should be the place where the logics of broader civic engagement are inculcated and made real no longer makes much sense.

It is important to see how the picture here is one that is determined by beliefs and values on the one hand and the hard realities of economic and social life on the other. These men worked within constraints as they attempted to define and express their lives. Constraints of time and of relationships, as well as conditioning constraints of what is culturally and socially meaningful and acceptable—all were part of the calculus. In a way, then, it is perhaps a bit misguided to expect that beliefs and values about masculinity—what we have called the "normative register" of masculinity—could be ultimately determinative. Neither a feminist project devoted to the establishment of egalitarian normativity nor a neo-traditionalist project devoted to reinvigorating essentialism could ultimately succeed. What each of them does is provide a kind of symbolic aspiration against which the realities of what is possible can be judged. It is perhaps good, then, that in this age wherein perfection of the self is the most important project, and the crafting of a plausible narrative of that self is reflexively constituted, men and women are more aware of the extent to which the building of cultural ideals as personal goals is in their own hands. While they might lament the failure of their churches or their families to give them all the tools they need and might contest the influences of the broader culture, including the media, they don't seem ultimately to expect that they should have found all the answers in those places. They think they know where the truth lies, in a turn toward personal, private, and domestic arrangements. And this may be the real crisis.

NOTES

INTRODUCTION

1 "Men in America," National Public Radio, All Things Considered, http://www.npr.org/series/323986426/men-in-america, accessed March 5, 2015.

2 The very first comment on the NPR board stands as a fascinating example of this fluidity (and an eloquent prefiguring of the accounts we will consider in these pages):

I am glad someone is finally talking about this. As a man I have often struggled with this very question. I am nearly forty and I still don't have a good answer. Having a one-year-old son, I'd like to find out those answers quick. Why do I think about sex so often? Society implies that this is bad and "piggish"[;] does this mean that I am a pig because I have such thoughts? I love and respect women and want them to be treated equally yet I still acknowledge the inherent differences between the genders both physically, and psychologically. Does this imply inequality? I grew up on stories and TV shows and movies and video games where male heroes rescued princesses and chivalry was a moral value considered good. Is this still true? Is it my duty and responsibility to provide for my wife and family? It feels good when I do. Is this a false belief laid on me from antiquated ideals that no longer fit into our culture? I feel the need to be physically strong and protect those I love. But do they really need protecting anymore? And do I even have the ability to do so against the dangers of today? Mass shootings? Drugs?

I love to go clothes shopping with my wife and hold her purse while she tries on clothes because she's gorgeous and I like to see her in different outfits and I like to see her smile and be happy, and shopping makes her happy. I like to talk baby talk to my son and hold him, kiss his little feet and hands and cheeks. And sometimes I watch him sleep at night and start crying because he is so beautiful and so precious to me. Yet I keep these things hidden because I am a man, or at least, trying to be.

From commenter "Captain Dave" at "The New American Man Doesn't Look Like His Father," http://www.npr.org/2014/06/23/323966448/the-new-american-man-doesnt-look-like-his-father, accessed March 5, 2015.

3 Tom Scocca, "Parsing the Narrow, Tribal Appeal of the Republican Nominee," Slate.com, November 2, 2012, http://www.slate.com/articles/news_and_politics/scocca/2012/11/mitt_romney_white_vote_parsing_the_narrow_tribal_appeal_of_the_republican.html/, accessed March 5, 2015.

4 Catherine Poe, "What Are White Guys Afraid Of?" *Washington Times*, November 2, 2012, http://communities.washingtontimes.com/neighborhood/ad-lib/2012/nov/2/election-2012-what-are-white-guys-afraid/, accessed March 5, 2015.

5 Rich Benjamin, "Whites-only GOP Meets Its Demographic Destiny," *Salon.com*, November 7, 2012, http://www.salon.com/2012/11/07/whites_only_gop_meets_its_demographic_destiny/, accessed March 5, 2015.

6 Derek Thompson, "The GOP Needs an Economic Plan for More than the "White Establishment," *The Atlantic*, November 7, 2012, http://www.theatlantic.com/business/archive/2012/11/the-gop-needs-a-economic-plan-for-more-than-the-whitewhite-establishment/264925/, accessed March 5, 2015.

7 See, for example, Michael Kimmel, *Manhood in America: A Cultural History* (Oxford: Oxford University Press, 2012), or Seth Dowland, "War, Sports and the Construction of Masculinity in American Christianity." *Religion Compass*, 5/7 (2011), 355–64.

8 *National Fatherhood Initiative*, http://www.fatherhood.org/, accessed September 6, 2013.

9 Then-Senator Barack Obama in 2008, for example, said,

Of all the rocks upon which we build our lives, we are reminded today that family is the most important. And we are called to recognize and honor how critical every father is to that foundation. They are teachers and coaches. They are mentors and role models. They are examples of success and the men who constantly push us toward it. But if we are honest with ourselves, we'll admit that what too many fathers also are is missing—missing from too many lives and too many homes. They have abandoned their responsibilities, acting like boys instead of men. And the foundations of our families are weaker because of it.

For the full transcript, see Politico Staff, "Text of Obama's Fatherhood Speech," http://www.politico.com/news/stories/0608/11094.html, accessed March 5, 2015.

10 Don Eberly, "Families, Fathers, and the Making of Democratic Citizens." *Civil Society Project Essays on Civil Society* 99 (1999), no. 1, http://www.civilsocietyproject.org/_files/FathersDemocraticCitizens.pdf, accessed October 7, 2008.

11 Randy Wilson, "Chosen for Fatherhood." *Focus on the Family*, 2007, http://www.focusonthefamily.com/parenting/parenting_roles/fatherhood/chosen_for_fatherhood.aspx, accessed September 6, 2013; Mark Driscoll, *Pastor Dad* (2001), http://theresurgence.com/books/pastor_dad, accessed September 6, 2013.

12 "New Warrior Training Adventure." *The Mankind Project International*, 2014, http://mankindproject.org/, accessed March 5, 2015.

13 See examples below, and for recent examples of the discourse about fathers and the media, see Matthew Philbin, "Deadbeats, Duds, and Doofusses: Dads in the Media," *NewsBusters*, June 16, 2011, http://newsbusters.org/blogs/matthew-philbin/2011/06/16/deadbeats-duds-and-doofusses-dads-media, accessed May 12, 2014; Wayne Parker, "Turn Off the TV and Tune into Your Family," About.com/Family Page, 2014, http://fatherhood.about.com/od/activities/a/turnofftv.htm, accessed May 12, 2014.

14 Robert Putnam, *Bowling Alone: The Collapse and Revival of American Community* (New York: Simon & Schuster, 2001).

15 We introduced Glenn Donegal in an earlier work. Stewart M. Hoover, *Religion in the Media Age* (London: Routledge, 2006).

16 Glenn was only one of several of our male informants who identified so heavily with *The Andy Griffith Show.*

17 Anthony Giddens, *Modernity and Self-Identity* (Stanford: Stanford University Press, 1991).

18 National Public Radio, "Laura Bush: Putting Boys in the Spotlight," *All Things Considered, NPR,* February 9, 2005.

19 Hilde Lövdahl, "Family Matters: James Dobson and Focus on the Family's Message to American Evangelicals" (Ph.D. diss., University of Oslo, 2012).

20 Gertrude Himmelfarb, *The Demoralization of Society: From Victorian Virtues to Modern Values* (New York: Knopf, 1995).

21 Bill Berkowitz, "Don Eberly's Conservative Civil Society," *MediaTransparency.org,* February 5, 2005, http://www.mediatransparency.org/personprofile.php?personID=124, accessed October 7, 2008.

22 Don Eberly and Ryan Streeter, *The Soul of Civil Society: Voluntary Associations and the Public Value of Moral Habits* (Lanham, Md.: Lexington Books, 2002).

23 Eberly and Streeter, *The Soul of Civil Society,* 40.

24 Eberly, *The Faith Factor in Fatherhood,* 6.

25 Don Eberly, "Families, Fathers, and the Making of Democratic Citizens." *Civil Society Project Essays on Civil Society,* Vol. 99, no. 1, 1999, http://www.civilsocietyproject.org/_files/FathersDemocraticCitizens.pdf, accessed October 7, 2008.

26 Eberly and Streeter, *The Soul of Civil Society,* 90.

27 Cf. Putnam, *Bowling Alone.*

28 Eberly and Streeter, *The Soul of Civil Society.*

29 Eberly, *The Faith Factor in Fatherhood,* 31.

30 Eberly and Streeter, *The Soul of Civil Society,* p. 40.

31 Barack Obama, "White House Address" (speech, Washington, D.C., June 19, 2009).

32 Barack Obama, "Father's Day Speech" (speech, Apostolic Church, Chicago, June 15, 2008), http://my.barackobama.com/page/community/post/stateupdates/gG5nFK, accessed February 23, 2009.

33 Ronald F. Levant, "The Masculinity Crisis." *Journal of Men's Studies* 5, no. 3 (1997): 221–31.

34 Joseph H. Pleck, *The Myth of Masculinity* (Cambridge, Mass.: MIT Press, 1983).

35 Laura Sessions Stepp, "What Does It Mean to Be Manly?" *Washington Post,* May 29, 2007, HE01; Eduardo Porter and Michelle O'Donnell, "The New Gender Divide: Still Single," *The New York Times,* August 6, 2006, 1; Jackson Katz and Sut Jhally, "Crisis in Masculinity," *Boston Globe,* May 2, 1999.

36 Stepp, "What Does It Mean to Be Manly?"

37 John Eldredge, *Wild at Heart: Discovering the Secret of a Man's Soul* (Nashville: Thomas Nelson, 2010).

38 Joseph Gelfer, *Numen, Old Men: Contemporary Masculine Spiritualities and the Problem of Patriarchy* (London: Equinox, 2009).

39 See, for example, Richard Rohr, *From Wild Man to Wise Man: Reflections on Male Spirituality* (Cincinnati: St. Anthony Messenger Press, 2005).

40 Reported here are the results of in-depth and detailed individual and group interviews with fifty-five Protestant men. Twenty-four of the men were Evangelicals. Sixteen of these had participated in "family interviews" wherein they were interviewed first along with their spouses, and then individually. The other Evangelical men were participants in a focus group drawn from a men's group at an "emerging" Evangelical church. Thirty-one non-Evangelical or "Ecumenical Protestant" men were interviewed—twenty in four separate focus groups, eleven in individual and family interviews (as with the Evangelicals, first with their spouses, then individually). The focus groups took place with men from two different Ecumenical Protestant churches. Additional interviews with non-Christian men were also conducted in the overall project but were not included in this study. Finally, interviews used in this study were conducted in the following regions in the United States: Mountain West, Pacific Northwest, Upper Midwest, and South.

41 Cf. Frank Furstenburg, "Can Marriage Be Saved?" *Dissent* 52, no. 3 (2005): 66–70.

42 See, for example, literatures reviewed in Judith Kegan Gardiner, "Men, Masculinities, and Feminist Theory," in *Handbook of Studies on Men and Masculinities*, ed. Michael Kimmel, Jeff Hearn, and R. W. Connell. Thousand Oaks, Calif.: Sage, 2005: 35–50.

43 Steven Goldberg, *Why Men Rule: A Theory of Male Dominance* (Chicago: Open Court Press, 1993).

44 John Gray, *Men Are from Mars, Women Are from Venus* (London: HarperCollins, 2002).

45 Catherine Hakim, "Dancing with the Devil? Essentialism and Other Feminist Heresies," *The British Journal of Sociology* 58, no. 1 (2007): 123–32.

46 Ibid.

47 Rosemary Crompton and Clare Lyonette, "The New Gender Essentialism— Domestic and Family Choices and Their Relation to Attitudes," *The British Journal of Sociology* 56, no. 4 (2005): 601–20.

48 Ibid.; Rosemary Crompton and Fiona Harris, "Explaining Women's Employment Patterns: Orientations to Work Revisited," *The British Journal of Sociology* 49 (1998): 148–70; Rosemary Crompton, "Gender Inequality and the Gendered Division of Labour," in *The Future of Gender*, ed. J. Browne (Cambridge: Cambridge University Press, 2007).

49 Hakim, "Dancing with the Devil?"

50 Susan McRae, "Constraints and Choices in Mothers' Employment Careers: A Consideration of Hakim's Preference Theory," *The British Journal of Sociology* 54, no. 3 (2003): 317–38.

51 Hakim, "Dancing with the Devil?" 127.

52 Stewart M. Hoover, *Religion in the Media Age* (London: Routledge, 2006).

53 Giddens, *Modernity and Self-Identity*.

54 David Gauntlett, "Gender Resources," *Theory.org*, 2012, http://www.theory.org. uk/ctr-iden.htm, accessed September 16, 2012.

55 Harvey C. Mansfield, *Manliness* (New Haven, Conn.: Yale University Press, 2006).

CHAPTER 1. THE NEW CHRISTIAN PATRIARCHS

1 We tend to make this distinction based on denominational choice, but we recognize that individuals can be more or less Evangelical, following Nancy Ammerman, "Golden Rule Christianity: Lived Religion in the American Mainstream," in *Lived Religion in America*, ed. David Hall (Princeton, N.J.: Princeton University Press, 1997). We also make note of the recent evolution of a robust scholarship devoted to "liberal Protestantism" as the contrasting category, though the leading voice in that discourse, David Hollinger, prefers "Ecumenical Protestantism" as the label. See David Hollinger, *After Cloven Tongues of Fire: Protestant Liberalism in Modern American History* (Princeton, N.J.: Princeton University Press, 2013).

2 Eighteen of thirty-one Ecumenical Protestant men interviewed expressed egalitarian narratives. However, only nine of the eighteen expressed strong gender constructivism. Five others oscillated between constructivism and essentialism in their narratives, so fewer than half of the men in the Ecumenical group expressed some form of constructivism (as compared with a single constructivist in the Evangelical cohort). Thus, feminism has clearly made significant gains in Ecumenical Protestantism, particularly in terms of egalitarianism. Constructivist feminism, however, has been less successful, because most of these men still express a form of masculine elementalism, particularly concerning the notion of male purpose.

3 This "received idea" is, of course, one of the central dimensions of the "essentialism" of religion that have come under such scrutiny in the field of religious studies in recent decades. But it remains an important taken-for-granted idea in the culture. It is implied in the "God-centered masculinity" called for by Don Eberly, for example.

4 Pierre Bourdieu, "Structures, Habitus, Power: Basis for a Theory of Symbolic Power," in *Culture/Power/History: A Reader in Contemporary Social Theory*, ed. Nicholas Dirks et al. (Princeton, N.J.: Princeton University Press, 1994).

5 Ibid., 161.

6 In a church site visit in 2012, the Ephesians 5 proof text was, in fact, used explicitly in a sermon. This was surprising given what we had heard from men about the lack of teachings on gender (about this text). However, the sermon using this text was not about gender per se. Rather, it was about how the marriage relationship in this text was an example of one's relationship with Christ. The gendered nature of this text was not elaborated. Rather, gender was taken for granted. It was naturalized. This suggests that the teachings on gender, at least in this Evangelical church, are still closer to the realm of Bourdieu's doxa, or as we mention later in the book, closer to "feelings of structure,"

as Robert Peaslee, "Media Conduction: Exploring power at the intersection of media, tourism, and festival studies" (paper presented at Society for Media and Cinema Studies, Chicago, 2013), would have it. Gender norms, roles, and essentials are implicit. They are the starting point or ground from which to discuss other theological matters, for example one's relationship with Christ.

7 Paul Heelas and Linda Woodhead, *The Spiritual Revolution: Why Religion Is Giving Way to Spirituality* (London: Blackwell, 2005).

8 In our study, 92 percent of Evangelicals and 71 percent of Ecumenical Protestants were strong, unambiguous gender essentialists.

9 We use this term self-consciously to contrast with the notion of "soft patriarchy" identified by W. Bradford Wilcox in his influential work *Soft Patriarchs, New Men: How Christianity Shapes Fathers and Husbands* (Chicago: University of Chicago Press, 2004). As we shall see, our cohort is nearly the same as Wilcox's and articulates many of the same senses of the situation. The difference, as we see it, is that here we are talking about church and Wilcox was talking about the domestic sphere. As will be seen later, we would also use the term *soft patriarchy* to describe the sensibility we encountered, with these same men, when they talked about their approach to marital relationships and roles in domestic life. However, with regard to church, the situation is different for these men. Patriarchy is clearly established in church structure with very definite roles for men and women.

10 Wilcox, *Soft Patriarchs, New Men*.

11 Curtis Coats, "God, Men, Then . . . Wait, How Does That Go? Emerging Gender Identities in 20-something Evangelicals," *Journal of Men, Masculinities and Spirituality* 3 no. 1 (2009): 64–79.

12 Wilcox, *Soft Patriarchs, New Men*.

13 This term comes from the title of a landmark book on Evangelical masculinity: Stu Weber, *Tender Warriors: God's Intention for Man* (Colorado Springs: Multnomah Books, 1999).

14 Weber's work was influential in the Evangelical Promise Keeper's organization, which stressed that true Christian leadership must be "servant" or "tender" leadership. See John Bartkowski, *The Promise Keepers: Servants, Soldiers and Godly Men* (New Brunswick, N.J.: Rutgers University Press, 2004), 101–2.

15 This is a position argued by such sources as Susan K. Gallagher and Christian Smith, "Symbolic Traditionalism and Pragmatic Egalitarianism: Contemporary Evangelicals, Families, and Gender." *Gender & Society* 13, no. 2 (1999): 211–33 and Judith Stacey, *Brave New Families: Stories of Domestic Upheaval in Late-Twentieth-Century America* (Berkeley: University of California Press, 1998).

16 Michael A. Messner, *Politics of Masculinities: Men in Movements* (Thousand Oaks, Calif.: Sage, 1997), 31.

17 Though we did not interview women individually, it is possible that one of the definitive sources of masculinity for these men is their spouses. While many of these men take issue with women's teaching men, it is likely that women, are, in fact, instrumental in teaching them about something so elemental as manhood.

18 Gallagher and Smith, "Symbolic Traditionalism"; Stacey, *Brave New Families.*

19 This highlights a tendency for Ecumenical men, egalitarian Evangelicals, and even academics to think that gender is central to Evangelical Christianity, whereas traditionalist Evangelical men tend to not see gender as much in their faith tradition.

20 For a comprehensive review of the literature, see Karin L. Brewster and Irene Padavic, "Change in Gender-Ideology, 1977–1996: The Contributions of Intracohort Change and Population Turnover," *Journal of Marriage and Family*, Volume 62, Issue 2, 62, no. 2 (2000): 477–87. Of course, for a less halcyon view of some of the same trends, see Susan Faludi, *Backlash: The Undeclared War Against American Women* (New York: Random House, 1991).

21 Of course, this is not new. Critiques of the feminized church (and Jesus) date, at least, to the mid–nineteenth century in America. See Clifford Putney, *Muscular Christianity: Manhood and Sports in Protestant America, 1880–1920* (Cambridge, Mass.: Harvard University Press, 2009); Nick Watson, Stuart Weir, and Stephen Friend, "The Development of Muscular Christianity in Victorian Britain and Beyond," *Journal of Religion and Society* 7, no. 1 (2005): 1–25; Donald Hall, ed., *Muscular Christianity: Embodying the Victorian Age,* Vol. 2 (Cambridge: Cambridge University Press, 2006); Jeffery A. Smith, "Hollywood Theology: The Commodification of Religion in Twentieth-Century Films," *Religion and American Culture* 11, no. 2 (2001): 191–231.

22 This is a significant matter. In fact, this sort of self-conscious distinction is a major point of differentiation between Evangelical Protestants and the "liberal" or "mainline" Protestants whom David Hollinger prefers to label "Ecumenical Protestants." His choice of this term is deliberate and definitive: " 'ecumenical' has emerged as the least confusing term to identify the liberal side in the division that has rent American Protestantism from the 1940s through the early twenty-first century. The liberalizing Protestants of that era put much more energy into transdenominational projects and shifted the emphasis of their foreign missions from conversion to social service." In David Hollinger, *After Cloven Tongues of Fire: Protestant Liberalism in Modern American History* (Princeton, N.J.: Princeton University Press, 2013), xiii. More significantly, according to Hollinger, this revealed an underlying turn away from exclusivism and toward more openness to other traditions, both socially and theologically. If Hollinger is correct, then what marks our non-Evangelical informants (most of whom belonged to churches of these "ecumenical" denominations) is a commitment to ideas of inclusion, not exclusion, and a self-consciousness of the outlines of this distinction in the broad field of religious politics.

23 Janice Radway, "Identifying Ideological Seams: Mass Culture, Analytical Method, and Political Practice," *Communication* 9 (1986): 93–124. See also Michael Messner, *Politics of Masculinities: Men in Movements* (Thousand Oaks, Calif.: Sage, 1997).

CHAPTER 2. THE MEDIA THAT MATTER

1 This aphorism is generally attributed to the pioneering mass communication theorist George Gerbner.

2 Certainly, this is partly related to the themes of our interviews, but the relative ease with which our respondents talked about media compared with their talk about religion was notable and persistent throughout this process. We would also point out that prominent literatures focused on masculinity, such as Eldredge's *Wild at Heart*, are rife with references to films and other popular culture. John Eldredge, *Wild at Heart: Discovering the Secret of a Man's Soul* (Nashville: Thomas Nelson, 2010).

3 Stuart Hall, "Cultural Studies and Its Theoretical Legacies," in *Stuart Hall: Critical Dialogues in Cultural Studies*, ed. David Morley and Kuan-Hsing Chin (New York: Routledge, 1996).

4 Raymond Williams, "Culture Is Ordinary," in *Cultural Theory: An Anthology*, ed. Imre Szeman and Timothy Kaposy (Oxford: Wiley-Blackwell, 2010).

5 Diane Winston, ed., *Small Screen, Big Picture: Television and Lived Religion* (Waco, Tex.: Baylor University Press, 2009).

6 Cf. Tracy Fessenden, *Culture and Redemption: Religion, the Secular and American Literature* (Princeton, N.J.: Princeton University Press, 2011).

7 Cf. David Morgan, "Warner Sallman and the Visual Culture of American Protestantism," in *Icons of American Protestantism: The Art of Warner Sallman*, ed. David Morgan (New Haven, Conn.: Yale University Press, 1996); Fessenden, *Culture and Redemption*, op. cit.; William F. Fore, *Television and Religion: The Shaping of Faith, Values, and Culture* (Minneapolis: Augsberg Press, 1987); Michele Rosenthal, *American Protestants and TV in the 1950s: Responses to a New Medium* (New York: Palgrave Macmillan, 2007).

8 Stewart Hoover, Lynn Schofield Clark, and Diane Alters with Joe Champ and Lee Hood, *Media, Home and Family* (New York: Routledge, 2004).

9 Ibid.

10 Lynn Lövdal, "Sex Role Messages in Television Commercials: An Update," *Sex Roles* 21 (1989): 715–24; Linda J. Busby, "Sex-role Research on the Mass Media," *Journal of Communication* 25 (1975): 107–31; Steve Craig, ed., *Men, Masculinity, and the Media* (Newbury Park, Calif.: Sage, 1992).

11 R. W. Connell, *The Men and the Boys* (Berkeley: University of California Press, 2001).

12 Harvey C. Mansfield, *Manliness* (New Haven, Conn.: Yale University Press, 2006); J. R. Macnamara, *Media and Male Identity: The Making and Remaking of Men* (New York: Palgrave Macmillan, 2006). See also, for discussion, Warren Farrell, *The Myth of Male Power* (New York: Penguin, 2001). For a popular-press treatment, see Kathleen Parker, *Save the Males: Why Men Matter and Why Women Should Care* (New York: Random House, 2010). We should make it clear here, if it is not obvious, that the authors of this volume do *not* subscribe to this view of the relationship between feminism and whatever "crisis" may be underway.

13 Macnamara, *Media and Male Identity*.

14 Judith Butler, *Gender Trouble: Feminism and the Subversion of Identity* (New York: Routledge, 2006).

15 David Gauntlett, *Media, Gender, and Identity* (London: Routledge, 2002); Margaret Wetherell and Nigel Edley, "Negotiating Hegemonic Masculinity: Imaginary Positions and Psycho-Discursive Practices," *Feminism & Psychology* 9 (1999): 335–56.

16 Mia Consalvo, "The Monsters Next Door: Media Constructions of Boys and Masculinity," *Feminist Media Studies* 3 (2003): 27–45.

17 For reviews of this literature, see Consalvo, "The Monsters Next Door," and Susan Faludi, *Stiffed: The Betrayal of the American Man* (New York: Harper, 2000).

18 Craig, *Men, Masculinity, and the Media.*

19 Macnamara, *Media and Male Identity*, 166.

20 Robert Hanke, "Redesigning Men: Hegemonic Masculinity in Transition," in *Men, Masculinity, and the Media*, ed. Steve Craig (Newbury Park, Calif.: Sage, 1992).

21 See, in particular, Gauntlett, *Media, Gender, and Identity*; David Gauntlett, *Creative Explorations: New Approaches to Identities and Audiences* (London: Routledge, 2007).

22 Gauntlett, *Media, Gender, and Identity*, 103.

23 The word *today* may also be relevant here. Throughout our discussions, we've observed that changing cultural norms of gender greatly condition the contexts and languages that surround it. For many men, it may be that their fathers' experiences and models are no longer relevant today.

24 Richard Pitt, "God Built This: Religion Entrepreneurship, Church-Founding, and Risk Perception" (Paper presented at the Annual Meeting of the Society for the Scientific Study of Religion, 2013). Pitt discussed the ways in which women negotiate patriarchal structures of ministry. We borrow this term to indicate, on the one hand, the stable "essentials" of masculinity yet, on the other hand, the fluidity of movement within these essential zones and the ambiguity about the sources from which these zones emerge.

25 See Erving Goffman, *The Presentation of Self in Everyday Life* (Garden City, N.Y.: Doubleday Anchor Books, 1959); Herbert Blumer, *Symbolic Interactionism: Perspective and Method* (Berkeley: University of California Press, 1986); Norman Denzin, *Symbolic Interactionism and Cultural Studies: The Politics of Interpretation* (Oxford: Blackwell, 1992); Norman Denzin, *Interpretive Interactionism*, Second Edition (Thousand Oaks, Calif.: Sage, 2001).

26 This is a long scholarly, professional, and popular discourse about effects of sexualization and violence in the media. Scholarly examples include Jean Kilbourne, *DEADLY PERSUASION: Why Women and Girls Must Fight the Addictive Power of Advertising* (New York: Free Press, 1999), and Kyle Kontour, "Revisiting Violent Videogames Research: Game Studies Perspectives on Aggression, Violence, Immersion, Interaction, and Textual Analysis," *Digital Culture and Education* 1 (2009): 6–30. Also see Vasilis K. Povios, Praveen R. Kambam, and H. Eric Bender, "Does Media Violence Lead to the Real Thing?" *New York Times*, August 23, 2013, http://www.nytimes.com/2013/08/25/opinion/sunday/does-media-violence-lead-to-the-real-thing.html?_r=0, accessed June 11, 2014.

27 For a more complete discussion of the relationship between religious viewers and the "common culture," see Stewart Hoover, *Religion in the Media Age* (New York: Routledge, 2006).

28 Cf., for example, Hoover et al., *Media, Home, and Family*, 3–17.

29 We use *perceived* intentionally in this discussion of representations of homosexuality in media. While LGBTQ *visibility* in media has increased, these portrayals are often still marginalized and stereotypical. See Brian Ott and Robert Mack, *Critical Media Studies: An Introduction* (Oxford: Wiley-Blackwell, 2010); and Bradley Bond, "Sex and Sexuality in Media Popular with Lesbian, Gay, and Bisexual Adolescents," *Mass Communication and Society* 17 (2014): 98–120.

30 Readers should keep in mind that the interviews on which this book is based took place before the widely reported allegations of sexual coercion against Bill Cosby surfaced. Thus, it was the earlier, more-respected Bill Cosby to whom our informants refer in these pages.

31 We base this assertion on our perception of the relative number and length of pauses in this portion of the interview compared with the number and length of pauses in other portions of the interview.

32 Interestingly, one of Gibson's most notable and controversial films, *The Passion of the Christ*, came up only once unsolicited. Other references to this film came up in our focus groups, some of which took place only a few years after its release and much more recently than his iconic film *Braveheart*.

33 Slasher films were frequently panned by our respondents. For Evangelicals, who had much more tolerance for violence, these films were gratuitous, providing no positive message that would make the violence morally acceptable.

34 The notable exception listed in both groups is Bill Cosby. However, Rebecca Abbott has argued that Cosby is a complex figure (and text), one that intersects with empowerment and assimilation into white culture. See Rebecca Abbott, "Television and Children: Issues in Black and White," *Sacred Heart University Review* 15 (Fall 1994/Spring 1995): Article 8, http://digitalcommons.sacredheart.edu/shureview/vol15/iss1/8, accessed June 11, 2014; see also Sut Jhally and Justin Lewis, *Enlightened Racism: The Cosby Show, Audiences and the Myth of the American Dream* (Boulder, Colo.: Westview Press, 1992).

35 Robert Jewett and John Lawrence, *The Myth of the American Superhero* (Grand Rapids, Mich.: W. B. Eerdmans Publishing, 2002).

36 See note 34 above. Also note that Ecumenicals listed President Obama and Dev Patel as media personalities they admired.

37 See Brian Ott, "Television as Lover, Part 1: Writing Dirty Theory," *Cultural Studies/Critical Methodologies* 7 (2007): 26–47.

CHAPTER 3. ELEMENTAL MASCULINITY, THE DOMESTIC IDEAL, AND EVERYDAY LIFE

1 Nancy Cordes, "Obama: Paul Ryan 'good man,' but has 'wrong vision for America,'" *CBS This Morning*, 2012, http://www.cbsnews.com/news/obama-paul-ryan-good-man-but-has-wrong-vision-for-america/, accessed June 12, 2014.

2 Anne Swidler, *Talk of Love: How Culture Matters* (Chicago: University of Chicago Press, 2000).

3 As part of our interviews and focus group meetings, we frequently presented—as a provocation—the titles of the derived dimensions of the "Male Role Norms Inventory" developed by Levant and his associates. This Inventory is a normed index of conventionalized descriptions of masculinity. The dimensions we presented were: Avoidance of Femininity; Fear and Hatred of Homosexuality; Self-Reliance; Aggression; Achievement/Status; Non-relational Attitudes Toward Sex; and Restrictive Emotionality. We found much disagreement with and resistance to these as subjective descriptions of normative masculinity. Men did not think these norms represented them, proposing formulations that elided some of the more socially problematic dimensions, particularly "fear and hatred of homosexuality," and "avoidance of femininity." Ronald F. Levant and Katherine Richmond, "A Review of Research on Masculinity Ideologies Using the Male Role Norms Inventory," *The Journal of Men's Studies* 15, no. 2 (2007): 130–46.

4 R. Marie Griffith, *God's Daughters: Evangelical Women and the Power of Submission* (Berkeley: University of California Press, 2000) (see especially Ch. 6).

5 Anthony Giddens, *Modernity and Self-Identity* (Stanford: Stanford University Press, 1991).

6 We've noted above how this worked with our informants when we presented them with such a list in the Male Role Norms Inventory; Levant and Richmond, "A Review of Research."

7 Robert Putnam, *Bowling Alone: The Collapse and Revival of American Community* (New York: Simon & Schuster, 2001). Also, for an account of Putnam's "social capital" in relation to civic engagement, see Nels Lindal, *Graduation with Civic Honors: Unlock the Power of Community Opportunity* (Bloomington: Indiana University Press, 2006).

8 Jeff Jackson, a Southern Evangelical, for example, noted that part of his role as a man was physical protection, if needed. He said, "If someone was to get into my house at night, I expect that it will be me who confronts that person, protect my family while my wife is trying to get my kids out of the house or call the police or whatever, but that's my job to do that. I don't think it is because I am physically stronger; I think it is my job to sacrifice myself for my family."

9 Charlotte Allen, "Newtown Answers: An NRO Symposium," *National Review Online*, December 19, 2012, http://www.nationalreview.com/articles/335996/newtown-answers-nro-symposium.

10 Meredith Bennett-Smith, "James Dobson: Connecticut Shooting Linked to Gay Marriage." *Huffington Post*, December 17, 2012.

11 To wit, Dobson argues that homosexuality is caused by early developmental problems linked to a male child's inability to differentiate from his mother by attaching to his father. On a post about homosexuality on Dobson's *Family Talk* blog, a contributor sums up Dobson's thoughts on homosexuality thus:

> It's Dr. Nicolosi's firm belief that "mothers make boys [but] fathers make men." In other words—unlike a girl—a boy must accomplish the extra

developmental task of disidentifying from his primary caregiver of infancy (mother) and identifying with his father in an effort to formulate a masculine identity. As early as eighteen months of age and most usually by the third year of life, a boy will begin this process known as "disconnection and differentiation." The child begins to observe gender differences and decides, albeit subconsciously, which gender he is going to be. In the vast majority of incidences, the young boy starts to see his father (or perhaps other significant males in his life) as a model of masculinity and sameness. However, as Dr. Nicolosi points out, this natural and healthy progression of gender identification can go awry—especially if the father is absent, rejecting, or abusive and there is no sufficient male substitute in the boy's life. A boy who is turned off by his dad's (or other men's) representation of maleness can gravitate back to his mother and take on more of her characteristics. Such gender confusion and feelings of alienation may be exacerbated when a child is ridiculed and rejected by same gender peers who perceive that he is "different." "Roots of Homosexuality," *Dr. James Dobson's Family Talk*, http:// drjamesdobson.org/Solid-Answers/Answers?a=4f397b0d-326a-4dc3-8d0c-598a5a88e05c, accessed June 12, 2014.

12 Amanda Hess, "The Pickup Artist Community's Predictable, Horrible Response to a Mass Murder," *Slate*, May 24, 2014, http://www.slate.com/blogs/xx_factor/2014/05/24/elliot_rodger_the_pick_up_artist_community_s_predictable_horrible_response.html, accessed June 5, 2014. Hess details the original discourse that emerged after the shootings on sites devoted to the so-called "Pick Up Artist (PUA) culture." These types of websites are peopled by men who practice a particular kind of misogyny decrying the contemporary culture of quick pickups and "hookups" because of their own relative lack of success and blaming women for this state of affairs.

13 Rebecca Solnit, "The Secret to Fighting Male Fury: Why the #YesAllWomen Discussion Is So Important," *Salon.com*, June 2, 2014, www.salon.com/2014/06/02/the_secret_to_fighting_male_fury_why_yesallwomen_is_so_important_partner/, accessed June 5, 2014.

14 Brian Tashman, "Family Research Council Spokesman links Isla Vista Shooting Spree to Gay Marriage," *Right Wing Watch*, 2014, http://www.rightwingwatch.org/content/family-research-council-spokesman-links-isla-vista-shooting-spree-gay-marriage, accessed June 12, 2014.

15 See, for example, Devin Kuhn-Choi, "Conservative Christianity's 'Come to Jesus' Moment in the Wake of Elliot Rodger Shootings," *Religion Dispatches*, May 27, 2014, http://www.religiondispatches.org/archive/sexandgender/7898/conservative_christianity_s__come_to_jesus__moment_in_wake_of_elliot_rodger_shootings, accessed June 9, 2014.

16 Gene Robinson, "#YesAllWomen Should Have the Church on Their Side," *The Daily Beast*, June 1, 2014, http://www.thedailybeast.com/articles/2014/06/01/yesallwomen-should-have-the-church-on-their-side.html, accessed June 5, 2014.

17 Ibid.

18 Ibid.

19 Chelsen Vicari, "Men, Sin and the #YesAllWomen Campaign," *The Ethics and Religious Liberty Commission*, 2014, http://erlc.com/article/men-sin-and-the-yesallwomen-campaign.

20 Chelsen Vicari, "Men, Sin, and the 'YesAllWomen' Campaign," *Juicy Ecumenism*, May 28, 2014, http://juicyecumenism.com/2014/05/28/men-sin-and-the-yesallwomen-campaign/.

21 See, for example, Jeff Zeleny and Jim Rutenberg, "G.O.P. 'Super PAC' Weighs Hard-Line Attack on Obama," *New York Times*, May 17, 2012, http://www.nytimes.com/2012/05/17/us/politics/gop-super-pac-weighs-hard-line-attack-on-obama.html, accessed September 20, 2013.

22 See Scott Mayerwitz, "Red, Lite and Blue: The Beers Obama, Gates and Crowley Will Drink at White House," *ABC News*, July 29, 2009, http://abcnews.go.com/Business/Politics/story?id=8204574, accessed September 20, 2013.

23 See, for example, Catherine Bennett, "Isn't It Time We Ditched This Bogus Notion of 'Real Manhood'?" *Observer*, September 22, 2012, http://www.theguardian.com/commentisfree/2012/sep/23/catherine-bennett-maleness-ranulph-fiennes, accessed June 9, 2014.

24 See chapter 2 and this chapter.

25 Cf. W. Bradford Wilcox, *Soft Patriarchs, New Men: How Christianity Shapes Fathers and Husbands* (Chicago: University of Chicago Press, 2004).

26 Recall in the previous chapter how men talked about media and work. Media do not represent this balance at all. Work either is nonexistent or causes alienation in domestic relations. The media provided salient resources with which to discuss this tension among the elements of provision and purpose, the domestic and the public.

27 Cf. Wilcox, *Soft Patriarchs, New Men*.

28 It is notable, of course, that a minority in our study did embrace egalitarian gender relations and did, by and large, reject "traditional manhood." Such a subject-position is possible in Evangelical or Ecumenical religious communities, though it is much more prevalent in Ecumenical circles. In Evangelical communities, a gender orthodoxy of masculine servant-leadership and feminine complementarianism has replaced the unchallenged gender traditionalism of the past. This orthodoxy carries incredible cultural capital and power. Thus, while it is possible to take up a subject-position of full egalitarianism in Evangelical cultural space, doing so still comes with considerable cultural risk, threatening one's position in this community. In Ecumenical circles, a space of gender heterodoxy dominates, where it is "normal" to express egalitarianism and softer forms of patriarchy in the same cultural space. We do not mean to overstate the egalitarianism of Ecumenical religious communities, however. In our focus groups, for example, there was considerable cultural pressure to "fit" into some form of gender essentialism. The point here is that these Ecumenical cultural spaces were quite different from Evangelical circles, where the pressure was stronger to maintain the orthodox position on gender.

The difference between the Evangelicals and Ecumenicals in relation to elementalism was subtle. While both groups accepted and negotiated with the notion that there are natural or elemental characteristics which define men and masculinity, this was clearly more salient for the Evangelicals than the Ecumenicals. With the latter cohort, elementalism served as a kind of backdrop against which they compared their aspirations to more egalitarian ideals. Tellingly, rather than fully reject the whole notion of elementalism, they instead chose to suggest that whatever characteristics of men and women are "natural" (and most seemed to assume that there are such essential characteristics to both genders), they seemed to be saying that men and women today should each aspire to take on some of the characteristics of the "other." While provision, protection, and purpose have been traditionally thought of as more or less exclusively male, they want to empower women to take up those characteristics, just as they want to challenge men to explore their "feminine" sides. Evangelical men also sought to explore what they perceived to be feminine traits, for example affection and emotion, and they encouraged a measure of egalitarianism in family life and in religious structure. Further, they certainly thought women provided certain things, should be protected in certain ways, and should be purposeful. But Evangelicals were more apt to set limits on such explorations and encouragements and to specifically "gender" as "male" aspirations of provision, purpose, and protection than their Ecumenical peers.

29 See Sally K. Gallagher and Christian Smith, "Symbolic Traditionalism and Pragmatic Egalitarianism: Contemporary Evangelicals, Families, and Gender," *Gender & Society* 13, no. 2 (1999): 211–33.

30 Cf. Ulrich Beck, *Risk Society: Towards a New Modernity*, trans. Mark Ritter (London: Sage, 1992).

31 Cf. J. R. Macnamara, *Media and Male Identity: The Making and Remaking of Men* (New York: Palgrave Macmillan, 2006).

32 Michael S. Kimmel, ed., *The Politics of Manhood: Profeminist Men Respond to the Mythopoetic Men's Movement (and the Mythopoetic Leaders Answer)* (Philadelphia: Temple University Press, 1995).

33 Cf. Harvey Mansfield, *Manliness* (New Haven, Conn.: Yale University Press, 2005).

34 Frederick Jackson Turner, *The Frontier in American History* (New York: H. Holt and Company, 1920); Richard Slotkin, *The Fatal Environment: The Myth of the Frontier in the Age of Industrialization 1800–1890* (New York: Atheneum, 1985); John S. Lawrence and Robert Jewett, *The Myth of the American Superhero* (Grand Rapids, Mich.: W. M. Eerdmans Publishing Co., 2002).

35 We are not arguing, of course, that threats are imaginary. Certainly, there are threats in the risk society of late modern America. The point is that protection is articulated as part of the masculine domain.

36 There is, of course, a longstanding theoretical discourse about the role of the media in social expectations of violence. What he called the "Mean World Syndrome"

was identified by George Gerbner and his associates as part of their long-term studies of the "cultivation" effects of media exposure. Studies have supported the notion that television viewers' exposure to violence in news and entertainment leads them to overestimate their own chances of experiencing crime. George Gerbner, Larry Gross, Michael Morgan, Nancy Signorielli, and James Shanahan, "Growing up with Television: Cultivation Effects," in *Media Effects: Advances in Theory and Research*, Second Edition, ed. Jennings Bryant and Dolf Zillmann (Mahwah, N.J.: Lawrence Erlbaum Associates, Inc., 2002), 43–67.

37 We acknowledge that these concerns about the effects of television have a long, deep, and current history in American public discourse. Debates over the effects of television and other media on children have been common for most of the past century, with extensive academic and educational resources devoted to studying and addressing the issue. These men and women, as parents, are thus far from alone or unique in these concerns.

38 Stewart M. Hoover, Lynn Schofield Clark, and Diane F. Alters, with Joseph Champ and Lee Hood, *Media, Home, and Family* (New York: Routledge, 2003).

39 Certainly, women share this concern and partner in protection. What is notable for our purposes here is how this narrative can function for men as a key practice to fulfill their essentialist need for protection. To the extent that men express essentialist masculine ideals, the threat of media culture provides them with a practical way to engage normative ideal of manhood.

40 Hoover et al., *Media, Home, and Family.*

41 See Stewart M. Hoover and Curtis D. Coats, "The Media and Male Identities: Audience Research in Media, Religion and Masculinities," *Journal of Communication* 61 (2011): 877–95.

42 Mansfield, *Manliness.*

43 Notable proof texts might include Matthew 10:35–38 (NIV): "For I have come to turn a man against his father, a daughter against her mother, a daughter-in-law against her mother-in-law—a man's enemies will be the members of his own household. Anyone who loves their father or mother more than me is not worthy of me; anyone who loves their son or daughter more than me is not worthy of me. Whoever does not take up their cross and follow me is not worthy of me."

CONCLUSION

1 "Fox's Hume: Christie Seen as a Bully Because He's an 'Old Fashioned Guy's Guy' in Today's 'Feminized Atmosphere,'" *Media Matters Foundation*, January 12, 2014, http://mediamatters.org/video/2014/01/12/foxs-hume-christie-seen-as-a-bully-because-hes/197548, accessed May 5, 2014.

2 Robert M. Peaslee, "Media Conduction" (paper presented at Society for Media and Cinema Studies, Chicago, 2013). Peaslee used this inversion of Raymond Williams's "structure of feeling" to describe the ways in which individuals "embody a boundary discourse." For a discussion on Williams's "structure of feeling," see Raymond Williams, *Marxism and Literature* (Oxford: Oxford University Press, 1978).

3 See Trevin Wax, "The Crazy Culture of Complementarianism," *The Gospel Coalition*, May 16, 2013, http://thegospelcoalition.org/blogs/trevinwax/2013/05/16/the-crazy-culture-of-complementarianism/, accessed June 14, 2014.

4 For a discussion on the complexities of Evangelical feminism, see Marie Griffith, "The New Evangelical Feminism of Bachmann and Palin," *Huffington Post*, July 6, 2011, http://www.huffingtonpost.com/marie-griffith/evangelical-feminism_b_891579.html, accessed June 14, 2014. See also "Rachel Held Evans," www.rachelheldevans.com, accessed June 14, 2014.

5 See Ray Suarez, "For One Gay Christian, a Search for Understanding While Hanging on to Faith," *PBSNewsHour*, June 21, 2013, http://www.pbs.org/newshour/bb/religion-jan-june13-chu_06-21/, accessed June 14, 2014.

6 See Robert Jones, Daniel Cox, and Juhem Navarro-Rivera, "A Shifting Landscape: A Decade of Change in American Attitudes about Same-Sex Marriage and LGBT Issues," *Public Religion Research Institute*, February 26, 2014, http://publicreligion.org/site/wp-content/uploads/2014/02/2014.LGBT_REPORT.pdf, accessed June 14, 2014. See also "Changing Attitudes on Gay Marriage," *Pew Research Religion and Public Life*, March 2014, http://features.pewforum.org/same-sex-marriage-attitudes/slide3.php, accessed June 14, 2014.

7 David Sessions, "How Rachel Held Evans Beat the Evangelical Decency Police." *The Daily Beast*, October 26, 2012, http://www.thedailybeast.com/articles/2012/10/26/how-rachel-held-evans-beat-the-evangelical-decency-police.html, accessed June 13, 2014.

8 This is, in a way, a measure of the effects of structural social change. Many of the Ecumenical or liberal Protestant groups have long had female clergy—for so long, in fact, that this has become an uncontested commonplace even for more conservative members. In Evangelicalism, where it is still a "live" question in many places, the question of female church leadership can become a point of contention.

9 Joseph Gelfer, *Numen, Old Men: Contemporary Masculine Spiritualities and the Problem of Patriarchy* (London: Equinox, 2009).

10 Ibid., 175.

11 See, for example, bell hooks, *Outlaw Culture: Resisting Representations* (New York: Routledge, 2006); Harry Benshoff and Sean Griffin, *America on Film: Representing Race, Class, Gender and Sexuality at the Movies*, Second Edition (West Sussex, England: Wiley-Blackwell, 2009).

12 For a review of this history, see Todd Gitlin, *Inside Prime Time* (Berkeley: University of California Press, 2000), 250ff.

13 Thus, this is not about the earlier media theory that focused on the "uses and gratifications" of various media. For a recent review, see Alan M. Rubin, "The Uses-and-Gratifications Perspective of Media Effects," in *Media Effects: Advances in Theory and Research*, ed. Jennings Bryant and Dolf Zillmann (Mahwah, N.J.: Lawrence Erlbaum Associates, Inc., 2002), 525–48.

14 Brian Ott, "(Re)locating Pleasure in Media Studies: Toward an Erotics of Reading," *Communication and Critical/Cultural Studies* 1, no. 2 (2004): 194–212.

15 Stewart M. Hoover, *Religion in the Media Age* (London: Routledge, 2006).

16 See Stanley Fish, *Is There a Text in This Class* (Cambridge, Mass.: Harvard University Press, 1980) 147–74. With reference to media, see John Fiske, "The Codes of Television," in *Media Studies: A Reader*, Second Edition, ed. Paul Marris (New York: New York University Press, 2000), 220–30; and Klaus Bruhn Jensen, "Television Futures: A Social Action Methodology for Studying Interpretive Communities," *Critical Studies in Mass Communication* 7 (1990): 129–46.

17 Ott, "(Re)locating Pleasure," 196.

18 This suggests that, even in the realm of *plaisir*, a cognitive framing of experience still may enter in. The rejection of Gibson by this group seemed to be a kind of political distancing from a celebrity who had publicly embraced both conservative or traditionalist religious values and has exhibited some controversial social opinions.

19 An online search reveals a large number of examples. For a typical one, see "Braveheart: Becoming a Man of Passion and Commitment," 2014, http://www.adabible.org/media_player/braveheart-becoming-a-man-of-passion-and-commitment/, accessed June 10, 2014.

20 Ott, "(Re)locating Pleasure," 203.

21 Ibid., 204.

22 See Julie Ingersoll, *Evangelical Women: War Stories in the Gender Battles* (New York: New York University Press, 2003).

23 It is, of course, possible that for some men, *Every Man's Battle* also constitutes a kind of case study of our category of "guilty pleasure." This would of course be much more controversial and troubling, and we suspect we would have been unlikely to have heard such narratives.

24 This might be explained in part by some probing we did in interviews on the question of whether Jesus might be a masculine role model. Interestingly, this was a problematic idea, particularly for Evangelical men. Ecumenical Protestant men were a little more prone to think of Jesus that way, but for all men, and for the Evangelicals in particular, Jesus was simply in another category, not accessible as a trope to negotiations of male identity. There was also a subtler discourse among our Evangelical men that connected Jesus as a model to struggles over feminization of the church. There is a longstanding ambivalence about the way Jesus has been commonly depicted and portrayed as too "effeminate," and this seemed to factor into some of our informants' ideas about this question. As the Evangelical cohort would have been the most likely one to have seen *The Passion of the Christ*, their ambivalence about Jesus and gender would perhaps explain how that film did not come up in our interviews.

25 See note 19 above.

26 We must also note the one dimension of the film that undoubtedly adds to its currency for Evangelicals: its realist, obvious, and unequivocal gestures toward religion. These are, of course, much more consistent with Gibson's own elemental Catholicism than the Evangelical Protestant imaginary, but their elementalism in symbolic terms no doubt makes them accessible as powerful markers of religion.

27 See Tim Edensor, "Mediating William Wallace," in *The Media and the Tourist Imagination: Converging Cultures*, ed. David Crouch, Rhona Jackson, and Felix Thompson (New York: Routledge, 2005).

28 See, in particular, Robert Putnam, *Bowling Alone: The Collapse and Revival of American Community* (New York: Simon & Schuster, 2001).

29 Anthony Giddens, *Modernity and Self-Identity* (Stanford: Stanford University Press, 1991).

30 In religion, several decades of important research have demonstrated this in the emergence of religious "seeking" as the central mode of religious practice today, at least for the Baby Boom and post–Baby Boom generations. See, in particular, Wade Clark Roof, *Spiritual Marketplace: Baby Boomers and the Remaking of American Religion* (Princeton, N.J.: Princeton University Press, 2001).

31 Cf. Stephanie Coontz, "'Til Children Do Us Part," *New York Times*, February 5, 2009, Section A, 31; Sandra Tsing Loh, "Let's Call the Whole Thing Off," *Atlantic*, July–August, 2009.

32 Tsing Loh, "Let's Call the Whole Thing Off."

33 Putnam, *Bowling Alone*.

BIBLIOGRAPHY

Abbott, Rebecca. "Television and Children: Issues in Black and White." *Sacred Heart University Review* 15, no.1 (Fall 1994/Spring 1995), http://digitalcommons.sacred-heart.edu/shureview/vol15/iss1/8, accessed March 10, 2015.

Ammerman, Nancy. "Golden Rule Christianity: Lived Religion in the American Mainstream," in *Lived Religion in America: Toward a History of Practice*, ed. David Hall. Princeton, N.J.: Princeton University Press, 1997.

Bartkowski, John. *The Promise Keepers: Servants, Soldiers and Godly Men*. New Brunswick, N.J.: Rutgers University Press, 2004.

Beck, Ulrich. *Risk Society: Towards a New Modernity*, trans. Mark Ritter. London: Sage, 1992.

Benshoff, Harry, and Sean Griffin. *America on Film: Representing Race, Class, Gender and Sexuality at the Movies*, Second Edition. West Sussex, England: Wiley-Blackwell, 2009.

Blumer, Herbert. *Symbolic Interactionism: Perspective and Method*. Berkeley: University of California Press, 1986.

Bond, Bradley. "Sex and Sexuality in Media Popular with Lesbian, Gay, and Bisexual Adolescents." *Mass Communication and Society* 17, no. 1 (January 2014): 98–120.

Bourdieu, Pierre. "Structures, Habitus, Power: Basis for a Theory of Symbolic Power," in *Culture/Power/History: A Reader in Contemporary Social Theory*, ed. Nicholas Dirks, Geoff Eley, and Sherry Ortner. Princeton, N.J.: Princeton University Press, 1994.

Brewster, Karin L., and Irene Padavic. "Change in Gender-Ideology, 1977–1996: The Contributions of Intracohort Change and Population Turnover." *Journal of Marriage and Family* 62, no. 2 (May 2000): 477–87.

Busby, Linda J. "Sex-role Research on the Mass Media." *Journal of Communication* 25 (1975): 107–31.

Butler, Judith. *Gender Trouble: Feminism and the Subversion of Identity*. New York: Routledge, 2006.

"Changing Attitudes on Gay Marriage," *Pew Research Religion and Public Life*, March 2014, http://features.pewforum.org/same-sex-marriage-attitudes/slide3.php, accessed March 10, 2015.

Coats, Curtis. "God, Men, Then . . . Wait, How does that go? Emerging Gender Identities in 20-something Evangelicals." *Journal of Men, Masculinities and Spirituality* 3, no. 1 (2009): 64–79.

Connell, R. W. *The Men and the Boys*. Oxford: Blackwell, 2000.

Consalvo, Mia. "The Monsters Next Door: Media Constructions of Boys and Masculinity." *Feminist Media Studies* 3, no. 1 (2003): 27–45.

Couldry, Nick, "Media Meta-Capital: Extending the Range of Bourdieu's Field Theory." *Theory and Society* 32, no. 5–6 (2003): 653–77.

Craig, Steve. *Men, Masculinity, and the Media*. London: Sage, 1992.

Crompton, Rosemary, and Fiona Harris. "Explaining Women's Employment Patterns: 'Orientations to Work' Revisited." *The British Journal of Sociology* (1998): 118–36.

Crompton, Rosemary, and Clare Lyonette. "The New Gender Essentialism—Domestic and Family Choices and Their Relation to Attitudes." *The British Journal of Sociology* 56, no. 4 (2005): 601–20.

Denzin, Norman. *Symbolic Interactionism and Cultural Studies: The Politics of Interpretation*. Oxford: Blackwell, 1992.

———. *Interpretive Interactionism*, Second Edition. Thousand Oaks, Calif.: Sage, 2001.

Dowland, Seth. "War, Sports and the Construction of Masculinity in American Christianity." *Religion Compass* 5/7 (2011): 355–64.

Eberly, Don. "Families, Fathers, and the Making of Democratic Citizens," *Civil Society Project Essays on Civil Society* 99, no. 1 (1999).

Eberly, Don, ed. *The Faith Factor in Fatherhood: Renewing the Sacred Vocation of Fatherhood*. New York: Lexington Books, 1999.

Eberly, Don, and Ryan Streeter. *The Soul of Civil Society: Voluntary Associations and the Public Value of Moral Habits*. Lanham, Md.: Lexington Books, 2002.

Edensor, Tim. "Mediating William Wallace," in *The Media and the Tourist Imagination: Converging Cultures*, ed. David Crouch, Rhona Jackson, and Felix Thompson. New York: Routledge, 2005.

Faludi, Susan. *Backlash: The Undeclared War Against American Women*. New York: Random House, 1991.

Farrell, Warren. *The Myth of Male Power: Why Men Are the Disposable Sex*. New York: Finch, 2001.

Fessenden, Tracy. *Culture and Redemption: Religion, the Secular, and American Literature*. Princeton, N.J.: Princeton University Press, 2011.

Fish, Stanley Eugene. *Is There a Text in This Class? The Authority of Interpretive Communities*. Cambridge, Mass.: Harvard University Press, 1980.

Fore, William F. *Television and Religion: The Shaping of Faith, Values, and Culture*. Minneapolis: Augsberg Press, 1987.

Gallagher, Susan K., and Christian Smith. "Symbolic Traditionalism and Pragmatic Egalitarianism: Contemporary Evangelicals, Families, and Gender." *Gender & Society* 13, no. 2 (1999): 211–33.

Gauntlett, David. Creative Explorations: New Approaches to Identities and Audiences. London: Routledge, 2007.

———. "Gender Resources," *Theory.org*, 2012, http://www.theory.org.uk/ctr-iden.htm, accessed September 16, 2012.

———. *Media, Gender and Identity*. New York: Routledge, 2002.

Gelfer, Joseph. *Numen, Old Men: Contemporary Masculine Spiritualities and the Problem of Patriarchy.* London: Equinox, 2009.

Gerbner, George, Larry Gross, Michael Morgan, Nancy Signorielli, and James Shanahan. "Growing up with Television: Cultivation Effects," in *Media Effects: Advances in Theory and Research*, Second Edition, ed. Jennings Bryant and Dolf Zillmann. Mahwah, N.J.: Lawrence Erlbaum Associates, Inc., 2002.

Giddens, Anthony. *Modernity and Self-Identity.* Stanford, Calif.: Stanford University Press, 1991.

Gitlin, Todd. *Inside Prime Time.* Berkeley: University of California Press, 2000.

Goffman, Erving. *The Presentation of Self in Everyday Life.* Garden City, N.Y.: Doubleday Anchor Books, 1959.

Goldberg, Steven. Why Men Rule: A Theory of Male Dominance. Chicago: Open Court Publishing, 1993.

Griffith, R. Marie. *God's Daughters: Evangelical Women and the Power of Submission.* Berkeley: University of California Press, 2000.

———. "The New Evangelical Feminism of Bachmann and Palin." *Huffington Post*, July 6, 2011, http://www.huffingtonpost.com/marie-griffith/evangelical-feminism_b_891579.html, accessed March 10, 2015.

Hall, Donald, ed. *Muscular Christianity: Embodying the Victorian Age.* Cambridge: Cambridge University Press, 2006.

Hall, Stuart. "Cultural Studies and Its Theoretical Legacies," in *Stuart Hall: Critical Dialogues in Cultural Studies*, ed. David Morley and Kuan-Hsing Chin. New York: Routledge, 1996.

Hanke, Robert. "Redesigning Men: Hegemonic Masculinity in Transition," in *Men, Masculinity, and the Media*, ed. Steve Craig. Newbury Park, Calif.: Sage, 1992.

Heelas, Paul, and Linda Woodhead. *The Spiritual Revolution: Why Religion Is Giving Way to Spirituality.* London: Wiley-Blackwell, 2005.

Himmelfarb, Gertrude. *The Demoralization of Society: From Victorian Virtues to Modern Values.* New York: Knopf, 1995.

Hollinger, David. *After Cloven Tongues of Fire: Protestant Liberalism in Modern American History.* Princeton, N.J.: Princeton University Press, 2013.

hooks, bell. *Outlaw Culture: Resisting Representations.* New York: Routledge, 2006.

Hoover, Stewart. *Religion in the Media Age.* London, Routledge, 2006.

Hoover, Stewart, and Curtis Coats. "The Media and Male Identities: Audience Research in Media, Religion and Masculinities." *Journal of Communication* 61 (2011): 877–95.

Hoover, Stewart, Lynn Clark, and Diane Alters with Joe Champ and Lee Hood. *Media, Home, and Family.* New York: Routledge, 2003.

Ingersoll, Julie. *Evangelical Women: War Stories in the Gender Battles.* New York: New York University Press, 2003.

Jewett, Robert, and John S. Lawrence. *The Myth of the American Superhero.* Grand Rapids, Mich.: W. B. Eerdmans Publishing Co., 2002.

Jhally, Sut, and Justin Lewis. *Enlightened Racism: The Cosby Show, Audiences and the Myth of the American Dream.* Boulder, Colo.: Westview Press, 1992.

Jones, Robert, Daniel Cox, and Juhem Navarro-Rivera. "A Shifting Landscape: A Decade of Change in American Attitudes about Same-Sex Marriage and LGBT Issues." *Public Religion Research Institute*, February 26, 2014, http://publicreligion.org/site/wp-content/uploads/2014/02/2014.LGBT_REPORT.pdf, accessed March 10, 2015.

Kilbourne, Jean. *DEADLY PERSUASION: Why Women and Girls Must Fight the Addictive Power of Advertising.* New York: Free Press, 1999.

Kimmel, Michael S. *Manhood in America: A Cultural History*, Third Edition. Oxford: Oxford University Press, 2012.

———. Masculinity as Homophobia: Fear, Shame, and Silence in the Construction of Gender Identity. In *Theorizing Masculinities*. SAGE series on Men and Masculinity, ed. Harry Brod and Michael Kaufman. Thousand Oaks, Calif.: Sage, 1994.

Kimmel, Michael S., ed. *The Politics of Manhood: Profeminist Men Respond to the Mythopoetic Men's Movement (and the Mythopoetic Leaders Answer).* Philadelphia: Temple University Press, 1995.

Kontour, Kyle. "Revisiting Violent Videogames Research: Game Studies Perspectives on Aggression, Violence, Immersion, Interaction, and Textual Analysis." *Digital Culture and Education* 1, no. 1 (2009): 6–30.

Levant, Ronald F. "The Masculinity Crisis." *Journal of Men's Studies* 5, no 3 (1997): 221–31.

Levant, Ronald, and Katherine Richmond. "A Review of Research on Masculinity Ideologies Using the Male Role Norms Inventory." *The Journal of Men's Studies* 15, no. 2 (2007): 130–46.

Lindal, Nels. *Graduation with Civic Honors: Unlock the Power of Community Opportunity.* Bloomington: Indiana University Press, 2006.

Lovdal, Lynn. "Sex Role Messages in Television Commercials: An Update." *Sex Roles* 21 (December 1989): 715–24.

Macnamara, J. R. *Media and Male Identity: The Making and Remaking of Men.* New York: Palgrave Macmillan, 2006.

Mansfield, Harvey. *Manliness.* New Haven, Conn.: Yale University Press, 2005.

McRae, Susan. "Constraints and Choices in Mothers' Employment Careers: A Consideration of Hakim's Preference Theory." *The British Journal of Sociology* 54, no. 3 (2003): 317–38.

Messner, Michael A. *Politics of Masculinities: Men in Movements.* Thousand Oaks, Calif.: Sage, 1997.

Morgan, David, ed. *Icons of American Protestantism: The Art of Warner Sallman.* New Haven, Conn.: Yale University Press, 1996.

———. *The Sacred Gaze: Religious Visual Culture in Theory and Practice.* Berkeley: University of California Press, 2005.

———. *The Lure of Images: A History of Religion and Visual Media in America.* New York: Routledge, 2007.

Ott, Brian. "(Re)locating Pleasure in Media Studies: Toward an Erotics of Reading." *Communication and Critical/Cultural Studies* 1, no. 2 (2004): 194–212.

———. "Television as Lover, Part 1: Writing Dirty Theory." *Cultural Studies/Critical Methodologies* 7, no. 1 (2007): 26–47.

Ott, Brian, and Robert Mack. *Critical Media Studies: An Introduction*. Oxford: Wiley-Blackwell, 2010.

Peaslee, Robert. "Media Conduction: Exploring Power at the Intersection of Media, Tourism, and Festival Studies." Paper presented at Society for Media and Cinema Studies, Chicago, 2013.

Pitt, Richard. "From Intrepreneur to Entrepreneur: Mapping the Call to Founding Pastorates." Paper presented at Annual Meeting of the Society for the Scientific Study of Religion, Phoenix, Ariz., November 9–11, 2012.

Putnam, Robert. *Bowling Alone: The Collapse and Revival of American Community*. New York: Simon & Schuster, 2001.

Putney, Clifford. *Muscular Christianity: Manhood and Sports in Protestant America, 1880–1920*. Cambridge, Mass.: Harvard University Press, 2009.

Radway, Janice. "Identifying Ideological Seams: Mass Culture, Analytical Method, and Political Practice." *Communication* 9 (1986): 93–124.

Rosenthal, Michele. *American Protestants and TV in the 1950s: Responses to a New Medium*. New York: Palgrave Macmillan, 2007.

Rubin, Alan M. "The Uses-and-Gratifications Perspective of Media Effects," in *Media Effects: Advances in Theory and Research*, ed. Jennings Bryant and Dolf Zillmann. Mahwah, N.J.: Lawrence Erlbaum Associates, Inc., 2002.

Slotkin, Richard. *The Fatal Environment: The Myth of the Frontier in the Age of Industrialization, 1800–1890*. New York: Atheneum, 1985.

Smith, Jeffery A. "Hollywood Theology: The Commodification of Religion in Twentieth-Century Films." *Religion and American Culture* 11, no. 2 (2001): 191–231.

Stacey, Judith. *Brave New Families: Stories of Domestic Upheaval in Late-Twentieth-Century America*. Berkeley: University of California Press, 1998.

Swidler, Anne. *Talk of Love: How Culture Matters*. Chicago: University of Chicago Press, 2000.

Turner, Frederick Jackson. *The Frontier in American History*. New York: H. Holt and Company, 1920.

Watson, Nick, Stuart Weir, and Stephen Friend. "The Development of Muscular Christianity in Victorian Britain and Beyond." *Journal of Religion and Society* 7, no. 1 (2005): 1–25.

Wetherell, Margaret, and Nigel Edley. "Negotiating Hegemonic Masculinity: Imaginary Positions and Psycho-Discursive Practices." *Feminism & Psychology* 9, no. 3 (1999): 335–56.

Wilcox, W. Bradford. *Soft Patriarchs, New Men: How Christianity Shapes Fathers and Husbands*. Chicago: University of Chicago Press, 2004.

Williams, Raymond. "Culture Is Ordinary," in *Cultural Theory: An Anthology*, ed. Imre Szeman and Timothy Kaposy. Oxford: Wiley-Blackwell, 2010.

Winston, Diane, ed. *Small Screen, Big Picture: Television and Lived Religion*. Waco, Tex.: Baylor University Press, 2009.

INDEX

Aaron, Barry, 58–59, 93–94

Abbott, Rebecca, 198n34

Absence: father absence, 4, 10, 180; rites of passage, 4

According to Jim (television show), 95, 166

"Accounts *of* media," 67, 70, 71, 107

Advertising, in media, 143

After Cloven Tongues of Fire: Protestant Liberalism in Modern American History (Hollinger), 195n22

Aggression, 117–18

Allen, Charlotte, 117–18

All Things Considered (radio show), 1

Ambiguity. *See* "Zones of ambiguity"

American Idol (television show), 101–2, 103

Ammerman, Nancy, 193n1

Andrews, Mike, 60, 129; media and, 81–82, 92–93, 141–42; on men and fathers, 92–93; provision and, 134–36; purpose and, 151; on sex and violence, 81–82

Andrews, Sally (wife), 93, 141–42

The Andy Griffith Show (television show), 91, 106

Arterburn, Steven, 172

The Atlantic online, 3

Atonement (film), 83–84

Authority: "final say," 38–39; men with clerical, 32–35; "subjective turn" and, 28. *See also* Headship

Autonomous Self, 9

Baby Boomers, 206n30

Barthes, Roland, 168, 170

Beck, Glenn, 3, 8, 12

Belushi, Jim, 95, 104

Benjamin, Rich, 3

the Bible: Ephesians, 26, 43–44, 47, 48, 193n6; headship in, 26, 43; Matthew, 203n43

The Biggest Loser (television show), 103

Billings, Jeremy, 60, 92

Blackwell, Ken, 119, 121

Boldness, 34–35

"Born-again," 14

Bourdieu, Pierre, 27, 158, 193n6

Bowling Alone (Putnam), 5, 183

Boys: with fathers, 11–12; masculinity crisis and, 3–4, 8. *See also* Children

Bradford, Matt, 61

Braveheart (film): as family drama, 150–51, 175–77; influence, 168, 176–77; men in, 57, 93, 103–4, 106, 138, 166, 175–79; with *Wild at Heart*, 57, 172

Brewer, Tim, 38, 90–91, 99–100

British Cultural Studies, 66

British Journal of Sociology, 20

Burke, Edmund, 10

Bush, George W., 3, 8, 9

Bush, Laura (wife), 8

Butler, Judith, 2, 22, 23, 69, 154

Caldwell, Clark: on "dumb dads," 90; gender stereotypes in media and, 85; on men's role in family, 56–57, 115, 150, 175; with work and media, 98–99

Calhoun, Denton: background, 14; calling and, 148; domestic ideal and, 123, 125–27, 129; family and, 15–17, 27, 179; gender relations and, 37–38; at home, 28, 125–26; with masculine identity, 27, 126–27; masculinity crisis and, 6, 25; with media and masculinity, 15, 86–87, 140; provision and, 131–32; purpose and, 151; with religion, 14–15, 36–37; work and, 15–16, 28–29

Calhoun, Nancy (wife), 14

Calling (vocation): domestic ideal and, 129–30, 134, 147–48; work as, 99, 100, 125, 128, 148–50

Cane, Larry: domestic ideal and, 123, 127–29; family and, 179; media and, 73–75, 83, 90, 141, 143; provision and, 132–33; with work as calling, 128, 148–49

Cane, Linda (wife), 83–84, 143–44, 149

Carter, Jimmy, 103

Children, 91, 104; boys, 3–4, 8, 11–12; fathers and relationship with, 11–12, 134–35; girls, 12; media and, 73–78, 81, 84, 102, 140, 141–44, 202n37. See also Families

Christianity, 194n9; Christian media, 173–74; Hollywood and, 15, 165, 198n32, 205n24, 205n26; with identity and masculinity crisis, 5. See also Ecumenical Protestants; Evangelical Protestants; Roman Catholics

Christie, Chris, 153

Citizenship, 5, 9, 10, 15, 179, 180

Civic engagement, 4–5; domestic purpose and, 179–80, 184, 187; families and, 10, 183; manhood and, 7, 10–12, 17, 116, 123; politics and, 116, 179–80; with social capital, 116, 199n7

Civil society, 4, 9–10, 12–13

Civil Society Project, 9

Clegg, Nick, 121–22

Coats, Curtis, 41–42, 45

Complementarianism, 160, 161, 163, 201n28

Consalvo, Mia, 69

Corbin, Jeff, 100

Cosby, Bill, 90, 93, 103, 168, 198n30, 198n34

The Cosby Show (television show), 90, 91, 93, 106

Courage, 105, 147

Crime, 202n36

Crisis. See Masculinity crisis

Crompton, Rosemary, 20–21

Crowe, Russell, 103

Culture: British Cultural Studies, 66; cultural traditionalism, 42; "culture warrior," 148; feminization of, 153–54; headship and culture war, 158, 165, 167; multiculturalism, 9; "PUA culture," 200n12; with white male decline, 3

Decline: religion, 4; social capital, 179; of white males, 3

Denzin, Norman, 22

Dobson, James, 9, 12, 118, 199n11

Domestic ideal: calling and, 129–30, 134, 147–48; with elementalism, 124–31; elemental masculinity and, 111–24; masculine purpose and, 146–52; politics and, 124; protection in, 138–47, 199n8; provision in, 131–37, 146; public realm and, 124–29, 151–52. See also Home

Domestic purpose, 179–80, 184, 187. See also Home

Donegal, Glenn: background, 6–7; with fathers on television, 7, 13; at home, 28; with masculine identity, 27, 28; masculinity crisis and, 6–8, 12, 25; work and, 28–29

Doxa, 27, 158, 193n6

Driscoll, Mark, 159, 160, 161, 171

"Dumb dads." See Fathers

Eastwood, Clint, 103

Eberly, Don, 12, 13, 193n3; families and, 9–10, 180, 183; on religion and social capital, 10–11

Ecumenical Protestants: egalitarianism
and, 53–55, 59–60, 193n2, 201n28;
elementalism and, 201n28; essentialism and, 56, 62, 193n2; Evangelical and,
42, 52, 55–56, 59, 63–64, 136–37, 162–63,
192n40, 195n22, 201n28; fathers and
media, 91–95; gender and, 42, 44, 55,
162–64, 194n8, 195n19; headship and,
53, 55, 58, 59–60, 75, 91, 94, 129, 136, 155,
162; media and, 75–77, 79–82, 91–95,
103–5, 142; as new Christian patriarchs, 25–26, 28, 31, 42, 44, 52–62; with
religion, 25–26, 108; role models and
media, 103–5; sex and media, 75–77,
79–82, 142; "subjective turn" and, 28;
television and family, 102–3; traditionalism and, 55; violence and media, 79;
work and, 97
Egalitarianism: Ecumenical Protestants
and, 53–55, 59–60, 193n2, 201n28;
elementalism and, 42; Evangelical
Protestants and, 41–42, 201n28; with
gender, 41–42, 201n28; masculine
identity and, 54; politics and, 42
Eldredge, John, 36, 161; criticism of, 58;
influence, 57–58, 168, 172. See also
Wild at Heart
Elementalism, 22; domestic ideal with,
124–31; Ecumenical Protestants and,
201n28; egalitarianism and, 42; essentialism and, 19–20, 24, 28, 193n3;
Evangelical Protestants and, 42, 62,
201n28; feminism and, 32–33, 117–18,
193n2; manhood and, 48, 68; with
public elementalism, 121
Elemental masculinity: domestic ideal
and, 111–24; manhood and, 19–20, 28,
72–73, 123; protection and, 19, 23, 25,
62–63, 68, 73, 114–17, 155, 202n35; provision and, 19, 23, 25, 62, 68, 73, 114–17,
155; purpose and, 19, 23, 25, 30–31, 63,
68, 73, 114–17, 155; religion and, 29–33,
50–51

Emasculation, 86–87, 94, 161
Engalls, Andrea (wife), 102
Engalls, Shane, 101–2
Ephesians. See the Bible
Essentialism: Ecumenical Protestants and,
56, 62, 193n2; elementalism and, 19–20,
24, 28, 193n3; gender essentialism and,
20, 56, 59–60, 194n8; with "preference theory," 20–21; protection as, 23,
203n39; provision as, 23; purpose as,
23, 56
Ethics. See Morality; Work
Evangelical Protestants: Ecumenical and,
42, 52, 55–56, 59, 63–64, 136–37, 162–63,
192n40, 195n22, 201n28; egalitarianism
and, 41–42, 201n28; elementalism and,
42, 62, 201n28; fathers and media, 91–
92, 94–95; feminism and, 161; gender
and, 41–44, 194n8, 195n19; with hard
patriarchy, 55; headship and, 25–27,
34–35, 38–41, 53, 55, 58, 59–60, 62, 63,
72, 73, 75, 81–82, 87–89, 91, 94–95, 108,
113, 129, 136–37, 155–62; literature, 61–
62, 122, 155, 159, 167, 194n13; media and,
75–80, 82–85, 91–92, 94–95, 103–5; as
new Christian patriarchs, 25–28, 31–36,
40–52, 55–56, 58–60, 62–64; with religion, 14–15, 25, 108; role models and
media, 103–5; sex and media, 75–80,
82–85; "subjective turn" and, 28; television and family, 103; traditionalism
and, 41–43, 48; violence and media,
79–80, 83; work and, 97–98, 156; with
"zones of ambiguity," 73–74
Evans, Rachel Held, 161, 171
Everly, Ned, 84, 86
Everly, Stacy (wife), 84
Everybody Loves Raymond (television
show), 88, 104
Every Man's Battle (Stoeker), 172, 174,
205n23
"Experiences in media," 67, 70
Extreme Makeover (television show), 102

Families: *Braveheart* as family drama,
150–51, 175–77; children, 3–4, 8, 11–12,
73–78, 81, 84, 91, 102, 104, 134–35, 140–
44, 202n37; civic engagement and, 10,
183; in civil society, 9–10; Focus on the
Family, 9; headship and, 6–7, 14–15, 26,
38, 45–48, 51, 62, 87–89, 91, 95, 121, 129,
131; home and, 4, 5, 27–28, 40, 45, 111–
52, 179–81, 184, 187; as "little platoons,"
10, 123, 180, 183; media and, 75, 101–2,
141–42; men's roles in, 15–17, 27, 56–57,
63, 115, 150, 175, 179–80, 190n9; morality and, 10; politics and, 111, 115; with
sex and violence in media, 75; television and, 102–3, 140–42; women's roles
in, 57, 128; work and, 96, 100
Family Guy (television show), 142
Family Research Council, 119
Family Talk blog, 199n11
Farrakhan, Louis, 8
Fathers, 194n9; children and relationship with, 11–12, 134–35; as "dumb
dads," 86, 90, 91, 94–96, 165–66; father
absence, 4, 10, 180; with masculinity
crisis, 3, 6–9, 11–12, 25; in media, 82,
86–95, 99; of men, 72, 126–27, 132–33,
181–82, 186–87, 189n2, 197n23; National
Fatherhood Initiative, 9; Obama on,
11–12, 180, 190n9; religion and, 49–50;
as role models, 116, 126–27, 132–33; stereotypes, 4; on television, 7, 13, 86–95,
99–100, 166. *See also* Patriarchy
Feelings. *See* "Structure of feelings"
Feminism: elementalism and, 32–33, 117–
18, 193n2; Evangelical Protestants and,
161; headship and, 127; influence, 26;
masculinity and, 18–19, 27, 28, 89, 112,
185, 196n12; neo-traditionalism and,
10; religion and, 39
Feminization: of culture, 153–54; emasculation with, 86–87, 94, 161; Jesus
with, 205n24; passivity with, 117–18; of
religion, 29–33, 40, 51, 60, 159, 195n21

Fight Club (film), 58
Films: Hollywood and Christianity, 15,
165, 198n32, 205n24, 205n26; influ-
ence, 15, 58, 73–74, 102, 150–51, 168, 172,
176–77, 196n2, 198n32; language of, 74;
men in, 13, 57, 93, 103–4, 106, 138–39,
164, 166, 175–79; sex in, 83–84; slasher,
198n33; violence in, 80, 198n33. *See also*
Media
"Final say," 38–39
Focus on the Family, 9
Foul language, 79, 82, 142
Fox, Matthew, 103, 168
Frames, media, 67–68, 70
French, Emory, 46–47, 95
French, Jessica (wife), 95
Friends (television show), 15, 76–78, 84,
104, 140

Gallagher, Susan K., 194n15
Gates, Henry Louis, 121
Gauntlett, David, 23, 70–71
Gelfer, Joseph, 13, 163
Gender: Ecumenical Protestants and,
42, 44, 55, 162–64, 194n8, 195n19;
egalitarianism with, 41–42, 201n28;
Evangelical Protestants and, 41–44,
194n8, 195n19; with feminization,
29–33, 40, 51, 60, 86–87, 94, 117–18,
153–54, 159, 161, 195n21, 205n24; gender
essentialism and, 20, 56, 59–60, 194n8;
gender trouble, 2, 23, 117, 121, 160–61;
as gifts, 44; hierarchy, 41–44, 55; home
and gender roles, 45; media and, 23,
68–71, 85–88; politics and, 1, 2, 121–22;
religion and gender relations, 37–39,
49–50, 54, 119, 178, 193n6; sexism and,
28; sex-role strain and, 12; stereotypes,
85–86; violence with, 1–2; work and, 4
Gerbner, George, 195n1, 202n36
Gibson, Mel: with *Braveheart*, 57, 93,
103–4, 106, 138, 150–51, 166, 168, 172,
175–79; influence, 198n32, 205n18;

Patriarchy: Ecumenical Protestants as new Christian, 25–26, 28, 31, 42, 44, 52–62; Evangelical Protestants as new Christian, 25–28, 31–36, 40–52, 55–56, 58–60, 62–64; "hard patriarchy," 36, 44, 50, 55; headship and soft, 46–47, 51, 60; media and, 166; "patriarchal bargains," 44; "soft patriarchy," 39, 43–44, 46–47, 51, 60, 112, 171, 194n9; traditionalists and, 41

Peaslee, Robert, 193n6, 203n2

Peck, Gregory, 103

Personal preferences, social norms and, 21–22

"Philosophical courage," 147

"Pick Up Artist (PUA) culture," 200n12

Pitt, Richard, 197n24

Pittman, Frank, 10

Plaisir (pleasure), 168, 169, 205n18

Platoons, little. *See* Families

Plausible narratives of self, 22, 160, 164

Pleasure: guilty pleasure, 78, 103, 104–5, 145, 170–71, 205n23; *jouissance*, 168, 170; media and, 16, 98, 106, 144, 157, 167–75; *plaisir*, 168, 169, 205n18

Pleck, Joseph, 12

Poe, Catherine, 2–3

Politics: civic engagement, 116, 179–80; with culture feminized, 153–54; domestic ideal and, 124; egalitarians as apolitical, 42; family and, 111, 115; gender and, 1, 2, 121–22; multiculturalism and, 9; with public elementalism, 121; with white male voters, 2–3; women and, 2

Pornography, 80–81, 172

Practical masculinity, 108

Practical models, of manhood, 159–60

Preferences: "preference theory," 20–21; social norms and personal, 21–22

Private realm, 4–5. *See also* Home

Promise Keepers, 15, 36, 43, 173, 194n14

Protection: in domestic ideal, 138–47, 199n8; with elemental masculinity, 19,

23, 25, 62–63, 68, 73, 114–17, 155, 202n35; as essentialism, 23, 203n39; media and, 157; violence and, 139–40; *Wild at Heart* and, 138–39

Provision: in domestic ideal, 131–37, 146; with elemental masculinity, 19, 23, 25, 62, 68, 73, 114–17, 155; as essentialism, 23; purpose and, 149; work and, 97, 100, 156

"PUA culture." *See* "Pick Up Artist culture"

Public elementalism, 121

Public realm: domestic ideal and, 124–29, 151–52; private and, 4–5. *See also* Politics; Work

Publishing industry, 43. *See also* Media

Purity, sex and, 78

Purpose: civic engagement and, 179–80, 184, 187; domestic ideal and masculine, 146–52; with elemental masculinity, 19, 23, 25, 30–31, 63, 68, 73, 114–17, 155; as essentialism, 23, 56; headship and, 34–35; manhood and, 56–58; provision and, 149; with work, 96–97, 156

The Purpose Driven Life, 14

Putnam, Robert, 5, 116, 183

Queer Eye for the Straight Guy (television show), 85–86

Race, 2–3

"Rational choice" theory, 20

"Reflexive project of the self," 8, 70, 125, 180

Religion: the Bible, 26, 43–44, 47, 48, 193n6, 203n43; decline, 4; Ecumenical Protestants with, 25–26, 108; elemental masculinity and, 29–33, 50–51; Evangelical Protestants with, 14–15, 25, 108; fathers and, 49–50; feminism and, 39; feminization of, 29–33, 40, 51, 60, 159, 195n21; gender relations and, 37–39, 49–50, 54, 119, 178, 193n6; hus-

Stewart M. Hoover is Professor of Media Studies and Professor Adjoint of Religious Studies and Director of the Center for Media, Religion, and Culture at the University of Colorado. He has lectured and conducted research in more than twenty countries and is the author, co-author, or editor of twelve books and numerous essays, reviews, journal articles, and online publications. An expert on media audiences, he is particularly interested in how evolving media practices change the prospects and practices of religion, spirituality, and religious authority.

Curtis D. Coats is Associate Professor of Communication Studies at Millsaps College. He joined the English faculty at Millsaps College in 2009 to help launch the new Communication Studies major. He earned his doctorate in Communication from the University of Colorado, Boulder, in 2008, and he was a postdoctoral research fellow at the Center for Media, Religion, and Culture at the University of Colorado until August 2009. His research explores media and religion in everyday life, with particular emphases on religious/spiritual tourism and the role of media and religion on gender identity.